T0331713

Constraint logic programming lies at the intersection of logic programming, optimisation and artificial intelligence. It has proved a successful tool for application in a variety of areas including production planning, transportation scheduling, numerical analysis and bioinformatics. Its migration from academic discipline to software development has been due in part to the availability of software systems that realise the underlying methodology; ECL^{i}PS^e is one of the leading such systems. It is exploited commercially by Cisco, and is freely available and used for teaching and research in over 500 universities.

This book has a two-fold purpose. It's an introduction to constraint programming, appropriate for a one-semester course for upper undergraduate or graduate students of computer science or for programmers wishing to master the practical aspects of constraint programming. By the end of the book, the reader will be able to understand and write constraint programs that solve complex problems.

Second, it provides a systematic introduction to the ECL^{i}PS^e system through carefully chosen examples that guide the reader through the language, illustrate its power and versatility, and clarify the gain achieved by this approach, which, ultimately allows the reader to better understand the proper use of constraints in solving real-world problems.

Krzysztof R. Apt received his PhD in 1974 in mathematical logic from the University of Warsaw in Poland. He is a senior researcher at Centrum voor Wiskunde en Informatica, Amsterdam and Professor of Computer Science at the University of Amsterdam. He is the author of three other books: *Verification of Sequential and Concurrent Programs* (with E.-R. Olderog), *From Logic Programming to Prolog*, and *Principles of Constraint Programming*, and has published 50 journal articles and 15 book chapters.

He is the founder and the first editor-in-chief of the ACM Transactions on Computational Logic, and past president of the Association for Logic Programming. He is a member of the Academia Europaea (Mathematics and Informatics Section).

After completing a degree at Oxford in Mathematics and Philosophy, Mark Wallace joined the UK computer company ICL, who funded his PhD at Southampton University, which was published as a book: *Communicating with Databases in Natural Language*.

He has been involved in the ECL^{i}PS^e constraint programming language since its inception and has led several industrial research collaborations exploiting the power of constraint programming with ECL^{i}PS^e. Currently he holds a chair in the Faculty of Information Technology at the Monash University, Victoria, Australia and is involved in a major new constraint programming initiative funded by National ICT Australia (NICTA), and in the foundation of a Centre for Optimisation in Melbourne. He has published widely, chaired the annual constraint programming conference, and is an editor for three international journals.

Advance praise for *Constraint Logic Programming using ECL^{i}PS^e*

The strength of *Constraint Logic Programming using ECL^{i}PS^e* is that it simply and gradually explains the relevant concepts, starting from scratch, up to the realisation of complex programs. Numerous examples and ECL^{i}PS^e programs fully demonstrate the elegance, simplicity, and usefulness of constraint logic programming and ECL^{i}PS^e.

The book is self-contained and may serve as a guide to writing constraint applications in ECL^{i}PS^e, but also in other constraint programming systems. Hence, this is an indispensable resource for graduate students, practioners, and researchers interested in problem solving and modelling.

Eric Monfroy, Université de Nantes

ECL^{i}PS^e is a flexible, powerful and highly declarative constraint logic programming platform that has evolved over the years to comprehensively support constraint programmers in their quest for the best search and optimisation algorithms. However, the absence of a book dedicated to ECL^{i}PS^e has presented those interested in this approach to programming with a significant learning hurdle. This book will greatly simplify the ECL^{i}PS^e learning process and will consequently help ECL^{i}PS^e reach a much wider community.

Within the covers of this book readers will find all the information they need to start writing sophisticated programs in ECL^{i}PS^e. The authors first introduce ECL^{i}PS^e's history, and then walk the reader through the essentials of Prolog and Constraint Programming, before going on to present the principal features of the language and its core libraries in a clear and systematic manner.

Anyone learning to use ECL^{i}PS^e or seeking a course book to support teaching constraint logic programming using the language will undoubtedly benefit from this book.

Hani El-Sakkout, Cisco Systems, Boston, Massachusetts

It has been recognized for some years now within the Operations Research community that Integer Programming is needed for its powerful algorithms, but that logic is a more flexible modelling tool. The case was made in most detail by John Hooker, in his book *Logic-Based Methods for Optimization: Combining Optimization and Constraint Satisfaction*.

The ECL^{i}PS^e system is a highly successful embodiment of these ideas. It draws on ideas coming from logic programming, constraint programming, and the Prolog language. I strongly recommend this book as a systematic account of these topics. Moreover, it gives a wealth of examples showing how to deploy the power thus made available via the ECL^{i}PS^e system.

Maarten van Emden, University of Victoria, Canada

This is an impressive introduction to Constraint Logic Programming and the ECL^{i}PS^e system by two pioneers in the theory and practice of CLP. This book represents a state-of-the-art and comprehensive coverage of the methodology of CLP. It is essential reading for new students, and an essential reference for practioners.

Joxan Jaffar, National University of Singapore

CONSTRAINT LOGIC PROGRAMMING
USING ECL^{i}PS^e

KRZYSZTOF R. APT AND MARK WALLACE

CAMBRIDGE
UNIVERSITY PRESS

CAMBRIDGE
UNIVERSITY PRESS

University Printing House, Cambridge CB2 8BS, United Kingdom

One Liberty Plaza, 20th Floor, New York, NY 10006, USA

477 Williamstown Road, Port Melbourne, VIC 3207, Australia

314-321, 3rd Floor, Plot 3, Splendor Forum, Jasola District Centre, New Delhi - 110025, India

103 Penang Road, #05-06/07, Visioncrest Commercial, Singapore 238467

Cambridge University Press is part of the University of Cambridge.

It furthers the University's mission by disseminating knowledge in the pursuit of education, learning and research at the highest international levels of excellence.

www.cambridge.org
Information on this title: www.cambridge.org/9780521866286

© Cambridge University Press 2007

First published 2007

A catalogue record for this publication is available from the British Library

ISBN 978-0-521-86628-6 Hardback

Contents

v

Introduction

The subject of this book is constraint logic programming, and we will present it using the open source programming system ECL^iPS^e, available at http://www.eclipse-clp.org. This approach to programming combines two programming paradigms: logic programming and constraint programming. So to explain it we first discuss the origins of these two programming paradigms.[1]

Logic programming

Logic programming has roots in the influential approach to automated theorem proving based on the resolution method due to Alan Robinson. In his fundamental paper, Robinson [1965], he introduced the resolution principle, the notion of unification and a unification algorithm. Using his resolution method one can *prove* theorems formulated as formulas of first-order logic, so to get a 'Yes' or 'No' answer to a question. What is missing is the possibility to *compute* answers to a question.

The appropriate step to overcome this limitation was suggested by Robert Kowalski. In Kowalski [1974] he proposed a modified version of the resolution that deals with a a subset of first-order logic but allows one to generate a substitution that satisfies the original formula. This substitution can then be interpreted as a result of a computation. This approach became known as **logic programming**. A number of other proposals aiming to achieve the same goal, viz. to compute with the first-order logic, were proposed around the same time, but logic programming turned out to be the simplest one and most versatile.

In parallel, Alain Colmerauer with his colleagues worked on a program-

---

[1] In what follows we refer to the final articles discussing the mentioned programming languages. This explains the small discrepancies in the dateline.

ming language for natural language processing based on automated theorem proving. This ultimately led in 1973 to creation of **Prolog**. Kowalski and Colmerauer with his team often interacted in the period 1971–1973, which explains the relation between their contributions, see Colmerauer and Roussel [1996]. Prolog can be seen as a practical realisation of the idea of logic programming. It started as a programming language for applications in natural language processing, but soon after, thanks to contributions of several researchers, it was successfully transformed into a general purpose programming language.

Colmerauer, when experimenting with Prolog, realised some of its important limitations. For example, one could solve in it equations between terms (by means of unification) but not equations between strings. Using the current terminology, Prolog supports only one constraint solver. This led Colmerauer to design a series of successors, Prolog II, Prolog III, and Prolog IV. Each of them represents an advance in the logic programming paradigm towards constraint programming. In particular Prolog III, see Colmerauer [1990], included a support in the form of solving constraints over Booleans, reals and lists and can be viewed as the first realisation of constraint logic programming.

Constraint programming

Let us turn now our attention to **constraint programming**. The formal concept of a **constraint** was used originally in physics and combinatorial optimisation. It was first adopted in computer science by Ivan Sutherland in Sutherland [1963] for describing his interactive drawing system Sketchpad. In the seventies several experimental languages were proposed that used the notion of constraints and relied on the concept of constraint solving. Also in the seventies, in the field of artificial intelligence (AI), the concept of a **constraint satisfaction problem** was formulated and used to describe problems in computer vision. Further, starting with Montanari [1974] and Mackworth [1977], the concept of **constraint propagation** was identified as a crucial way of coping with the combinatorial explosion when solving constraint satisfaction problems using top-down search.

Top-down search is a generic name for a set of search procedures in which one attempts to construct a solution by systematically trying to extend a partial solution through the addition of constraints. In the simplest case, each such constraint assigns a value to another variable. Common to most top-down search procedures is **backtracking**, which can be traced back to the nineteenth century. In turn, the **branch and bound search**, a top-down search concerned with optimisation, was defined first in the context of combinatorial optimisation.

In the eighties the first constraint programming languages of importance were proposed and implemented. The most significant were the languages based on the logic programming paradigm. They involve an extension of logic programming by the notion of constraints. The main reason for the success of this approach to constraint programming is that constraints and logic programming predicates are both, mathematically, relations; backtracking is automatically available; and the variables are viewed as unknowns in the sense of algebra. The latter is in contrast to the imperative programming in which the variables are viewed as changing, but each time known entities, as in calculus.

The resulting paradigm is called *constraint logic programming*. As mentioned above, Prolog III is an example of a programming language realising this paradigm. The term was coined in the influential paper Jaffar and Lassez [1987] that introduced the operational model and semantics for this approach and formed a basis for the CLP($\mathcal{R}$) language that provided support for solving constraints on reals, see Jaffar et al. [1992].

Another early constraint logic programming language is CHIP, see Dincbas et al. [1988] and for a book coverage Van Hentenryck [1989]. CHIP incorporated the concept of a constraint satisfaction problem into the logic programming paradigm by using constraint variables ranging over user-defined finite domains. During the computation the values of the constraint variables are not known, only their current domains. If a variable domain shrinks to one value, then that is the final value of the variable. CHIP also relied on top-down search techniques originally introduced in AI.

The language was developed at the European Computer-Industry Research Centre (ECRC) in Munich. This brings us to the next stage in our historical overview.

ECL^{i}PS^e

ECRC was set up in 1984 by three European companies to explore the development of advanced reasoning techniques applicable to practical problems. In particular three programming systems were designed and implemented. One enabled complex problems to be solved on multiprocessor hardware, and eventually on a network of machines. The second supported advanced database techniques for intelligent processing in data-intensive applications. The third system was CHIP. All three systems were built around a common foundation of logic programming.

In 1991 the three systems were merged and ECL^{i}PS^e was born. The constraint programming features of ECL^{i}PS^e were initially based on the CHIP system, which was spun out from ECRC at that time in a separate company. Over the next 15 years the constraint solvers and solver interfaces supported by ECL^{i}PS^e have been continuously extended in response to users' requirements.

The first released interface to an external state-of-the-art linear and mixed integer programming package was in 1997. The integration of the finite domain solver and linear programming solver, supporting hybrid algorithms, came in 2000. In 2001 the `ic` library was released. It supports constraints on Booleans, integers and reals and meets the important demands of practical use: it is sound, scalable, robust and orthogonal. ECL^{i}PS^e also includes as libraries some constraint logic programming languages, for example CLP($\mathcal{R}$), that were developed separately. By contrast with the constraint solving facilities, the parallel programming and database facilities of ECL^{i}PS^e have been much less used, and over the years some functionality has been dropped from the system.

The ECL^{i}PS^e team was involved in a number of European research projects, especially the Esprit project CHIC – Constraint Handling in Industry and Commerce (1991–1994). Since the termination of ECRC's research activities in 1996, ECL^{i}PS^e has actively been further developed at the Centre for Planning and Resource Control at Imperial College in London (IC-Parc), with funding from International Computers Ltd (ICL), the UK Engineering and Physical Sciences Research Council, and the Esprit project CHIC-2 – Creating Hybrid Algorithms for Industry and Commerce (1996–1999). The Esprit projects played an important role in focussing ECL^{i}PS^e development. In particular they emphasised the importance of the end user, and the time and skills needed to learn constraint programming and to develop large scale efficient and correct programs.

In 1999, the commercial rights to ECL^{i}PS^e were transferred to IC-Parc's spin-off company Parc Technologies, which applied ECL^{i}PS^e in its optimisation products and provided funding for its maintenance and continued development. In August 2004, Parc Technologies, and with it the ECL^{i}PS^e platform, was acquired by Cisco Systems.

ECL^{i}PS^e is in use at hundreds of institutions for teaching and research all over the world, and continues to be freely available for education and research purposes. It has been exploited in a variety of applications by academics around the world, including production planning, transportation scheduling, bioinformatics, optimisation of contracts, and many others. It is also being used to develop commercial optimisation software for Cisco.

Overview of the book

In this book we explain constraint logic programming using ECL^iPS^e. Since ECL^iPS^e extends Prolog, we explain the latter first. The reader familiar with Prolog may skip the first five chapters or treat them as a short reference manual.

In Part I of the book we focus on the logic programming paradigm. We begin by introducing in **Chapter 1** a subset of Prolog called pure Prolog and explaining the underlying computation model. In **Chapter 2** we clarify the programming features implicitly supported by pure Prolog by discussing a toy procedural programming language and explaining how pure Prolog can be translated into it.

Part II is devoted to a short exposition of Prolog. In **Chapter 3** we explain the Prolog approach to arithmetic. In particular, arithmetic constraints are allowed, but only for testing. We call constraints used in this way *passive*. In **Chapter 4** we discuss control in Prolog. Also, we explain there how Prolog supports meta-programming, i.e., the possibility of writing programs that use other programs as data. Next, in **Chapter 5** we explain how Prolog allows us to inspect, compare and decompose terms. This exposition of Prolog is incomplete: the standard Prolog has 102 built-ins and we cover only those we need later.[2]

Part III begins with a primer on constraint programming, provided in **Chapter 6**. We introduce here the concepts of constraints, constraint satisfaction problems (CSPs) and constraint optimisation problems (COPs), and discuss the basic techniques used to solve CSPs and COPs. Then in **Chapter 7** we return to ECL^iPS^e by introducing a large suite of iterators that allow us to write programs without recursion. They are extensively used in the remainder of the book. Next, in **Chapter 8** we study the top-down search in presence of passive constraints by considering search algorithms for both complete and incomplete search.

One of the limitations of Prolog is that arithmetic constraints, when selected too early cause a run-time error. In **Chapter 9** we introduce the **suspend** library of ECL^iPS^e that allows us to circumvent this problem by automatically delaying various types of constraints, including arithmetic constraints, until they reduce to tests.

Part IV forms the main part of the book. We begin by introducing in **Chapter 10** two ECL^iPS^e libraries, **sd** and **ic**, that treat constraints as *active constraints*, by allowing their evaluation to affect their variables.

---

[2] For those wishing to acquire the full knowledge of Prolog we recommend Bratko [2001] and Sterling and Shapiro [1994].

This is achieved through the process of **constraint propagation**. In **Chapter 11** we explain how to combine the constraint propagation with ECL^{i}PS^e facilities that support top-down search. Next, in **Chapter 12** we discuss the `branch_and_bound` library that allows us to solve COPs using ECL^{i}PS^e.

The last two chapters deal with constraints on continuous variables. In **Chapter 13** we explain how the approach to solving CSPs and COPs based on the constraint propagation and top-down search can be modified to deal with such constraints. Finally, in **Chapter 14** we consider linear and non-linear constraints over continuous and integer variables. In ECL^{i}PS^e they are solved using the `eplex` library that provides an interface to a package for solving mixed integer programming problems.

Resources on ECL^{i}PS^e

The main website of ECL^{i}PS^e is `www.eclipse-clp.org`. It provides a substantial body of documentation to aid users in getting the most out of the system.

There are a tutorial and three manuals: a User Manual, a Reference Manual and a Constraint Library Manual. There are documents about ECL^{i}PS^e embedding and interfacing, and about applications development in ECL^{i}PS^e. Also there are example ECL^{i}PS^e programs for solving a variety of puzzles and applications in planning and scheduling. Finally, there is a great deal of on-line help available, covering all (currently 2644) built-in predicates.

The programs presented in this book can be found at `www.cwi.nl/~apt/eclipse`.

Acknowledgements

Krzysztof Apt would like to thank his colleagues who during their stay at CWI used ECL^{i}PS^e and helped him to understand it better. These are: Sebastian Brand, Sandro Etalle, Eric Monfroy and Andrea Schaerf. Also, he would like to warmly thank three people who have never used ECL^{i}PS^e but without whose support this book would never have been written. These are: Alma, Daniel and Ruth.

Mark Wallace offers this book as a testament both to the ECRC CHIP team, who set the ball rolling, to Micha Meier at ECRC, and to the IC-Parc ECL^{i}PS^e team, including Andy Cheadle, Andrew Eremin, Warwick Harvey, Stefano Novello, Andrew Sadler, Kish Shen, and Helmut Simonis – of both the CHIP and ECL^{i}PS^e fame – who have designed, built and maintained the functionality described herein. Last but not least, he thanks Joachim Schimpf, a great colleague, innovative thinker and brilliant software engineer, who has shaped the whole ECL^{i}PS^e system.

Since dragging his reluctant family halfway round the world to Australia, Mark has buried himself in his study and left them to it. With the completion of this book he looks forward to sharing some proper family weekends with Duncan, Tessa and Toby and his long-suffering wonderful wife Ingrid.

The authors acknowledge helpful comments by Andrea Schaerf, Joachim Schimpf, Maarten van Emden and Peter Zoeteweij. Also, they would like to thank the School of Computing of the National University of Singapore for making it possible for them to meet there on three occasions and to work together on this book. The figures were kindly prepared by Ren Yuan using the **xfig** drawing program.

*To Alma, Daniel and Ruth and
to Duncan, Tessa, Toby and Ingrid*

Part I

Logic programming paradigm

1

Logic programming and pure Prolog

1.1 Introduction

L OGIC PROGRAMMING (LP in short) is a simple yet powerful formalism suitable for computing and for knowledge representation. It provides a formal basis for **Prolog** and for **constraint logic programming**. Other successful applications of LP include **deductive databases**, an extension of relational databases by rules, a computational approach to machine learning called **inductive logic programming**, and a computational account of various forms of reasoning, in particular of **non-monotonic reasoning** and **meta-reasoning**.

The **logic programming paradigm** substantially differs from other programming paradigms. The reason for this is that it has its roots in automated theorem proving, from which it borrowed the notion of a deduction. What is new is that in the process of deduction some values are computed. When stripped to the bare essentials, this paradigm can be summarised by the following three features:

- any variable can stand for a number or a string, but also a list, a tree, a record or even a procedure or program,

- during program execution variables are constrained, rather than being assigned a value and updated,
- program executions include choice points, where computation can take alternative paths; if the constraints become inconsistent, the program backtracks to the previous open choice point and tries another path.

In this chapter we discuss the logic programming framework and the corresponding small subset of Prolog, usually called **pure Prolog**. This will allow us to set up a base over which we shall define in the successive chapters a more realistic subset of Prolog supporting in particular arithmetic and various control features. At a later stage we shall discuss various additions to Prolog provided by ECL^iPS^e, including libraries that support constraint programming.

We structure the chapter by focussing in turn on each of the above three items. Also we clarify the intended meaning of pure Prolog programs.[1] Consequently, we discuss in turn

- the objects of computation and their syntax,
- the meaning of pure Prolog programs,
- the accumulation of constraints during program execution, and
- the creation of choice points during program execution and backtracking.

1.2 Syntax

Syntactic conventions always play an important role in the discussion of any programming paradigm and logic programming is no exception in this matter. In this section we discuss the syntax of Prolog.

Full Prolog syntactic conventions are highly original and very powerful. Their full impact is little known outside of the logic programming community. We shall discuss these novel features in Chapters 3 and 4.

By the 'objects of computation' we mean anything that can be denoted by a Prolog variable. These are not only numbers, lists and so on, but also compound structures and even other variables or programs.

Formally, the objects of computation are **base terms**, which consists of:

- **variables**, denoted by strings starting with an upper case letter or '_' (the underscore), for example X3 is a variable,
- **numbers**, which will be dealt with in Chapter 3,

---

[1] To clarify the terminology: **logic programs** are pure Prolog programs written using the logical and not Prolog notation. In what follows we rather focus on Prolog notation and, as a result, on pure Prolog programs.

- **atoms**, denoted by sequences of characters starting with a lower case letter, for example x4 is an atom. Any sequence of characters put between single quotes, even admitting spaces, is also an atom, for example 'My Name',

and **compound terms**, which comprise a **functor** and a number of **arguments**, each of which is itself a (base or compound) **term**.

By a **constant** we mean a number or an atom. Special case of terms are **ground terms** which are terms in which no variable appears. In general, the qualification 'ground', which we will also use for other syntactic objects, simply means 'containing no variables'.

In Chapter 4 we shall explain that thanks to the **ambivalent syntax** facility of Prolog programs can also be viewed as compound terms. This makes it possible to interpret **programs as data**, which is an important feature of Prolog.

In the standard syntax for compound terms the functor is written first, followed by the arguments separated by commas, and enclosed in round brackets. For example the term with functor f and arguments a, b and c is written f(a,b,c). Similarly, a more complex example with functor h and three arguments:

  (i) the variable A,
  (ii) the compound term f(g,'Twenty',X),
  (iii) the variable X,

is written h(A,f(g,'Twenty',X),X).

Some compound terms can be also written using an infix notation. Next, we define goals, queries, clauses and programs. Here is a preliminary overview.

- A program is made up of procedures.
- A procedure is made up of clauses, each terminated by the period '.'.
- A **clause** is either a fact or a rule.
- There is no special procedure such as main and a user activates the program by means of a query.

Now we present the details.

- First we introduce an **atomic goal** which is the basic component from which the clauses and queries are built. It has a **predicate** and a number of arguments. The predicate has a **predicate name** and a **predicate arity**. The predicate name is, syntactically, an atom. The arguments are placed after the predicate name, separated by commas and surrounded by round brackets. The number of arguments is the arity of the predicate.

An example of an atomic goal is `p(a,X)`. Here the predicate name is `p` and its arity is 2. We often write `p/n` for the predicate with name `p` and arity n.

- A **query** (or a **goal**) is a sequence of atomic goals terminated by the period '`.`'. A query is called **atomic** if it consists of exactly one atomic goal.
- A **rule** comprises a **head**, which is an atomic goal, followed by '`:-`', followed by the **body** which is a non-empty query, and is terminated by the period '`.`'.

 An example of a rule is

```
p(b,Y) :- q(Y), r(Y,c).
```

A rule contributes to the definition of the predicate of its head, so this example rule contributes to the definition of `p/2`. We also call this a rule for `p/2`. Rule bodies may contain some atomic goals with a binary predicate and two arguments written in the infix form, for example `X = a`, whose predicate is `=/2`.

- A **fact** is an atomic goal terminated by the period '`.`'. For example

```
p(a,b).
```

 is a fact. This fact also contributes to the definition of `p/2`.

- A sequence of clauses for the same predicate makes a **procedure**. The procedure provides a **definition** for the predicate.

 For example, here is a definition for the predicate `p/2`:

```
p(a,b).
p(b,Y) :- q(Y), r(Y,c).
```

- A **pure Prolog program** is a finite sequence of procedures, for example

```
p(a,b).
p(b,Y) :- q(Y), r(Y,c).
q(a).
r(a,c).
```

So a program is simply a sequence of clauses.

In what follows, when discussing specific queries and rules in a running text we shall drop the final period '`.`'.

Before leaving this discussion of the syntax of pure Prolog, we point out a small but important feature of variable naming. If a variable appears more than once in a query (or similarly, more than once in a program clause), then each occurrence denotes the *same* object of computation. However, Prolog also allows so-called **anonymous variables**, written as '_' (underscore). These variables have a special interpretation, because each occurrence of '_' in a query or in a clause is interpreted as a *different* variable. That is why we talk about the anonymous variable*s* and not about the anonymous variable. So by definition each anonymous variable occurs in a query or a clause only once.

Anonymous variables form a simple and elegant device and, as we shall see, their use increases the readability of programs in a remarkable way. ECL^{i}PS^e and many modern versions of Prolog encourage the use of anonymous variables by issuing a warning if a non-anonymous variable is encountered that occurs only once in a clause. This warning can be suppressed by using a normal variable that starts with the underscore symbol '_', for example _X.

Prolog has several (about one hundred) built-in predicates, so predicates with a predefined meaning. The clauses, the heads of which refer to these built-in predicates, are ignored. This ensures that the built-in predicates cannot be redefined. Thus one can rely on their prescribed meaning. In ECL^{i}PS^e and several versions of Prolog a warning is issued in case an attempt at redefining a built-in predicate is encountered.

So much about Prolog syntax for a moment. We shall return to it in Chapters 3 and 4 where we shall discuss several novel and powerful features of Prolog syntax.

1.3 The meaning of a program

Pure Prolog programs can be interpreted as statements in the first-order logic. This interpretation makes it easy to understand the behaviour of a program. In particular, it will help us to understand the results of evaluating a query w.r.t. to a program. In the remainder of this section we assume that the reader is familiar with the first-order logic.

Let us start by interpreting a simple program fact, such as p(a,b). It contributes to the definition of the predicate p/2. Its arguments are two atoms, a and b.

We interpret the predicate p/2 as a relation symbol p of arity 2. The atoms a and b are interpreted as logical constants a and b. A logical constant denotes a value. Since, in the interpretation of pure Prolog programs, different constants denote different values, we can think of each constant denoting itself. Consequently we interpret the fact p(a,b) as the atomic formula $p(a, b)$.

The arguments of facts may also be variables and compound terms. Consider for example the fact `p(a,f(b))`. The interpretation of the compound term `f(b)` is a logical expression, in which the unary function f is applied to the logical constant b. Under the interpretation of pure Prolog programs, the denotations of any two distinct ground terms are themselves distinct.[2] Consequently we can think of ground terms as denoting themselves, and so we interpret the fact `p(a,f(b))` as the atomic formula $p(a, f(b))$.

The next fact has a variable argument: `p(a,Y)`. We view it as a statement that for all ground terms t the atomic formula $p(a, t)$ is true. So we interpret it as the universally quantified formula $\forall Y. \, p(a, Y)$.

With this interpretation there can be no use in writing the procedure

```
p(a,Y).
p(a,b).
```

because the second fact is already covered by the first, more general fact.

Finally we should mention that facts with no arguments are also admitted. Accordingly we can assert the fact `p`. Its logical interpretation is the proposition p.

In general, we interpret a fact by simply changing the font from `teletype` to *italic* and by preceding it by the universal quantification of all variables that appear in it.

The interpretation of a rule involves a logical ***implication***. For example the rule

```
p :- q.
```

states that if q is true then p is true.

As another example, consider the ground rule

```
p(a,b) :- q(a,f(c)), r(d).
```

Its interpretation is as follows. If $q(a, f(c))$ and $r(d)$ are both true, then $p(a, b)$ is also true, i.e., $q(a, f(c)) \wedge r(d) \rightarrow p(a, b)$.

Rules with variables need a little more thought. The rule

```
p(X) :- q.
```

states that if q is true, then $p(t)$ is true for any ground term t. So logically this rule is interpreted as $q \rightarrow \forall X. \, p(X)$. This is equivalent to the formula $\forall X. \, (q \rightarrow p(X))$.

If the variable in the head also appears in the body, the meaning is the same. The rule

---

[2] This will no longer hold for arithmetic expressions which will be covered in Chapter 3.

```
p(X) :- q(X).
```

states that for any ground term t, if $q(t)$ is true, then $p(t)$ is also true. Therefore logically this rule is interpreted as $\forall X.\,(q(X) \to p(X))$.

Finally, we consider rules in which variables appear in the body but not in the head, for example

```
p(a) :- q(X).
```

This rule states that if we can find a ground term t for which $q(t)$ is true, then $p(a)$ is true. Logically this rule is interpreted as $\forall X.\,(q(X) \to p(a))$, which is equivalent to the formula $(\exists X.\,q(X)) \to p(a)$.

Given an atomic goal A denote its interpretation by $\tilde{A}$. Any ground rule H :- $B_1, \ldots, B_n$ is interpreted as the implication $\tilde{B}_1 \wedge \ldots \wedge \tilde{B}_n \to \tilde{H}$. In general, all rules H :- $B_1, \ldots, B_n$ have the same, uniform, logical interpretation. If $\mathbf{V}$ is the list of the variables appearing in the rule, its logical interpretation is $\forall \mathbf{V}.\,(\tilde{B}_1 \wedge \ldots \wedge \tilde{B}_n \to \tilde{H})$.

This interpretation of ',' (as $\wedge$) and ':-' (as $\to$) leads to so-called ***declarative interpretation*** of pure Prolog programs that focusses – through their translation to the first-order logic – on their semantic meaning.

The computational interpretation of pure Prolog is usually called ***procedural interpretation***. It will be discussed in the next section. In this interpretation the comma ',' separating atomic goals in a query or in a body of a rule is interpreted as the semicolon symbol ';' of the imperative programming and ':-' as (essentially) the separator between the procedure header and body.

1.4 Computing with equations

We defined in Section 1.2 the computational objects over which computations of pure Prolog programs take place. The next step is to explain how variables and computational objects become constrained to be equal to each other, in the form of the answers. This is the closest that logic programming comes to assigning values to variables.

1.4.1 Querying pure Prolog programs

The computation process of pure Prolog involves a program P against which we pose a query Q. This can lead to a successful, failed or diverging computation (which of course we wish to avoid).

A successful computation yields an *answer*, which specifies constraints on the query variables under which the query is true. In this subsection we describe how these constraints are accumulated during query processing. In the next subsection we will describe how the constraints are checked for consistency and answers are extracted from them.

The constraints accumulated by Prolog are equations whose conjunction logically entails the truth of the query. To clarify the discussion we will use the following simple program:

```
p(X) :- q(X,a).
q(Y,Y).
```

Let us first discuss the answer to the atomic query

```
q(W,a).
```

The definition of the predicate q/2 comprises just the single fact q(Y,Y). Clearly the query can only succeed if W = a.

Inside Prolog, however, this constraint is represented as an equation between two atomic goals: q(W,a) = q(Y1,Y1). The atomic goal q(W,a) at the left-hand side of the equation is just the original query. For the fact q(Y,Y), however, a new variable Y1 has been introduced. This is not important for the current example, but it is necessary in general because of possible variable clashes. This complication is solved by using a different variable each time. Accordingly, our first query succeeds under the constraint q(W,a) = q(Y1,Y1).

Now consider the query

```
p(a).
```

This time we need to use a rule instead of a fact. Again a new variable is introduced for each use of the rule, so this first time it becomes:

```
p(X1) :- q(X1,a).
```

To answer this query, Prolog first adds the constraint p(a) = p(X1), which constrains the query to match the definition of p/1. Further, the query p(a) succeeds only if the body q(X1,a) succeeds, which it does under the additional constraint q(X1,a) = q(Y1,Y1). The complete sequence of constraints under which the query succeeds is therefore p(a) = p(X1), q(X1,a) = q(Y1,Y1). Informally we can observe that these constraints hold if all the variables take the value a.

Consider now the query:

```
p(b).
```

Reasoning as before, we find the query would succeed under the constraints: p(b) = p(X1), q(X1,a) = q(Y1,Y1). In this case, however, there are no possible values for the variables which would satisfy these constraints. Y1 would have to be equal both to a and to b, which is impossible. Consequently the query fails.

Next consider a non-atomic query

p(a), q(W,a).

The execution of this query proceeds in two stages. First, as we already saw, p(a) succeeds under the constraints p(a) = p(X1), q(X1,a) = q(Y1,Y1), and secondly q(W,a) succeeds under the constraint q(W,a) = q(Y2,Y2). The complete sequence of constraints is therefore: p(a) = p(X1), q(X1,a) = q(Y1,Y1), q(W,a) = q(Y2,Y2). Informally these constraints are satisfied if all the variables take the value a.

A failing non-atomic query is:

p(W), q(W,b).

Indeed, this would succeed under the constraints p(W) = p(X1), q(X1,a) = q(Y1,Y1), q(W,b) = q(Y2,Y2). However, for this to be satisfied W would have to take both the value a (to satisfy the first two equations) and b (to satisfy the last equation), so the constraints cannot be satisfied and the query fails.

Operationally, the constraints are added to the sequence during computation, and tested for consistency immediately. Thus the query

p(b), q(W,b).

fails already during the evaluation of the first atomic query, because already at this stage the accumulated constraints are inconsistent. Consequently the second atomic query is not evaluated at all.

1.4.2 Most general unifiers

The Prolog system has a built-in algorithm which can detect whether a sequence of equations between atomic goals is consistent or not. In general, two outcomes are possible. Either the algorithm returns a failure, because some atomic goals cannot be made equal (for example p(X,a) = p(b,X)), or it yields a positive answer in the form of a **substitution**, which is a set of equations of the form *Variable = Term* such that each variable occurs at most once at a left-hand side of an equation. The resulting set of equations is called a **unifier**.

For example, the equation p(X,f(X,Y),c) = p(V,W,V) has a unifier {V = c, X = c, W = f(c,Y)}. Also {V = c, X = c, W = f(c,a)} is a unifier but the first one is *more general* in a sense that can be made precise. Such a most general substitution that subsumes all others is called a ***most general unifier*** (usually abbreviated to ***mgu***). If an equation between two atomic goals has a unifier, the atomic goals are called ***unifiable***.

The problem of deciding whether a sequence of equations between atomic goals has a unifier is called the ***unification problem***. The following result was established by A. Robinson.

Unification theorem *An algorithm exists, called a **unification algorithm**, that for a sequence of equations between atomic goals determines whether they are consistent and if they do, it produces their mgu.*

An ***answer*** to a query is then any most general unifier of the sequence of constraints accumulated during query evaluation.

An elegant unification algorithm was introduced by M. Martelli and U. Montanari. Given a term t we denote here the set of its variables by $Var(t)$.

MARTELLI–MONTANARI ALGORITHM

Non-deterministically choose from the set of equations an equation of a form below and perform the associated action.

(1) $f(s_1, ..., s_n) = f(t_1, ..., t_n)$ *replace by the equations* $s_1 = t_1, ..., s_n = t_n,$

(2) $f(s_1, ..., s_n) = g(t_1, ..., t_m)$ where $f \not\equiv g$ *halt with failure,*

(3) $x = x$ *delete the equation,*

(4) $t = x$ where t is not a variable   *replace by the equation* $x = t,$

(5) $x = t$ where $x \notin Var(t)$ and x occurs elsewhere   *perform the substitution* $\{x/t\}$ *on all other equations*

(6) $x = t$ where $x \in Var(t)$ and $x \not\equiv t$ *halt with failure.*

The algorithm starts with the original sequence of equations and terminates when no action can be performed or when failure arises. In case of success we obtain the desired mgu.

Note that in the borderline case, when $n = 0$, action (1) includes the case $c = c$ for every constant c which leads to deletion of such an equation. In addition, action (2) includes the case of two different constants and the cases where a constant is compared with a term that is neither a constant or a variable.

To illustrate the operation of this algorithm consider some examples. To facilitate the reading the selected equations are underlined.

(i) Consider the equation

```
p(k(Z, f(X,b,Z))) = p(k(h(X), f(g(a),Y,Z))).
```

Applying action (1) twice yields the set

$$\{Z = h(X), \underline{f(X, b, Z) = f(g(a), Y, Z)}\}.$$

Choosing the second equation again action (1) applies and yields

$$\{Z = h(X), X = g(a), \underline{b = Y}, Z = Z\}.$$

Choosing the third equation action (4) applies and yields

$$\{Z = h(X), X = g(a), Y = b, \underline{Z = Z}\}.$$

Now, choosing the last equation action (3) applies and yields

$$\{Z = h(X), \underline{X = g(a)}, Y = b\}.$$

Finally, choosing the second equation action (5) applies and yields

$$\{Z = h(g(a)), X = g(a), Y = b\}.$$

At this stage no action applies, so $\{Z = h(g(a)), X = g(a), Y = b\}$ is an mgu of the atomic goals `p(k(Z, f(X,b,Z)))` and `p(k(h(X), f(g(a),Y,Z)))`.

(ii) Consider now the equation

```
p(k(h(a), f(X,b,Z))) = p(k(h(b), f(g(a),Y,Z))).
```

Again applying action (1) twice yields the set

$$\{\underline{h(a) = h(b)}, f(X, b, Z) = f(g(a), Y, Z)\}.$$

Next, choosing the first equation action (1) applies again and yields

$$\{\underline{a = b}, f(X, b, Z) = f(g(a), Y, Z)\}.$$

Choosing again the first equation action (2) applies and a failure arises. So the atomic goals `p(k(h(a), f(X,b,Z)))` and `p(k(h(b), f(g(a),Y,Z)))` are not unifiable.

(iii) Finally, consider the equation

```
p(k(Z, f(X,b,Z))) = p(k(h(X), f(g(Z),Y,Z))).
```

Let us try to repeat the choices made in (i). Applying action (1) twice we get the set

$$\{Z = h(X), f(X, b, Z) = f(g(Z), Y, Z)\}.$$

Next, choosing the second equation action (1) applies again and yields

$$\{Z = h(X), X = g(Z), \underline{b = Y}, Z = Z\}.$$

Choosing the third equation action (4) applies and yields

$$\{Z = h(X), X = g(Z), Y = b, \underline{Z = Z}\}.$$

Now, choosing the fourth equation action (3) applies and yields

$$\{Z = h(X), \underline{X = g(Z)}, Y = b\}.$$

Finally, choosing the second equation action (5) applies and yields

$$\{\underline{Z = h(g(Z))}, X = g(Z), Y = b\}.$$

But now choosing the first equation action (6) applies and a failure arises. Hence the atomic goals `p(k(Z, f(X,b,Z)))` and `p(k(h(X),f(g(Z),Y,Z)))` are not unifiable.

1.4.3 Choice points and backtracking

Until now we did not fully explain what happens during a program execution when an equation, for instance `q(b,a) = q(Y,Y)`, fails. When such an equation is generated during the execution of a query, backtracking is triggered, a process we first illustrate using the following simple program:

```
p(X) :- X = a.
p(X) :- X = b.
```

Each of the two rules in this program has a body consisting of an atomic goal, with predicate `=/2` written in the infix form. The behaviour of this predicate is built into the underlying implementation and will be discussed in the next section. Its logical interpretation is, of course, equality. When we pose the query

```
p(a).
```

against this program, it therefore succeeds, returning the answer "Yes".

Next, consider what happens when we pose the query

```
p(b).
```

According to the computation process explained in Subsection 1.4.1, using the first rule we accumulate two equations, p(b) = p(X1), X1 = a, which are inconsistent. This might suggest that the answer to the query p(b) is "No". However, this disregards the fact that in the program the predicate p/2 is defined by means of two clauses.

When the first equation, p(b) = p(X1), is considered a *choice point* is created, which consists of the second clause, p(X1) :- X1 = b, and the current state (in which values of all the variables are recorded). Now when the failure arises during the execution that starts with the selection of the first clause, the computation returns to the choice point, the state is restored to the one stored and the second clause is selected. So all the substitutions performed since the creation of this choice point are undone. Now we accumulate the equations p(b) = p(X1), X1 = b, which are consistent. So the answer is "Yes".

Finally, when we pose the query

p(c).

against this program, we get the answer "No" because both X1 = a and X1 = b fail under the initial condition X1 = c.

In general, if a predicate is defined by n clauses with $n > 1$, then upon selection of the first clause all the other clauses are kept in a choice point. When during the execution which starts by selecting the first clause a failure arises, the computation returns to the last created choice point and resumes in the state stored there but with the next clause stored in this choice point. If the last clause is selected, the choice point is removed. So when a failure arises during the execution that involves the last clause, the computation resumes at the one before last choice point, if such a choice point exists and otherwise a failure results. This computation process is called *backtracking*.

1.5 Prolog: the first steps

1.5.1 Prolog: how to run it

It is useful at this stage to get an idea how one interacts with a Prolog system. There are two ways of running a Prolog program using ECL^{i}PS^e. The first is using tkeclipse, which provides an interactive graphical user interface to the ECL^{i}PS^e compiler and system. The second is a more traditional command line interface accessed by invoking just eclipse.

To start TkECL^{i}PS^e, either type the command tkeclipse at an operating system command line prompt, or select TkECL^{i}PS^e from the program menu,

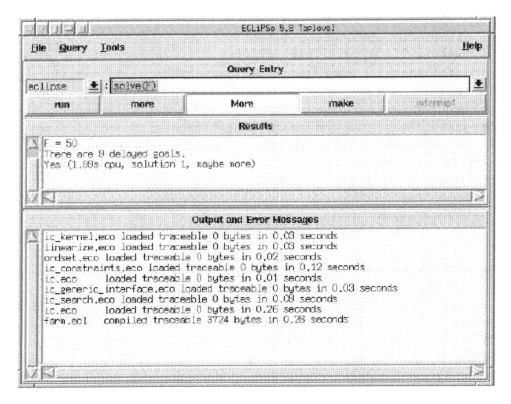

Fig. 1.1 Top level of TkECL^{i}PS^e

Help for TkECL^{i}PS^e and its component tools is available from the **Help** menu in the TkECL^{i}PS^e window.

To write your programs you need an editor. From the editor, save your program as a plain text file, and then you can compile the program into ECL^{i}PS^e. To compile the program in TkECL^{i}PS^e, select the **Compile** option from the **File** menu. This will bring up a file selection dialogue, from which you select the file you want to compile and click on the **Open** button. This will compile the file, and any other it depends on.

If you have edited a file and want to compile it again (together with any other files that may have changed), you just click on the **make** button. Now a query to the program can be submitted, by typing it into the **Goal Entry** field.

The idea is that the system evaluates the query with respect to the program read-in and reports an answer. There are three possible outcomes.

- The query succeeds.

  Then an answer is printed followed by "**Yes**". The answer corresponds to the logical answer, so it shows for what values of the variables the query becomes true.

  Assuming the query has one or more variables, another answer can be obtained by clicking on the **more** button.

- The query fails or a request to produce the next answer fails.

  Then the answer "**No**" is printed.

- The query diverges.

  You guessed it: then nothing happens. In this case, you can interrupt the execution by clicking on the **interrupt** button.

In the command line interface the interaction starts by typing `eclipse`. The ECL^{i}PS^e system replies by the prompt "`[eclipse 1]:`". Now, assuming that the program is stored in the file `filename.ecl` it can be read in by typing `[filename]` (so without the suffix '`.ecl`'), followed by the period '`.`'. (ECL^{i}PS^e also supports Prolog suffix '`.pl`'). Assuming that the program is syntactically correct, the system replies with the answer "**Yes**" followed by the prompt "`[eclipse 2]:`". Now a query to the program can be submitted (so with the period '`.`' at its end). If the query succeeds, typing the **Enter** key terminates the computation, whereas typing '`;`' is interpreted as the request to produce the next answer. Finally, typing "`halt.`" (which is a propositional built-in) finishes the interaction with the system.

To illustrate these matters let us return to the program

```
p(X) :- q(X,a).
q(Y,Y).
```

discussed in Subsection 1.4.1. Assume it is stored in the file `example1.ecl`. We have then the following interaction with ECL^{i}PS^e, where we reconsider the previously discussed queries.

```
[eclipse 1]: [example1].
example1.ecl   compiled traceable 72 bytes in 0.00 seconds

Yes (0.00s cpu)
[eclipse 2]: q(W,a).

W = a
```

```
Yes (0.00s cpu)
[eclipse 3]: p(a).

Yes (0.00s cpu)
[eclipse 4]: p(b).

No (0.00s cpu)
[eclipse 5]: p(a), q(W,a).

W = a
Yes (0.00s cpu)
[eclipse 6]: p(W), q(W,b).

No (0.00s cpu)
```

1.5.2 Unification in Prolog

Armed with the knowledge of how to execute Prolog programs let us discuss now how unification is available in Prolog. It is provided by means of the already mentioned built-in =/2 defined internally by the single fact presented in Figure 1.2.

```
% X = Y :- X and Y are unifiable.

X = X.
```

Fig. 1.2 The EQUALITY program

By ignoring the differences between the predicates and function symbols we can equally well consider equations between a pair of atomic queries. To illustrate the effect of =/2 let us return to the pairs of atomic queries discussed in Subsection 1.4.2. We have then:

```
[eclipse 7]: p(k(Z, f(X,b,Z))) = p(k(h(X), f(g(a),Y,Z))).

Z = h(g(a))
X = g(a)
Y = b
Yes (0.00s cpu)
```

For the second pair of atomic queries we get the same outcome as in Subsection 1.4.2, as well:

```
[eclipse 8]: p(k(h(a), f(X,b,Z))) = p(k(h(b), f(g(a),Y,Z))).
```

No (0.00s cpu)

However, for the third pair of atomic queries we get a puzzling answer:

```
[eclipse 9]: p(k(Z, f(X,b,Z))) = p(k(h(X), f(g(Z),Y,Z))).
```

```
Z = h(g(h(g(h(g(h(g(h(g(h(g(h(g(h(g(...)))))))))))))))))
X = g(h(g(h(g(h(g(h(g(h(g(h(g(h(g(h(...)))))))))))))))))
Y = b
Yes (0.00s cpu)
```

The point is that for the efficiency reasons unification in Prolog is implemented with the test $x \in Var(t)$ (so whether x occurs in t) in the actions (5) and (6) of the MARTELLI–MONTANARI algorithm omitted. This test is called an **occur check**. If x does occur in t, then instead of a failure a 'circular binding' is generated.

In ECL^{i}PS^e the situation is restored, by setting a specific flag on:

```
[eclipse 10]: set_flag(occur_check,on).
```

Yes (0.00s cpu)
```
[eclipse 11]: p(k(Z, f(X,b,Z))) = p(k(h(X), f(g(Z),Y,Z))).
```

No (0.00s cpu)

In practice it is very rare that this complication arises so the default is that this flag is not set.

Let us return now to the program

```
p(X) :- X = a.
p(X) :- X = b.
```

discussed in Subsection 1.4.3 and consider the query p(X):

```
[eclipse 12]: p(X).
```

```
X = a
Yes (0.00s cpu, solution 1, maybe more) ? ;
```

```
X = b
```

`Yes (0.00s cpu, solution 2)`

Here backtracking arises when the user requests more solutions by typing ';' after a solution is displayed. The computation then returns to the last created choice point. This leads to a second solution. In general, upon a request for more solutions, a computation can yield another solution, but does not have to, or it may diverge. If no choice point exists, the computation terminates.

1.5.3 Comparing unification to assignment

To better understand the unification process it is useful to reflect for a moment on the similarities and differences between the unification and the customary assignment statement present in the traditional programming languages. In the examples below, following the computational interpretation of Prolog programs we interpret the comma ',' separating the atomic goals in a query as the semicolon symbol ';'.

To avoid confusion, when discussing the assignment statement we use below the lower case letters to denote variables. Superficially, unification seems to be very similar to the assignment statement. Indeed, the query `X = 1, Y = 2` yields the same result as the sequence of the assignments `x = 1; y = 2` and in both cases we can reverse the order of the equations, respectively assignments, without affecting the outcome. However, this is about all one can say about the similarities between these two concepts. Here is a list of important differences.

- Unification can succeed or fail, while assignment can succeed or abort (for example when performing division by zero).

  However, from a failure the computation can 'recover' by backtracking (we shall clarify this matter in the next section), while abortion is 'fatal'.
- Using unification we can assign terms to variables, for example `f(a,b)`, or even terms with variables, for example `g(X,a)`.

  Variables that appear in the values assigned to other variables are called *logical variables*. The use of logical variables is a distinguishing feature of the logic programming paradigm. It is a powerful mechanism that allows us to compute a final object in stages, by passing a partially instantiated output computed by one procedure call as an input to another procedure call.
- Once a ground term, in particular, a constant, is assigned to a variable by means of unification, this variable cannot be modified anew. In contrast, if the assignment is used, then one can modify the values of the variables.

For example, the execution of the query X = 1, X = 2 yields a failure:

[eclipse 13]: X = 1, X = 2.

No (0.00s cpu)

while after performing the sequence of assignments x = 1; x = 2 the value of x is 2.

This feature of the unification is sometimes called a ***one time assignment***.

- The query of the form X = s, where X occurs in s but differs from s, always fails, while the corresponding assignment x = s succeeds or aborts.

  For example, the query X = X+1 fails, while the assignment x = x+1 leads to an increment of x. Further, the query X = X/0 fails, while the assignment x = x/0 aborts.

- Unification is symmetric, while assignment is not.

  In particular, the queries X = Y and Y = X have always the same effect, while the assignments x = y and y = x do not necessarily.

- Unification, in contrast to the assignment, can be used to assign values to several variables at the same time.

  For example, the query f(b,X) = f(Y,a) assigns a to X and b to Y (i.e., is equivalent to X = a, Y = b).

These differences between unification and the assignment statement reflect the different views of variables. In logic programming and pure Prolog variables are viewed as ***unknowns***, very much like in mathematics. This is in contrast to the imperative programming languages, such as C or Java, in which variables represent *known* but varying quantities.

1.5.4 Lists in Prolog

A data structure that supports use of sequences with a single operation on them – an insertion of an element at the front – is called a ***list***. Lists form a fundamental data structure and in Prolog special, built-in notational facilities for them are available. In particular, the pair consisting of a constant [] and a binary function symbol [.|..] is used to define them. Formally, lists in Prolog are defined inductively as follows:

- [] is a list, called the ***empty list***.
- if t is a list, then for any term h also [h | t] is a list; h is called its ***head*** and t is called its ***tail***.

For example, [s(0)|[]] and [0|[X|[]]] are lists, whereas [0|s(0)] is not, because s(0) is not a list. The tree depicted in Figure 1.3 represents the list [a|[b|[c|[]]]].

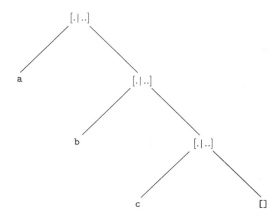

Fig. 1.3 A list

The list notation is not very readable and even short lists become difficult to parse, as the depicted list [a|[b|[c|[]]]] shows.

So the following shorthands are carried out internally in Prolog for $m \geq 1$ and $n \geq 0$, also within the subterms:

- $[s_0|[s_1, ..., s_m|t]]$ abbreviates to $[s_0, s_1, ..., s_m|t]$,
- $[s_1, ..., s_m|[t_1, ..., t_n]]$ abbreviates to $[s_1, ..., s_m, t_1, ..., t_n]$.

Thus for example, [a|[b|c]] abbreviates to [a,b|c], and the depicted list [a|[b|[c|[]]]] abbreviates to a more readable form, [a,b,c].

The following interaction with ECL^{i}PS^e shows that these simplifications are also carried out internally.

```
[eclipse 14]:  X = [a | [b | c]].

X = [a, b|c]
Yes (0.00s cpu)
[eclipse 15]: [a,b |c]  = [a | [b | c]].

Yes (0.00s cpu)
[eclipse 16]: f(X) = f([a,b,c | [d,e,f]]).

X = [a, b, c, d, e, f]
Yes (0.00s cpu)
```

```
[eclipse 17]: [a,b,c] = [a | [b, c | []]].
```

Yes (0.00s cpu)

These abbreviations are widely used in Prolog programs. Also, to enhance the readability, one uses in Prolog programs the names ending with 's' to denote variables which are meant to be instantiated to lists.

1.6 Two simple pure Prolog programs

To illustrate some basic features of Prolog programming we now consider two simple examples.

1.6.1 The BOOKS program

Consider the self-explanatory program given in Figure 1.4.

```
book(harry_potter, rowlings).
book(anna_karenina, tolstoy).
book(elements, euclid).
book(histories, herodotus).
book(constraint_logic_programming, apt).
book(constraint_logic_programming, wallace).

genre(harry_potter, fiction).
genre(anna_karenina, fiction).
genre(elements, science).
genre(histories, history).
genre(constraint_logic_programming, science).

author(Author, Genre) :- book(X, Author), genre(X, Genre).
```

Fig. 1.4 The BOOKS program

This program can be used both for testing:

```
[eclipse 18]: book(anna_karenina, tolstoy).
```

Yes (0.00s cpu)
```
[eclipse 19]: book(anna_karenina, rowlings).
```

```
No (0.00s cpu)
```

and to compute one or more solutions, like in the following two queries:

```
[eclipse 20]: author(Author, history).

Author = herodotus
Yes (0.00s cpu, solution 1, maybe more) ? ;

No (0.00s cpu)

[eclipse 21]: book(constraint_logic_programming, Author).

Author = apt
Yes (0.00s cpu, solution 1, maybe more) ? ;

Author = wallace
Yes (0.00s cpu, solution 2)
```

Recall that ';' is the user's request for more solutions.

1.6.2 The APPEND program

To illustrate the use of lists we now discuss the perhaps most often cited Prolog program. This program concatenates two lists. The inductive definition of concatenation is as follows:

- the concatenation of the empty list [] and the list ys yields the list ys,
- if the concatenation of the lists xs and ys equals zs, then the concatenation of the lists [x | xs] and ys equals [x | zs].

This translates into the program given in Figure 1.5.[3]

```
% app(Xs, Ys, Zs) :- Zs is the result of
%     concatenating the lists Xs and Ys.

app([], Ys, Ys).
app([X | Xs], Ys, [X | Zs]) :- app(Xs, Ys, Zs).
```

Fig. 1.5 The APPEND program

---

[3] append/3 is actually a built-in so we denote the defined predicate by app/3.

So the `app/3` predicate is defined by means of **recursion**, which is typical for Prolog programming style.

The `APPEND` program can be used not only to concatenate the lists:

```
[eclipse 22]: app([mon, wed], [fri, sun], Zs).

Zs = [mon, wed, fri, sun]
Yes (0.00s cpu)
```

but also to split a list in all possible ways:

```
[eclipse 23]: app(Xs, Ys, [mon, wed, fri, sun]).

Xs = []
Ys = [mon, wed, fri, sun]
Yes (0.00s cpu, solution 1, maybe more) ? ;

Xs = [mon]
Ys = [wed, fri, sun]
Yes (0.00s cpu, solution 2, maybe more) ? ;

Xs = [mon, wed]
Ys = [fri, sun]
Yes (0.00s cpu, solution 3, maybe more) ? ;

Xs = [mon, wed, fri]
Ys = [sun]
Yes (0.00s cpu, solution 4, maybe more) ? ;

Xs = [mon, wed, fri, sun]
Ys = []
Yes (0.01s cpu, solution 5)
```

By combining these two ways of using `APPEND` we can easily generate rotations of a list:

```
rotate(Xs, Ys) :- app(As, Bs, Xs), app(Bs, As, Ys).
```

The first call to `app/3` generates upon backtracking all possible splits of its last argument into two lists, while the second call concatenates these lists in the reverse order. By imposing an additional condition on the output we can then generate all rotations that satisfy some condition. For example, the following query generates in the variable Zs all rotations of a list of integers that begin with 2:

```
[eclipse 24]: Zs = [2|_], rotate([1,2,2,3,1,2], Zs).

Zs = [2, 2, 3, 1, 2, 1]
Yes (0.00s cpu, solution 1, maybe more) ? ;

Zs = [2, 3, 1, 2, 1, 2]
Yes (0.00s cpu, solution 2, maybe more) ? ;

Zs = [2, 1, 2, 2, 3, 1]
Yes (0.00s cpu, solution 3, maybe more) ? ;

No (0.00s cpu)
```

1.7 Summary

In this chapter we introduced pure Prolog programs and discussed their syntax, meaning and the computation process. In pure Prolog programs the values are assigned to variables by means of the unification algorithm.

To explain the execution model of pure Prolog we discussed computing with equations, choice points and backtracking. Finally, to clarify some basic features of Prolog programming we introduced two simple pure Prolog programs.

1.8 Exercises

Exercise 1.1 What is the ECL^{i}PS^e output to the following queries?

1. X = 7, X = 6.

2. X = 7, X = X+1.

3. X = X+1, X = 7.

4. X = 3, Y = X+1.

5. Y = X+1, X = 3.

Exercise 1.2 Consider the program BOOKS from Subsection 1.6.1. Using X \= Y to test whether X is different from Y, what query do you use to find the other author of the book by apt?

Exercise 1.3 Consider the following program:

```
q(X) :- Z = 1.
```

What is the ECL^{i}PS^e output to the following queries?

1. Z = 2, q(X).

2. Z = 2, q(Z).

3. Z = 2, q(X), Y = Z+1.

Exercise 1.4 Consider the following program:

```
p([prolog, works, for, nothing]).
p([prolog, is, pure, fantasy]).
p([prolog, works, for, solving(theories), only]).
p([prolog, works, for, solving(_), among, others]).
p([prolog, works, for, making(problems), and, others]).

q([programming, is, pure, fantasy]).
q([logic, works, in, some, cases]).
q([thanks, to, thierry, le, provost, for, this, example]).
q([prolog, works, for, solving(problems) | _]).
q([prolog, works, for, solving(_), between, others]).
```

What is the ECL^{i}PS^e output to the query p(Behold), q(Behold)?

Exercise 1.5 Reconsider the predicate **rotate/2** defined on page 25. Explain why in the following interaction with ECL^{i}PS^e the first solution is produced twice. (The query asks for all rotations of the list [1,2,2,3,1,2] that begin with 1.)

```
[eclipse 1]: Zs = [1|_], rotate([1,2,2,3,1,2], Zs).

Zs = [1, 2, 2, 3, 1, 2]
Yes (0.00s cpu, solution 1, maybe more) ? ;

Zs = [1, 2, 1, 2, 2, 3]
```

```
Yes (0.00s cpu, solution 2, maybe more) ? ;

Zs = [1, 2, 2, 3, 1, 2]
Yes (0.00s cpu, solution 3)
```

Suggest a modification of `rotate/2`, using \=, for which each solution is produced once.

2

A reconstruction of pure Prolog

2.1 Introduction

I N THE PREVIOUS chapter we discussed the basic aspects of the logic programming paradigm by focussing on pure Prolog. To provide a better insight into this paradigm we discuss in this chapter a translation of pure Prolog programs into a more conventional programming language. This translation allows us to clarify that pure Prolog implicitly supports a number of programming features, including sequencing, procedures and local variables.

Then we discuss the issue of declarative programming. We clarify in what sense both pure Prolog and the small programming language here introduced support declarative programming.

2.2 The programming language $\mathcal{L}_0$

In Subsection 1.5.3 we compared the equality interpreted as the unification to the assignment statement. But, so interpreted, equality is not explicitly present as a statement in logic programming and pure Prolog: it is 'hidden' in the computing process. Also the process of selection of the appropriate clauses during an execution of a query is implicit and no distinction is made between local and non-local variables.

To make these and other aspects of pure Prolog explicit we now define a translation of pure Prolog into a small programming language $\mathcal{L}_0$ that does include equality as an explicit atomic statement. Additionally, this language features a number of other programming constructs, including recursive procedures and an alternative choice statement. This interpretation of the pure Prolog programs within a more conventional programming language provides an alternative account of their semantics, a matter to which we return in Sections 2.4 and 2.5.

To start with, we assume the same set of terms as in the case of pure Prolog. The $\mathcal{L}_0$ programming language comprises

- four types of **atomic statements**:
  - the **equality** statement,
  - the `skip` statement,
  - the `fail` statement,
  - the **procedure call** statement,
- the **program composition**, written as ';',
- the **alternative choice** statement, written as

$$\texttt{begin } S_1 \texttt{ orelse } \ldots \texttt{ orelse } S_n \texttt{ end,}$$

where $n \geq 1$,
- the **block** statement in which a sequence of local variables is introduced, written as

$$\texttt{begin new } x_1, \ldots, x_n; S \texttt{ end,}$$

where $n \geq 1$,
- **procedure declarations**

$$p(x_1, \ldots, x_n) : S,$$

where $n \geq 0$, p is the *procedure identifier*, $x_1, \ldots, x_n$ are different variables called *formal parameters*, and S is the *procedure body*. If $n = 0$, we view this declaration as $p : S$.

By a **program** we mean a sequence of procedure declarations followed by a ('main') statement. We now explain the meaning of the programs written in this small language. All variables used range over the set of possible values, which are terms. A **state** is an answer in the sense of Subsection 1.4.2 but now viewed as a finite mapping that assigns to each variable a value which is a term. Each variable is interpreted in the context of the current state. The statements transform the states, i.e., the answers.

The meaning of the introduced statements relies on the concepts of a *choice point* and *failure*. The choice points are created by the alternative choice statement

$$\text{begin } S_1 \text{ orelse } \ldots \text{ orelse } S_n \text{ end,}$$

so we explain its meaning first.

For $n = 1$, that is for the statement begin S_1 end, its meaning coincides with the meaning of S_1. For $n = 2$ the statement begin S_1 orelse S_2 end is executed as follows. First a choice point is created which consists of the statement S_2 and the current state. Then the statement S_1 is executed. If it succeeds, the next statement after begin S_1 orelse S_2 end (if any) is executed. If the execution of S_1 results in a failure (a contingency to be discussed in a moment), then *backtracking* takes place. This means that the execution returns to the last created choice point from which the execution resumes. So, assuming that the execution of S_1 did not create any choice points, the execution continues with the S_2 statement executed in the state stored at this choice point. If this execution of S_2 succeeds, the next statement after begin S_1 orelse S_2 end (if any) is executed. If this execution also results in a failure, the backtracking to the previous choice point takes place. If no such choice point is present, the execution of begin S_1 orelse S_2 end ends in a failure.

Finally, we interpret the statement begin S_1 orelse $\ldots$ orelse S_n end for $n > 2$ inductively as

$$\text{begin } S_1 \text{ orelse begin } S_2 \text{ orelse } \ldots \text{ orelse } S_n \text{ end end.}$$

So the alternative choice statement can be seen as a means of providing the automatic backtracking.

Next, the skip statement is simply a 'non-action' statement. The fail statement causes a failure, upon which the backtracking to the most recent choice point takes place. If no such choice point is present, the execution ends in a failure.

In turn, the equality statement $s = t$ is executed by trying to unify the terms s and t. So this statement can lead to either a success or a failure. In the first case a substitution is generated that is an mgu of s and t. This substitution is then combined with the current state (which is an answer) to obtain a new state. In the second case a failure results, upon which the backtracking to the last choice point takes place. If no such choice point is present, the execution ends in a failure.

The program composition ';' has the usual meaning. Next, the block statement begin new $x_1, \ldots, x_n; S$ end is executed by renaming first $x_1, \ldots, x_n$ to the variables $x_1', \ldots, x_n'$ that are not present in the current state. This yields a renaming S' of S. Then S' is executed. If it succeeds, the equations involving the variables $x_1', \ldots, x_n'$ are removed from the state. If it fails, then backtracking takes place.

Finally, a procedure call $p(t_1, \ldots, t_n)$, where p is declared by

$$p(x_1, \ldots, x_n) : S$$

and $n > 0$, is interpreted by

- renaming the formal parameters $x_1, \ldots, x_n$ to variables $x_1', \ldots, x_n'$ that do not occur in $p(t_1, \ldots, t_n)$; this yields a renaming S' of the procedure body S,
- replacing each occurrence of x_i in S' by t_i; this yields a statement S'',
- executing the statement S''.

If $n = 0$, the procedure call simply results in executing the procedure body S. So the parameter passing is taken care of by means of a substitution, which is typical of ALGOL 60 **call-by-name** parameter mechanism.

A procedure call $p(t_1, \ldots, t_n)$, where no declaration of p is present, yields a failure. Note that in addition the failure can be also caused by the execution of the `fail` statement or by an unsuccessful execution of the equality statement.

The following example clarifies the above explanations. As the variables in pure Prolog start with the upper case letter, we adopt the same convention in the language $\mathcal{L}_0$. In (iii) and (v) during the program execution a backtracking takes place.

Example 2.1   Assume that the initial state is the empty answer, i.e., initially no variable has a value.

(i) The statement `X = f(Y); Y = a` successfully terminates in the state `X = f(a), Y = a`.

(ii) The statement `X = a; X = b` fails.

(iii) The statement `begin f(X) = g(b) orelse f(X) = f(a) end` successfully terminates in the state `X = a`.

(iv) The statement `X = a; begin new X; X = b end` successfully terminates in the state `X = a`.

(v) Assuming the procedure declaration

```
p(X,Y): begin X = a; Y = b orelse X = b; Y = a end
```

the procedure call p(b,a) successfully terminates in the empty state, while the procedure call p(a,a) fails.

2.3 Translating pure Prolog into $\mathcal{L}_0$

We now explain how to translate pure Prolog into the $\mathcal{L}_0$ programming language. We illustrate it first by means of an example. Consider the following pure Prolog program NUM defining numerals:

```
num(0).
num(s(X)) :- num(X).
```

We translate it by first rewriting it to the following equivalent pure Prolog program that uses the built-in =/2:

```
num(Y) :- Y = 0.
num(Y) :- Y = s(X), num(X).
```

Now both clauses have the same head, num(Y). In general, we shall rewrite first a pure Prolog program in such a way that, for each predicate p, all clauses that define p have the same head of the form $p(x_1,\ldots,x_n)$, where $x_1,\ldots,x_n$ are different variables.

Next, we translate the bodies of the above two clauses to the following two statements: Y = 0 and **begin new** X; Y = s(X); num(X) **end**. The latter reflects the fact that in the second clause X is a *local variable*, i.e., it does not occur in the clause head. These two statements are then put together by means of the alternative choice statement and the original program NUM is translated to the following procedure declaration:

```
num(Y): begin
          Y = 0
        orelse
          begin new X; Y = s(X); num(X) end
        end
```

The reader can now check that given this procedure declaration the procedure call num(s(s(X))) succeeds and assigns 0 to X, while the procedure call num(s(f(X))) fails. This coincides with the outcomes of the corresponding Prolog computations.

Let us define now the translation for an arbitrary pure Prolog program P. It will be translated into a sequence of procedure declarations. We perform successively the following steps, where $X_1, \ldots, X_n, \ldots$ are new variables:

Step 1: Transform each fact $p(t_1, \ldots, t_n)$ of P to the clause

$$p(X_1, \ldots, X_n) \; :\!- \; X_1 = t_1, \ldots, X_n = t_n.$$

Transform each rule $p(t_1, \ldots, t_n) \; :\!- \; \mathbf{B}$ of P to the clause

$$p(X_1, \ldots, X_n) \; :\!- \; X_1 = t_1, \ldots, X_n = t_n, \mathbf{B}.$$

Step 2: Translate each clause body $X_1 = t_1, \ldots, X_n = t_n, A_1, \ldots, A_l$ to the following program:

$$\textbf{begin new } Y_1, \ldots, Y_m; X_1 = t_1; \ldots; X_n = t_n; A_1; \ldots; A_l \textbf{ end},$$

where $Y_1, \ldots, Y_m$ are the variables that occur in $t_1, \ldots, t_n, A_1, \ldots, A_l$.

In the boundary case when the clause body is empty (so $n = 0$ and $l = 0$), translate it to the **skip** statement. If no variable occurs in $t_1, \ldots, t_n, A_1, \ldots, A_l$ (so $m = 0$), translate the clause body to

$$X_1 = t_1; \ldots; X_n = t_n; A_1; \ldots; A_l.$$

Step 3: Let

$$p(\mathbf{X}) \; :\!- \; \mathbf{B}_1.$$
$$\ldots$$
$$p(\mathbf{X}) \; :\!- \; \mathbf{B}_k.$$

where $k \geq 1$, be the definition of the predicate p obtained in step 1 and let $S_1, \ldots, S_k$ be the corresponding translations of the clause bodies $\mathbf{B}_1, \ldots, \mathbf{B}_k$ into the program statements defined in step 2.

Replace the above definition of p by the following procedure declaration:

$$p(\mathbf{X}) : \textbf{begin } S_1 \textbf{ orelse } \ldots \textbf{ orelse } S_k \textbf{ end}.$$

Step 4: For each predicate q that appears in the original pure Prolog program P but not in a head of a clause in P (that is, the definition of q is empty) add the following procedure declaration:

$$q(\mathbf{X}) : \textbf{fail}.$$

To clarify the boundary cases of the above translation consider the following pure Prolog program:

```
p.
p :- r.
r :- q.
u.
```

It translates to the following sequence of four procedure declarations:

```
p: begin skip orelse r end;
r: begin q end;
q: fail;
u: begin skip end;
```

2.4 Pure Prolog and declarative programming

As already stated in the previous chapter, there are two natural interpretations of a pure Prolog program. The first one, called a declarative interpretation, is concerned with the question *what* is being computed. According to this interpretation a pure Prolog program is simply viewed as a set of formulas. The second interpretation, called a procedural interpretation, explains *how* the computation takes place. Informally, we can say that the declarative interpretation is concerned with the *meaning*, whereas the procedural interpretation is concerned with the *method*.

These two interpretations of pure Prolog programs are closely related to each other by means of specific theorems that we omit here. The first interpretation helps us to better understand the second and explains why pure Prolog supports **declarative programming**. Loosely speaking, declarative programming can be described as follows. Programs can be interpreted in a natural way as formulas in some logic. Then the results of the program computations follow *logically* from the program.

Now 'thinking' declaratively is in general much easier than 'thinking' procedurally. For example, in the case of pure Prolog programs, to understand the declarative interpretation, we only need to know the semantics of the first-order logic. In contrast, to understand the procedural interpretation we need to be familiar with the notions of a most general unifier, substitutions and their applications, and answers.

So programs written in a formalism supporting declarative programming are often simpler to understand and to develop. In fact, in some situations the specification of a problem in an appropriate format already forms the algorithmic solution to the problem. In other words, declarative programming makes it possible to write executable specifications.

It should be added however, that in practice the programs obtained in this way are often inefficient. Moreover, the declarative interpretation does not address the issue of termination. In summary, to write efficient Prolog programs, a good understanding of the procedural interpretation is needed.

2.5 $\mathcal{L}_0$ and declarative programming

To better understand the idea of declarative programming we now show that the programming language $\mathcal{L}_0$ supports declarative programming, as well. So we explain how the programs written in it can be interpreted as first-order formulas. To this end we successively interpret

- the `skip` statement as *true*,
- the `fail` statement as *false*,
- each procedure call statement as an atomic formula,
- the program composition ';' as the conjunction ' $\wedge$ ',
- the alternative choice statement

$$\textbf{begin } S_1 \textbf{ orelse } \ldots \textbf{ orelse } S_n \textbf{ end}$$

as the disjunction $S_1 \vee \ldots \vee S_n$,
- the block statement

$$\textbf{begin new } x_1, \ldots, x_n; S \textbf{ end}$$

as the existentially quantified formula $\exists x_1 \ldots \exists x_n. S$,
- the procedure declaration

$$p(x_1, \ldots, x_n) : S$$

as the universally quantified formula $\forall x_1 \ldots \forall x_n. (S \rightarrow p(x_1, \ldots, x_n))$.

In general, each program in $\mathcal{L}_0$ corresponds to a first-order formula that can be viewed as its declarative interpretation. Now, consider an $\mathcal{L}_0$ program P that consists of the main statement S and a sequence *Proc* of the procedure declarations. Let $\tilde{S}$ be the first-order formula corresponding to S and $\tilde{Proc}$ the set of first-order formulas corresponding to *Proc*. Suppose that S succeeds and yields the state (i.e., the answer) E. One can prove that $\tilde{E} \rightarrow \tilde{S}$ then logically follows from $\tilde{Proc}$. In other words, the programming language $\mathcal{L}_0$ supports declarative programming.

Note that if we added to $\mathcal{L}_0$ the customary assignment statement, then $\mathcal{L}_0$ would no longer support declarative programming, since there is no natural way to interpret the assignment as a first-order formula.

It is instructive to compare the declarative interpretations of pure Prolog and $\mathcal{L}_0$ as they differ. To clarify matters let us return to the pure Prolog program `NUM` already discussed:

```
num(0).
num(s(X)) :- num(X).
```

Its declarative interpretation is the set (or equivalently conjunction) of the formulas

$$\{num(0), \ \forall X. \ (num(s(X)) \rightarrow num(X))\}.$$

Next, consider the procedure declaration

```
num(Y): begin
           Y = 0
        orelse
           begin new X; Y = s(X); num(X) end
        end
```

obtained earlier by translating the above program NUM into $\mathcal{L}_0$. It is interpreted as the following first-order formula:

$$\forall Y. \ ((Y = 0 \vee \exists X. \ (Y = s(X) \wedge num(X))) \rightarrow num(Y)).$$

So these two interpretations differ. However, it can be shown (see the reference in Chapter 14.9) that they imply logically the same atomic formulas. So there is no difference as far as the analysis of successful queries is concerned. In some sense the declarative interpretation of $\mathcal{L}_0$ is more explicit than that of pure Prolog.

2.6 Summary

In this chapter we defined the meaning of pure Prolog programs by translating them into a small programming language $\mathcal{L}_0$. This translation reveals the programming features implicitly present in the logic programming paradigm. In particular, it clarifies the following three points made in the previous chapter:

- computing takes place over the set of all terms,
- values are assigned to variables by means of the ***most general unifiers***,
- the control is provided by a single mechanism: automatic ***backtracking***.

Additionally, we note that

- the predicates correspond to the procedure identifiers,
- the variables present in the body of a clause but not in its head correspond to local variables,
- the definition of a predicate corresponds to a procedure declaration,
- the comma ',' separating the atomic goals in a query or in a clause body corresponds to the program composition ';'.

So this translation shows that pure Prolog is a very succinct yet highly expressive formalism.

Additionally, we clarified what it means that logic programming and pure Prolog support declarative programming. Finally we showed that the language $\mathcal{L}_0$ supports declarative programming, as well.

2.7 Exercises

Exercise 2.1 Assume the declaration of the procedure num introduced in Section 2.3. What is the result of executing the statement
num(s(Y)); num(X); Y = X?

Exercise 2.2 Assume the procedure declaration

```
p(X,Y): begin
            begin new X; X = b; Y = b end
        orelse
            X = b; Y = a
        end
```

What is the outcome of executing the following procedure calls:

(i) p(a,a),

(ii) p(a,b),

(iii) p(b,a).

Exercise 2.3 Translate to the language $\mathcal{L}_0$ the program APPEND from Figure 1.5 on page 24.

Part II

Elements of Prolog

3

Arithmetic in Prolog

3.1 Introduction

I N THIS CHAPTER we discuss Prolog support for arithmetic. In our presentation we focus on the essentials. In particular ECL^{i}PS^e has 64 built-ins that support arithmetic and we discuss only sixteen. The handling of arithmetic in Prolog boils down to two additions to pure Prolog. First, a mechanism for an *evaluation* of ground arithmetic expressions is offered. Second, a facility for a *comparison* of ground arithmetic expressions is provided. The latter is the first step towards integrating constraints into the logic programming paradigm. We shall discuss this matter in Section 3.4.

The handling of arithmetic in Prolog leads to a deviation from the computational model based on logic programming in that it introduces the possibility of run-time errors. This compromises the declarative character of the language. The problem is that, due to lack of types in Prolog, the facilities that support arithmetic can be used with arbitrary terms, in particular non-numeric ones.

On the other hand this lack of types turns out to be an advantage in the case of meta-programming that will be discussed in the next chapter.[1]

---

[1] Meta-programming usually stands for the possibility of writing programs that use other programs as data.

3.2 Arithmetic expressions and their evaluation

We begin the exposition with the arithmetic. In Prolog we have at our disposal infinitely many integer constants:

$$0, \ -1, \ 1, \ -2, \ 2, \ \ldots$$

and infinitely many floating point numbers, such as

$$0.0, \ -1.72, \ 3.141, \ -2.0, \ \ldots$$

Floating point numbers are the computer representable 'reals' and the number of digits allowed after the obligatory decimal point '.' depends on the implementation. Of course, in each implementation of Prolog only (very large) finite subsets of integer constants and floating point numbers are supported.

In what follows, by a ***number*** we mean either an integer constant or a floating point number.

In addition, Prolog provides various operations on the numbers. In the case of Prolog and ECL^{i}PS^e they include the following binary operations:

- addition, written as +,
- subtraction, written as -,
- multiplication, written as *,
- integer division, written as //, (rounding towards zero) or div (rounding towards negative infinity),
- remainder of the integer division, written as rem (rounding towards zero), or mod (rounding towards negative infinity),[2]
- exponentiation, written as ^,

and the following unary operations:

- unary minus, written as -,
- absolute value, written as abs.

We call the above operations ***arithmetic operators***.

According to the usual notational convention of logic programming and Prolog, function symbols and predicates are written in a ***prefix form***, that is in front of the arguments. In contrast, in accordance with the usage in arithmetic, the binary arithmetic operators are written in the ***infix form***, that is between the arguments, while the unary arithmetic operators are written in the prefix form. Moreover, unary minus of a number can be written in the ***bracketless prefix form***, that is without brackets surrounding its argument.

---

[2] x rem y is defined as x - y*(x//y).

Recall that the integer division is defined as the integer part of the usual division outcome and given two integers x and y such that $y \neq 0$, x mod y is defined as x - y*(x//y). The use of the infix and bracketless prefix form for arithmetic operators leads to well-known ambiguities. For example, 4+3*5 could be interpreted either as (4+3)*5 or 4+(3*5) and -3+4 could be interpreted either as (-3)+4 or -(3+4). Further, 12//4//3 could be interpreted either as (12//4)//3 or 12//(4//3), etc.

Such ambiguities are resolved in Prolog by stipulating the following *binding order* (written as $\prec$):

$$+, \ -(binary), -(unary) \prec *, \ // \ \text{div, rem, mod} \prec \hat{}$$

and assuming that the binary arithmetic operators are left associative. That is to say, '+' binds weaker than '*', so 4+3*5 is interpreted as 4+(3*5). In turn, 12//4*3 is interpreted as (12//4)*3, 12//4//3 is interpreted as (12//4)//3, etc.

The arithmetic operators and the above set of numbers uniquely determine a set of terms. We call terms defined in this language *arithmetic expressions* and introduce the abbreviation *gae* for *ground arithmetic expressions*, i.e., arithmetic expressions without variables.

As in every programming language we would like to evaluate the ground arithmetic expressions. For example, we would like to compute 3+4 in Prolog. In customary programming languages this is done by means of the assignment statement. In Prolog this is done by means of a limited counterpart of the assignment, the built-in is/2, written in the infix form. For example, we have

```
[eclipse 1]: X is 3+4.

X = 7
Yes (0.00s cpu)
```

We call is/2 the *arithmetic evaluator*. The above example represents the most common use of is/2. In general, s is t is executed by unifying s with the *value* of the ground arithmetic expression t. If t is not a gae, a run-time error arises. More precisely, the following possibilities arise.

- t is a gae.
  Let val(t) be the value of t.

  - s is a number identical to val(t).
    Then the arithmetic evaluator succeeds and the empty substitution is produced. For example,

```
[eclipse 2]: 7 is 3+4.
```

```
Yes (0.00s cpu)
```

— s is a number different from val(t).

Then the arithmetic evaluator fails. For example,

```
[eclipse 3]: 8 is 3+4.
```

```
No (0.00s cpu)
```

— s is a variable.

Then the arithmetic evaluator succeeds and the substitution s = val(t) is produced. For example,

```
[eclipse 4]: X is 4+3*5.
```

```
X = 19
Yes (0.00s cpu)
```

— s is not a number and not a variable.

Then a run-time error arises. For example,

```
[eclipse 5]: 3+4 is 3+4.
type error in +(3, 4, 3 + 4)
Abort
```

• t is not a gae.

Then a run-time error arises. For example,

```
[eclipse 6]: X is Y+1.
instantiation fault in +(Y, 1, X)
Abort
[eclipse 7]: X is X+1.
instantiation fault in +(X, 1, X)
Abort
```

So the is/2 built-in significantly differs from the assignment statement. In particular, as the last example shows, we cannot increment a variable using is/2. Because of this, typical uses of counting in Prolog are rather subtle and confusing for the beginners. Consider for instance the following trivial problem:

Problem Write a Prolog program that computes the length of a list.

The correct solution is presented in Figure 3.1.[3]

---

[3] length/2 is actually a built-in so we denote the defined predicate by len/2. The length/2 built-

```
% len(List, N) :- N is the length of the list List.

len([], 0).
len([_ | Ts], N) :- len(Ts, M), N is M+1.
```

Fig. 3.1 The LENGTH program

The program employs recursion to perform the iteration. In Chapter 7 we shall see an alternative solution that involves iteration constructs that are present in ECL^{i}PS^e. Note the use of the local variable M to compute the intermediate result being the length of the list Ts. We have then for example:

```
[eclipse 8]: len([a,b,c], X).

X = 3
Yes (0.00s cpu)
```

A naive solution in which instead of the second clause we use

```
len([_ | Ts], N+1) :- len(Ts, N).
```

generates unexpected results:

```
[eclipse 9]: len([a,b,c], X).

X = 0 + 1 + 1 + 1
Yes (0.00s cpu)
```

The problem is that the gaes can be evaluated only using the **is** statement. To compute the value of a gae defined inductively one needs to generate new local variables (like M in the LENGTH program) to store in them the intermediate results, and then use the **is** statement.

To save explicitly introducing such extra variables, ECL^{i}PS^e supports for is/2 a functional syntax. Let us suppose p/2 is a predicate whose last argument is numeric, viz.

```
p(a, 1).
p(b, 2).
```

in can be used both to compute the length of a list, and to build a list of different variables of a specified length.

Then p/1 can be used as a function when it occurs on the right-hand side of is, for example:

```
[eclipse 10]: X is p(a)+1.
```

```
X = 2
Yes (0.00s cpu)
```

In particular, both the len/2 predicate from the LENGTH program and the length/2 built-in can be used as a function, for example:

```
[eclipse 11]: X is length([a,b,c]).
```

```
X = 3
Yes (0.00s cpu)
```

As another example of the use of an arithmetic evaluator consider a predicate defining all the integer values in a given range. The appropriate definition is given in Figure 3.2.

```
% select_val(Min, Max, Val) :-
%     Min, Max are gaes and Val is an integer
%     between Min and Max inclusive.

select_val(Min, Max, Val) :- Min =< Max, Val is Min.
select_val(Min, Max, Val) :-
    Min < Max, Min1 is Min+1,
    select_val(Min1, Max, Val).
```

Fig. 3.2 The SELECT program

Note the use of a local variable Min1 in the arithmetic evaluator Min1 is Min+1 to compute the increment of Min. In this program the appropriate values are generated only 'upon demand', by means of backtracking. We shall see the usefulness of such a process in Section 7.6. We have for example:

```
[eclipse 12]: select_val(10, 13, Val).
```

```
Val = 10
Yes (0.00s cpu, solution 1, maybe more) ? ;
```

```
Val = 11
```

```
Yes (0.00s cpu, solution 2, maybe more) ? ;

Val = 12
Yes (0.00s cpu, solution 3, maybe more) ? ;

Val = 13
Yes (0.00s cpu, solution 4, maybe more) ? ;

No (0.00s cpu)
```

Note that, unlike in the customary programming languages, using this definition we can recognise as well as generate values. For example we have

```
[eclipse 13]: select_val(10, 13, 9).

No (0.00s cpu)
[eclipse 14]: select_val(10, 13, X), select_val(12, 15, X).

X = 12
Yes (0.00s cpu, solution 1, maybe more) ? ;

X = 13
Yes (0.00s cpu, solution 2, maybe more) ? ;

No (0.01s cpu)
```

3.3 Arithmetic comparison predicates

Prolog allows us not only to compute the values of gaes but also to compare them by means of the following six *arithmetic comparison predicates* (in short *comparison predicates*):

- 'less than', written as <,
- 'less than or equal', written as =<,
- 'equality', written as =:=,
- 'disequality', written as =\=,
- 'greater than or equal', written as >=,
- 'greater than', written as >.

The equality predicate =:=/2 between gaes should not be confused with the 'is unifiable with' predicate =/2 discussed in Section 1.4.

The comparison predicates work on gaes and produce the expected outcome. So for instance `>/2` compares the values of two gaes and succeeds if the value of the first argument is larger than the value of the second and fails otherwise. Thus, for example

```
[eclipse 15]: 5*2 > 3+4.
```

```
Yes (0.00s cpu)
[eclipse 16]: 7 > 3+4.
```

```
No (0.00s cpu)
```

However, when one of the arguments of the comparison predicates is not a gae, a run-time error arises. In particular, `=:=/2` cannot be used to assign a value to a variable. For example, we have

```
[eclipse 17]: X =:= 5.
instantiation fault in X =:= 5
Abort
```

As a simple example of the use of the comparison predicates consider the program in Figure 3.3 that checks whether a list is an ≤-ordered list of numbers.

```
% ordered(Xs) :- Xs is an =<-ordered list of numbers.

ordered([]).
ordered([H | Ts]) :- ordered(H, Ts).

% ordered(H, Ts) :- [H|Ts] is an =<-ordered list of numbers.

ordered(_, []).
ordered(H, [Y | Ts]) :- H =< Y, ordered(Y, Ts).
```

Fig. 3.3 The ORDERED program

We now have

```
[eclipse 18]: ordered([1,1.5,2,3]).
```

```
Yes (0.00s cpu)
```

but also

```
[eclipse 19]: ordered([1,X,3]).
instantiation fault in 1 =< X
Abort
```

Here a run-time error took place because during the computation the comparison predicate =</2 was applied to an argument that is not a number.

On the other hand, we also have

```
[eclipse 20]: ordered([a]).

Yes (0.00s cpu)
```

which shows that programs that use the arithmetic comparison predicates can be quite subtle. In this case, the ORDERED program correctly rejects (by means of a run-time error) some queries, such as ordered([1,X,3]) but incorrectly accepts some other queries, such as ordered([X]).

A possible remedy is to use the number/1 built-in of Prolog that tests whether its argument is a number and rewrite the program as follows.

```
ordered([]).
ordered([H | Ts]) :-
    number(H),
    ordered(H, Ts).

ordered(_, []).
ordered(H, [Y | Ts]) :-
    number(Y),
    H =< Y, ordered(Y, Ts).
```

However, we get then the uninformative 'No' answer to such queries as ordered([X]) or ordered([1,X,3]). We shall explain in the next chapter how more informative answers can be generated.

As another example of a Prolog program that employs the comparison predicates consider the Prolog version of the well-known **quicksort** procedure proposed in Hoare [1962]. According to this sorting procedure, a list is first partitioned into two sublists using an element X of it, one consisting of elements smaller than X and the other consisting of elements larger than or equal to X. Then each sublist is quicksorted and the resulting sorted sublists are appended with the element X put in the middle. This can be expressed in Prolog by means of the program in Figure 3.4, where X is chosen to be the first element of the given list.

```
% qs(Xs, Ys) :-
%      Ys is an =<-ordered permutation of the list Xs.

qs([], []).
qs([X | Xs], Ys) :-
    part(X, Xs, Littles, Bigs),
    qs(Littles, Ls),
    qs(Bigs, Bs),
    app(Ls, [X | Bs], Ys).

% part(X, Xs, Ls, Bs) :-
%      Ls is a list of elements of Xs which are < X,
%      Bs is a list of elements of Xs which are >= X.

part(_, [], [], []).
part(X, [Y | Xs], [Y | Ls], Bs) :-
    X > Y,
    part(X, Xs, Ls, Bs).
part(X, [Y | Xs], Ls, [Y | Bs]) :-
    X =< Y,
    part(X, Xs, Ls, Bs).
```

augmented by the APPEND program of Figure 1.5.

Fig. 3.4 The QUICKSORT program

In the part/4 predicate the first two arguments are used as inputs and the last two as outputs. Note that the list constructors are used both in the input positions and in the output positions.

We then have

```
[eclipse 21]: qs([7,9,8,1,5], Ys).

Ys = [1, 5, 7, 8, 9]
More (0.00s cpu) ? ;

No (0.00s cpu)
```

However, we also have

```
[eclipse 22]:  qs([3,X,0,1], Ys).
```

```
instantiation fault in 3 > X
Abort
```

because during the computation the comparison predicate >/2 is applied to non-gae arguments.

In the next chapter we shall return to this program to discuss a typical source of inefficiency in Prolog programs and a way of avoiding it.

3.4 Passive versus active constraints

Atomic goals that employ arithmetic comparison predicates, for example 3*X < Y+2, go beyond the syntax of pure Prolog. Like the goals that refer to the =/2 built-in, for example f(a,X) = f(Y,b), they impose a restriction on their variables. The important difference is that at present the first type of goals can be successfully processed *only* when all its variables are ground.

Both atomic goals can be viewed as constraints in the sense that they refer to some predefined predicate (here < and =), and hence restrict the set of values the variables can be assigned to. (A formal account of constraints will be given in Chapter 6.) We call the atomic goals that use the comparison predicates **arithmetic constraints**.

In what follows we distinguish between **active constraints** and **passive constraints**. This distinction refers to the way the constraints are used during the computation process. The evaluation of the former ones can affect the variables present in them, while the evaluation of the latter ones cannot. So f(a,X) = f(Y,b) is an active constraint, while at present 3*X < Y*Y+2 is a passive constraint.

In other words at this stage we can use arithmetic constraints only for testing. Moreover, these constraints can cause a run-time error, when their variables are not ground. In particular, the query ordered([1,X,3]) mentioned on page 49 yields a run-time error. The query ordered([X,2,1]) also yields a run-time error, even though it would fail for *any* value of X.

Later, in Chapter 9 we shall discuss an ECL^{i}PS^e library that allows us to use arithmetic constraints as passive constraints without causing a run-time error, so the last query can correctly fail instead of causing an error. Still later, in Chapter 10, we shall discuss an ECL^{i}PS^e library that allows us to express arithmetic constraints as active constraints, so the query ordered([2,X,2]) can succeed, *instantiating* X to 2.

3.5 Operators

Arithmetic operators are examples of function symbols that are written in the infix form (for example '+') or bracketless prefix form (the unary '-'). These forms are equivalent to the standard, prefix, form. For example in Prolog and ECL^{i}PS^e the expressions +(1,2) and 1+2 are indistinguishable:

```
[eclipse 23]: 1+2 = +(1,2).


Yes (0.00s cpu)
```

Prolog provides a means to declare a symbol so that it can be used in a form alternative to the standard one. Function symbols and predicates that are declared this way are called *operators*.

3.5.1 Binary operators: infix notation

Let us take as an example the predicate before/2. We wish to be able to write time1 before time2 instead of before(time1, time2). To allow it we use an *operator declaration*, which is written as follows:

```
:- op(700, xfx, before).
```

This declares before/2 as an infix binary operator. The first two arguments, 700 and xfx, will be explained later.

We can now write 10 before 11 anywhere we could previously write before(10, 11). For example we could write the following program:

```
10 before 11.
9 before 10.
X before Z :- X before Y, Y before Z.
```

and ask

```
[eclipse 24]: 9 before X.


X = 10
Yes (0.00s cpu, solution 1, maybe more) ? ;


X = 11
Yes (0.00s cpu, solution 2, maybe more) ?
% Asking for more here would start an infinite loop!
```

This query can still be written in the standard syntax, as before(9, X).

3.5.2 Binary operators: binding order

The drawback of using infix operators is the resulting ambiguity. To see this suppose we also want to write the time using an infix operator, thus 10:00. When we write 10:00 before 11:00 we intend this to be the same as before(:(10,00), :(11,00)). However, this expression could also be parsed in a different way that is equivalent to the expression

$$:(10, \ :(before(00,11), \ 00)).$$

One way to guide the parser is to introduce brackets, thus

$$(10:00) \ before \ (11:00).$$

Now there is no ambiguity. The last expression is parsed then as

$$before(:(10,00), \ :(11,00)).$$

To achieve the other form we would have to bracket the original expression thus:

$$10:((00 \ before \ 11):00).$$

This second bracketing specifies that ((00 before 11):00) is a single compound term. This term has the function symbol :/2 and two arguments, (00 before 11) and 00.

If such brackets were always required, however, then it would make arithmetic expressions quite unreadable. For example, we would have to write (2*3)-(4//((3*Y)+(2*Z))) instead of 2 * 3 - 4 // (3 * Y + 2 * Z). In order to guide the parser without the need for extra brackets, we associate a priority with each operator. In the declaration

```
:- op(700, xfx, before).
```

the priority is 700. In Prolog :/2 is already predeclared as an operator with the priority 600. A lower priority number indicates a tighter binding, so :/2 binds tighter than before/2. Consequently, in the context T1:T2 before T3 the parser implicitly inserts the bracketing resulting in (T1:T2) before T3.

Thus we can safely write a more natural version of our program as follows:

```
10:00 before 11:00.
9:00 before 10:00.
X before Z :- X before Y, Y before Z.
```

3.5.3 Binary operators: associativity

Operator priorities can be used to disambiguate terms involving different operators, but not multiple occurrences of the same operator. Consider the term 1+2+3+4. Since +/2 is associative this could be written equivalently as ((1+2)+3)+4 or 1+((2+3)+4) or in several other ways. The second argument of the operator declaration

```
:- op(700, xfx, before).
```

is used to handle terms like this. In fact xfx is the strictest form of infix binary operator and it does not allow such ambiguity. We shall return to this form in a moment.

To allow terms such as 1+2+3+4 the forms yfx and xfy are provided. They denote left associativity and right associativity. The operator +/2 is predeclared in Prolog as follows:

```
:- op(500, yfx, +).
```

With this declaration the term 1+2+3+4 is successfully parsed and is equivalent to the term ((1+2)+3)+4. The binary '-' is also declared as left associative:[4]

```
:- op(500, yfx, -).
```

We can also declare a right associative operator

```
:- op(500, xfy, ++).
```

and then the term 1++2++3++4 is parsed as 1++(2++(3++4)).

In turn, of/2 is declared as a non-associative operator:

```
:- op(650, xfx, of).
```

This rules out expressions such as a of b of c.

Similarly, on account of the declaration

```
:- op(700, xfx, before).
```

the expression t1 before t2 before t3 is rejected by the parser.

ECL^{i}PS^e also allows prefix binary operators to be declared using the forms fxx and fxy. For example, given the declaration

```
:- op(800, fxx, bin).
```

---

[4] This is regrettable since ambiguous terms such as 1-2+3 are then accepted, and – as explained below – are parsed as (1-2)+3. It would be better to use the declaration

```
:-op(500, xfx, -).
```

and require such terms as 1-2+3 to be explicitly bracketed by the user.

ECL^{i}PS^e will successfully parse the term `bin 2 2` as `bin(2,2)`.

3.5.4 Unary operators

In addition to binary operators, Prolog also admits unary prefix or postfix operators. For example the unary '-' is predeclared as a prefix operator, so we can write `-1 + 2`. The operator declaration for this prefix unary operator `-/1` is:

```
:- op(500, fx, -).
```

Because the priority of `before` is 700, the operator `-/1` binds tighter than `before`. Consequently the expression

```
- T1 before T2
```

is parsed like

```
(- T1) before T2.
```

In addition to the form `fx` also the forms `xf`, `fy` and `yf` are allowed. Together with the forms for binary operators they allow for ambiguous situations with operators with the same priority. In the specification of an operator (e.g. `xf`, `yfx`, `xfy`), 'x' represents an argument whose priority must be lower than that of the operator and 'y' represents an argument whose priority must be lower than or equal to that of the operator.

For example, `+/2` has the same priority as `-/1`. Because the declaration of `-/1` specifies `fx` and not `fy`, the term following '-' cannot have the form `X+Y`. Consequently

```
- X + Y
```

is parsed like

```
(- X) + Y.
```

Moreover, the form `fx` of `-/1` ensures that the expression

```
- - Y
```

is illegal.

3.6 Summary

In this chapter we discussed Prolog facilities for arithmetic. They consist of

- the `is/2` built-in that allows us to evaluate ground arithmetic expressions,

- the customary six comparison operators, written as

     `<, =<, =:=, =\=, >=,  >,`

- the `number/1` built-in that tests whether its argument is a number,
- the possibility of declaring a function symbol or a predicate in an infix or postfix form by means of an operator declaration. These declarations involve the following forms for the binary function symbols:

  - `xfx` (no associativity),
  - `xfy` (right associativity),
  - `yfx` (left associativity),
  - `fxx`,
  - `fxy`,

and for the unary function symbols:

  - `fx`,
  - `fy`,
  - `xf`,
  - `yf`.

The arithmetic operators mentioned in Section 3.2 are predeclared as

```
:- op(500, yfx, [+, -]).
:- op(500,  fx, -).
:- op(400, yfx, [*, //, div, rem, mod]).
:- op(200, xfy, ^).
```

This ensures the binding order and the associativity information stated in Section 3.2.

In turn, the comparison predicates introduced in Section 3.3 are predeclared as

```
:- op(700, xfx, [<, =<, =:=, =\=, >=, >]).
```

When discussing the comparison predicates we introduced the distinction between passive and active constraints to which we shall return in later chapters.

Finally, we would like to point out that the possibility of declaring a function symbol or a predicate in an infix or postfix form allows us to view programs as data and consequently to realise meta-programming in a straightforward way. We shall explain this in detail in the next chapter.

3.7 Exercises

Exercise 3.1 What is the ECL^{i}PS^e output to the following queries?

1.   X is 7, X is 6.

2.   X is 7, X is X+1.

3.   X is X+1, X is 7.

4.   X is 3, Y is X+1.

5.   Y is X+1, X is 3.

Exercise 3.2 Consider the following program:

q(X) :- Z is 1.

inc(X) :- Z is X+1.

What is the ECL^{i}PS^e output to the following queries?

1. Z is 2, q(X).

2. Z is 2, q(Z).

3. Z is 2, q(X), Y is Z+1.

4. Z = 2, inc(X), X = 2.

5. X = 2, inc(X), Z = 2.

Exercise 3.3 Consider the following two programs:

% min(X, Y, Z) :- Z is the minimum of the gaes X and Y.

min(X, Y, X) :- X < Y.
min(X, Y, Y) :- X >= Y.

and

% min(X, Y, Z) :- Z is the minimum of the gaes X and Y.

min(X, Y, Z) :- X < Y, Z is X.

```
min(X, Y, Z) :- X >= Y, Z is Y.
```

Find a query for which they yield different answers.

Exercise 3.4 Assume the following declarations:

```
:- op(500, yfx, have).
:- op(400, yfx, and).
```

What are the interpretations of the following terms (that is, what is their representation in the customary first-order logic syntax):

1. `she and he have luck`,
2. `they have time and money and luck`.

Exercise 3.5 Redefine the `len/2` predicate from Figure 3.1 on page 45 as an infix operator `has_length/2`, using an appropriate operator declaration.

4

Control and meta-programming

S O FAR, IT looks that Prolog syntax is just a syntactic sugar of the first-order logic syntax. This is, however, not the case and Prolog's novel use of syntax turns it into a powerful language. This is achieved by a combination of three Prolog features: operators, ambivalent syntax and meta-variables. We continue our presentation with the latter two.

4.1 More on Prolog syntax

4.1.1 Ambivalent syntax

The power of the operators in Prolog becomes apparent only when they are combined with two other syntactic features of Prolog, *ambivalent syntax* and *meta-variables*.

To explain the first one let us recall that in the first-order logic one assumes that the sets of used function symbols and predicates are disjoint. In Prolog this assumption is relaxed and there is no difference between function symbols and predicates. A function symbol or a predicate f of arity n is referred to as f/n and is called a *functor*. Once there is no difference between function symbols and predicates the difference between terms and atomic goals also disappears. A term or an atomic goal is called in Prolog a *structure*.

Moreover, also in contrast to first-order logic, the same name can be used to denote function symbols or predicates of different arity. For example, it is perfectly legal to use in a Prolog program functors p/1 and p/2 and build syntactically legal structures such as p(p(a,b),c,p(X)). Whether such a structure corresponds to a term or to an atomic goal depends on the context in which it is used. For example, in the clause

```
p(p(a,b), c, p(X)) :- q(a,b,X).
```

the above structure is used as an atomic goal and in the clause

```
q(X) :- r(p(p(a,b),c,p(X))).
```

it is used as a term. In both cases we have syntactically legal Prolog clauses.

In the presence of the ambivalent syntax we need to modify slightly the MARTELLI–MONTANARI unification algorithm of Section 1.4 by using instead of action (2) the following one:

$(2')$ $f(s_1,...,s_n) = g(t_1,...,t_m)$ $\qquad\qquad$ *halt with failure,*
$\qquad$ where $f \not\equiv g$ or $n \neq m$.

This takes care of equations such as f(s) = f(t,u) which are now syntactically allowed. (Here s,t,u are structures.)

In the previous chapter we explained using the example of the before/2 predicate that binary predicates can be turned into operators. Now that we have also introduced the ambivalent syntax only one small step is needed to realise meta-programming in Prolog. Namely, it suffices to identify queries and clauses with the structures. To this end we just view the comma ',' separating the atomic goals of a query as a right-associative, infix operator and ':-' as an infix operator. To ensure the correct interpretation of the resulting structures the following declarations are internally stipulated:

```
:- op(1000, xfy, ',').
:- op(1200, xfx, :-).
```

So when referring to the first operator we use quotes and write ','/2. .

To see how we can now view a clause as a structure consider for instance the clause

```
qs([X | Xs], Ys) :-
    part(X, Xs, Littles, Bigs),
    qs(Littles, Ls),
    qs(Bigs, Bs),
    app(Ls, [X | Bs], Ys)
```

of the QUICKSORT program. The reader can easily check that it is a structure with the priority 1200 and interpretation

```
:-(qs([X | Xs], Ys),
   (part(X, Xs, Littles, Bigs),
     (qs(Littles, Ls),
       (qs(Bigs, Bs),
          app(Ls, [X | Bs], Ys)
       )
     )
   )
 ).
```

Now that we have identified queries and clauses with structures we can naturally view programs as lists of clauses and pass them as arguments. However, it is much more convenient to be able to access the considered program directly. To this end Prolog provides a built-in that we shall discuss in Section 4.3.

4.1.2 Meta-variables

Another unusual syntactic feature of Prolog is that it permits the use of variables in the positions of atomic goals, both in the queries and in the clause bodies. Such a use of a variable is called a ***meta-variable***. Computation in the presence of the meta-variables is defined as for pure Prolog programs with the exception that the mgus employed now also bind the meta-variables. So for example, given the QUICKSORT program and the clause

```
solve(Q) :- Q.
```

the query solve(qs([7,9,8,1,5], Ys)) resolves in one step to the already considered (in Section 3.3) query qs([7,9,8,1,5], Ys) that succeeds and produces the answer Ys = [1,5,7,8,9].

Prolog requires that the meta-variables become instantiated before they are selected. Otherwise a run-time error arises. For example, the query solve(Q) ends up in a run-time error.

Meta-variables are useful in a number of ways as we shall see in the next two sections.

4.2 Control

So far the only control mechanism we introduced is the automatic back-tracking. Prolog provides several control statements that allow one to write more efficient and simpler programs.

if-then-else The familiar **if B then S else T** statement is present in Prolog and is written, in a somewhat awkward way, as

```
B -> S ; T.
```

It has the expected meaning: if B succeeds, then the execution proceeds with S and if B fails, then the execution proceeds with T. There is no separate provision for the **if B then S** statement. So it is written as **if B then S else true**, so as

```
B -> S ; true.
```

Further, `B -> S ; fail` abbreviates to `B -> S`.

The evaluation of B can lead to the side effects if at the moment of its evaluation it contains variables. For example we have

```
[eclipse 1]: X = a -> Y = a ; Y = b.

X = a
Y = a
Yes (0.00s cpu)
```

As a more meaningful example consider the problem of modifying the `ORDERED` program of Figure 3.3 so that in the case of a wrong input an appropriate information is printed. To this end we use the `number/1` built-in which tests whether its argument is a number and the `write/1` built-in which writes its argument (which can be a compound term, like `'wrong input':H`) below). This modification is presented in Figure 4.1.

We get then as desired

```
[eclipse 2]: ordered([1,a,0]).
wrong input : a
Yes (0.00s cpu)
```

Disjunction Next, we discuss two control mechanisms of Prolog inspired by the first-order logic. Both are powerful additions to Prolog. We shall discuss their merits later.

Disjunction is a Prolog's built-in written as an infix operator `;/2`. The query `Q ; R` is executed in a completely analogous way as the alternative

```
% ordered(Xs) :- Xs is an =<-ordered list of numbers.

ordered([]).
ordered([H | Ts]) :-
    ( number(H) ->
        ordered(H, Ts)
    ;
        write('wrong input':H)
    ).


% ordered(H, Ts) :- [H|Ts] is an =<-ordered list of numbers.

ordered(_, []).
ordered(H, [Y | Ts]) :-
    ( number(Y) ->
      H =< Y, ordered(Y, Ts)
    ;
        write('wrong input':Y)
    ).
```

Fig. 4.1 Another ORDERED program

choice statement discussed in Section 2.2. So the explanation of its meaning involves the already discussed there concept of a choice point. First, a choice point is created which consists of the query Q and the current substitution (state). Then the query Q executed. If it succeeds, the computed substitution is displayed. When a request for more solutions is issued, the backtracking to the last created choice point takes place. The same happens when Q fails but in that case of course no substitution is displayed. If R succeeds, the new computed substitution is displayed. If R fails a backtracking takes place to the last choice point created before the execution of the query Q ; R. If no such choice point is present, a failure results. So for example

```
[eclipse 3]: X = a ; X = b.

X = a
More (0.00s cpu) ? ;

X = b
```

```
Yes (0.00s cpu)

[eclipse 4]: X = a, (X = b ; Y = c).

X = a
Y = c
Yes (0.00s cpu)
```

Internally the disjunction is defined in a remarkably concise way thanks to the automatic backtracking and the presence of meta-variables. We just need the following declaration and clauses that employ the meta-variables:

```
:- op(1100, xfy, ;).
X ; _ :- X.
_ ; Y :- Y.
```

Negation In turn, *negation* is a unary functor not/1 written in the bracketless prefix form. To use a catchy phrase, not turns failure into a success. More precisely, the query not Q succeeds if and only if the query Q fails. Thus we have

```
[eclipse 5]: not a = b.

Yes (0.00s cpu)
[eclipse 6]: not a = a.

No (0.00s cpu)
```

Also note that we have

```
[eclipse 7]: not X = 1.

No (0.00s cpu)
```

The reason is that the query not X = 1 fails since the query X = 1 succeeds. However, there exists an instance of X that is different than 1, for example 2. So the use of not in the presence of variables can lead to counterintuitive answers. From the declarative point of view it is preferable to use it only as a test, so when the query in its scope, like a = b in not a = b, has no variables at the moment of the execution.

We shall discuss the internal definition of not once we introduce the so-called *cut* functor.

Once Next, Prolog provides the functor once/1. The query once Q is executed the same way as Q is with the exception that once a solution is found, the other solutions are discarded. So for example

```
[eclipse 8]: once (X = a ; X = b).
```

```
X = a
Yes (0.00s cpu)
```

```
[eclipse 9]: once(a = b).
```

```
No (0.00s cpu)
```

Again, we shall discuss the internal definition of once after we have introduced the *cut* functor.

Cut The most controversial control facility of Prolog is the nullary functor called **cut** and denoted by '!/0'. It is used to make the programs more efficient by pruning the computation tree over which the search for solutions takes place. Informally, the cut means 'commit to the current choice and discard other solutions', though the precise meaning is more complicated. To explain its effect, we explain first the implementation of two already introduced built-ins using cut.

The once/1 functor is internally defined by means of the following declaration and the single clause:

```
:- op(900, fy, once).
once Q :- Q, !.
```

So once Q is executed by executing Q first. If Q succeeds for the first time the cut functor '!' is executed. This has the effect that the execution of once Q successfully terminates without any attempt to explore whether other solutions to Q exist. If Q fails, then once Q fails, as well.

The implementation of the negation functor not/1 is equally short though much less easy to understand:

```
:- op(900, fy, not).
not Q :- Q, !, fail.
not _ .
```

Here fail/0 is a Prolog built-in with the empty definition. This cryptic two line program employs several discussed features of Prolog. Consider the call not Q, where Q is a query. If Q succeeds, then the cut '!' is performed.

This has the effect that all alternative ways of computing Q are discarded *and also* the second clause is discarded. Next, the built-in `fail` is executed and a failure arises. Since the only alternative clause was just discarded, the query `not Q` fails. If on the other hand the query Q fails, then the backtracking takes place and the second clause, `not _`, is selected. It immediately succeeds with the empty substitution and so the initial query `not Q` succeeds with the empty substitution.

After these two examples of the uses of cut let us provide its definition in full generality. Consider the following definition of a predicate p:

$$p(s_1) \; \text{:-} \; \mathbf{A}_1.$$

$$\ldots$$

$$p(s_i) \; \text{:-} \; \mathbf{B}, !, \mathbf{C}.$$

$$\ldots$$

$$p(s_k) \; \text{:-} \; \mathbf{A}_k.$$

Here the ith clause contains the cut '!'. Suppose now that during the execution of a query a call `p(t)` is encountered and eventually the ith clause is used and the indicated occurrence of the cut is executed. Then this occurrence of '!' succeeds immediately, but additionally

(i) all alternative ways of computing **B** are discarded, and

(ii) all computations of `p(t)` using the $i + 1$th to kth clause for **p** are discarded as backtrackable alternatives to the current selection of the ith clause.

The cut was introduced in Prolog to improve the efficiency of the programs. As an example let us return to the **QUICKSORT** program defined in Figure 3.4 of Section 3.3 and consider the execution of a typical query such as `qs([7,9,8,1,5], Ys)`. To see that the resulting computation is inefficient let us focus on the definition of the **part/4** predicate:

```
part(_, [], [], []).
part(X, [Y | Xs], [Y | Ls], Bs) :-
    X > Y,
    part(X, Xs, Ls, Bs).
part(X, [Y | Xs], Ls, [Y | Bs]) :-
    X =< Y,
    part(X, Xs, Ls, Bs).
```

The above query `qs([7,9,8,1,5], Ys)` leads to the call

```
part(7, [9,8,1,5], Littles, Bigs).
```

Now the execution of the second clause above fails when 7 is compared with 9 and subsequently the last, third, clause is tried. At this moment 7 is again compared with 9. The same redundancy occurs later when 1 is compared with 5. To avoid such inefficiencies the definition of part/4 can be rewritten using the cut as follows:

```
part(_, [], [], []).
part(X, [Y | Xs], [Y | Ls], Bs) :-
    X > Y, !,
    part(X, Xs, Ls, Bs).
part(X, [Y | Xs], Ls, [Y | Bs]) :-
    part(X, Xs, Ls, Bs).
```

So the cut is introduced after the test X > Y whereas the test X =< Y is deleted. The reader can easily check that the cut has the desired effect here.

The cut can also be used to ensure that only one solution is produced. Consider for example the MEMBER program defined in Figure 4.2.[1]

```
% mem(Element, List) :- Element is an element
%                       of the list List.

mem(X, [X | _]).
mem(X, [_ | Xs]) :- mem(X, Xs).
```

Fig. 4.2 The MEMBER program

This program can be used both to check whether an element is a member of a list or to generate all members of a list:

```
[eclipse 10]: mem(wed, [jan, wed, fri]).

More (0.00s cpu) ? ;

No (0.00s cpu)

[eclipse 11]: mem(X, [jan, wed, fri]).

X = jan
More (0.00s cpu) ? ;
```

[1] member/2 is actually a built-in so we denote the defined predicate by mem/2.

```
X = wed
More (0.00s cpu) ? ;

X = fri
More (0.00s cpu) ? ;

No (0.00s cpu)
```

To ensure that only one solution is produced we modify the MEMBER program by adding to the first clause the cut:

```
mem_check(X, [X | _]) :- !.
mem_check(X, [_ | Xs]) :- mem_check(X, Xs).
```

After this change we now have

```
[eclipse 12]: mem_check(wed, [jan, wed, fri]).

Yes (0.00s cpu)

[eclipse 13]: mem_check(X, [jan, wed, fri]).

X = jan
Yes (0.00s cpu)
```

Another use of the cut will be illustrated in the next section. In general, the cut is a powerful mechanism inherent to Prolog. Some of its uses can be replaced by employing other built-ins that are internally defined using the cut. For example, instead of the just discussed revision of the MEMBER program we could use the once/1 built-in and simply run the queries of the form once(mem(s,t)). Further, notice that the not/1 built-in can be defined in a much more intuitive way using the if-then-else statement as follows:

```
not Q :- (Q -> fail ; true).
```

The above clause simply formalises the intuitive meaning of negation, namely that it reverses failure and success. What is happening here is that the cut is absorbed in the if-then-else statement, which itself can be defined using the cut as follows:

```
if_then_else(B, Q, R) :- B,!,Q.
if_then_else(B, Q, R) :- R.
```

On the other hand, several natural uses of the cut can be modelled by means of other built-ins only at the cost of, sometimes considerable, rewriting of the program that can affect the readability. For example, in the case of the **part/4** predicate we can use the **if-then-else** operator and rewrite the second clause as

```
part(X, [Y | Xs], Ls, Bs) :-
   ( X > Y ->
      Ls = [Y | L1s], part(X, Xs, L1s, Bs)
   ;
      Bs = [Y | B1s], part(X, Xs, Ls, B1s)
   ).
```

The effect is the same as when using the cut but we had to introduce the explicit calls to the unification functor =/2.

Non-trivial complications arise during the interaction of the cut with other Prolog built-ins. In some situations cut is not allowed. For example, no cuts are allowed in the query B in the context of the **if-then-else** call B -> S ; T. Moreover, once the cut is used, the clause order becomes of crucial importance. For example, if we ignore the efficiency considerations, in the original **QUICKSORT** program the order of the clauses defining the **part/4** predicate was immaterial. This is no longer the case in the revised definition of **part/4** that uses the cut. In short, the cut has to be used with considerable care.

4.3 Meta-programming

4.3.1 Accessing programs directly

We explained in Section 4.1 how Prolog programs can be conveniently passed as data, in the form of a list of clauses. But it is much more convenient to be able to access the considered program directly. To this end Prolog provides the **clause/2** built-in.

In its call the first argument has to be a term that is neither a variable nor a number. This makes it possible to determine the functor to which the call refers to. So for example each of the calls **clause(X, Y)** and **clause(100, Y)** yields a run-time error, while the call **clause(p(X), Y)** may succeed or fail.

Given a call **clause(head, body)**, first the term **head** is unified with a head of a clause present in the considered program. If no such clause exists, the call **clause(head, body)** fails. Otherwise, the first such clause is picked and the term **head :- body** is unified with this clause. (It is assumed that **true** is the body of a unit clause. (**true/0** is a Prolog built-in that immediately succeeds.) Upon backtracking successive choices for **head** are considered and the corresponding alternative solutions are generated.

As an example of the use of **clause/2** assume that the file with the **QUICKSORT** program of Figure 3.4 from page 50 is read in. Then we have the following interaction:[2]

```
[eclipse 14]: clause(qs(U, V), Z).
```

```
U = []
V = []
Z = true
Yes (0.00s cpu, solution 1, maybe more) ? ;
```

```
U = [X|Xs]
V = V
Z = part(X, Xs, Littles, Bigs), qs(Littles, Ls),
    qs(Bigs, Bs), app(Ls, [X|Bs], V)
Yes (0.00s cpu, solution 2)
```

which shows how easily we can 'dissect' the definition of the **qs/2** predicate into parts that can be further analysed. Note three references to the ',' /2 operator in the structure assigned to Z.

To be able to access the definition of a functor **p/n** by means of the **clause/2** built-in, **p/n** has to be declared as a *dynamic predicate*. For example, the above interaction with the **QUICKSORT** program requires the presence of the declaration

```
:- dynamic qs/2.
```

4.3.2 Meta-interpreters

Using the **clause/2** built-in it is remarkably easy to write meta-interpreters, so programs that execute other programs. As an example consider the problem of writing in Prolog an interpreter for pure Prolog. The program is presented in Figure 4.3. It is strikingly concise and intuitive.

The first clause states that the built-in **true/0** succeeds immediately. The second clause states that a query of the form **A,B** succeeds if both A and B

---

[2] In ECL^{i}PS^e the values of all variables are displayed. This explains the superfluous equation V
   = V. In particular, the empty substitution is displayed as a sequence of such equalities for each
   variable present in the query.

```
% solve(X)   :-
%     The query X succeeds for the pure Prolog
%     program accessible by clause/2.

solve(true) :- !.
solve((A,B)) :- !, solve(A), solve(B).
solve(H) :- clause(H, Body), solve(Body).
```

Fig. 4.3 The META_INTERPRETER program

succeed. Here A,B is a structure the functor of which is ',' /2. Recall from page 60 that ',' /2 was declared by

```
:- op(1000, xfy, ',').
```

So ',' /2 is right associative and in A,B the first argument, A, denotes an atomic goal and the second argument, B, a sequence of the remaining goals. The additional pair of brackets around A,B is neccessary to ensure that A,B is passed as one argument to solve.

Finally, the last clause states that an atomic query H succeeds if there exists a clause of the form H :- Body such that the query Body succeeds. The cuts are used here to enforce the distinction 'by cases': either the argument of solve is true or else a non-atomic query or else an atomic one.

To illustrate the behaviour of the META_INTERPRETER program assume that APPEND is a part of the considered program. We then have

```
[eclipse 15]: solve((app(Xs, [_, _|Ys], [mon, wed, fri, sun]),
                      app(Xs, Ys, Zs))).

Xs = []
Ys = [fri, sun]
Zs = [fri, sun]
More (0.00s cpu) ? ;

Xs = [mon]
Ys = [sun]
Zs = [mon, sun]
More (0.00s cpu) ? ;

Xs = [mon, wed]
```

```
Ys = []
Zs = [mon, wed]
More (0.00s cpu) ? ;
```

```
No (0.00s cpu)
```

So we get the same results as when executing the query

```
app(Xs, [_, _|Ys], [mon, wed, fri, sun]), app(Xs, Ys, Zs)
```

directly.

The META_INTERPRETER program forms a basis for several non-trivial meta-programs written in Prolog, including debuggers, tracers, interpreters and partial evaluators. As an example of a simple extension of this program consider the problem of enhancing the answers to the queries with the length of the derivation. The appropriate modification of solve/1 is straightforward and is presented in Figure 4.4.

```
% solve(X, N)   :-
%      The query X succeeds for the pure Prolog
%      program accessible by clause/2 in N steps.

solve(true, 0) :- !.
solve((A, B), N) :- !, solve(A, N1), solve(B, N2),
                 N is N1+N2.
solve(H, N) :- clause(H, Body), solve(Body, M),
                 N is M+1.
```

Fig. 4.4 The SOLVE program

For the same query as above we now get the following answers:

```
[eclipse 16]: solve((app(Xs, [_, _|Ys], [mon, wed, fri, sun]),
                 app(Xs, Ys, Zs)), N).
```

```
Xs = []
Ys = [fri, sun]
Zs = [fri, sun]
N = 2
More (0.00s cpu) ? ;
```

```
Xs = [mon]
Ys = [sun]
Zs = [mon, sun]
N = 4
More (0.00s cpu) ? ;

Xs = [mon, wed]
Ys = []
Zs = [mon, wed]
N = 6
More (0.00s cpu) ? ;


No (0.00s cpu)
```

By using meta-variables we can easily extend the above program SOLVE so that it also deals with the programs that use the comparison predicates. To this end it suffices to modify it as in Figure 4.5.

```
solve(true, 0) :- !.
solve(A, 1) :- arithmetic(A), !, A.
solve((A, B), N) :- !, solve(A, N1), solve(B, N2),
                    N is N1+N2.
solve(H, N) :- clause(H, Body), solve(Body, M),
               N is M+1.

arithmetic(_ < _).
arithmetic(_ =< _).
arithmetic(_ =:= _).
arithmetic(_ =\= _).
arithmetic(_ >= _).
arithmetic(_ > _).
```

Fig. 4.5 The SOLVE2 program

In this program the calls of the arithmetic atomic queries are just shifted to the 'system level'. In other words, these calls are executed *directly* by the underlying Prolog system. We now have

```
[eclipse 17]: solve(qs([7,9,8,1,5], Ys), N).
```

```
Ys = [1, 5, 7, 8, 9]
N = 36
More (0.00s cpu) ? ;
```

```
No (0.00s cpu)
```

So it takes 36 derivation steps to compute the answer to the query

`qs([7,9,8,1,5], Ys).`

4.4 Summary

In this chapter we discussed in turn:

- ambivalent syntax and meta-variables,
- various control constructs,
- meta-programming.

In the process we introduced the following built-ins:

- the `if-then-else` statement written in Prolog as B -> S ; T,
- `write/1`,
- disjunction: `;/2`,
- negation: `not/1`,
- `fail/0`,
- `once/1`,
- cut: `!/0`,
- `clause/2`.

In particular we showed how the syntactic features of Prolog (and the absence of types) make it easy to write various meta-programs. The ambivalent syntax goes beyond the first-order logic syntax. It is useful to realise that there is an alternative syntactic reading of Prolog programs in which the first-order logic syntax is respected and the ambivalent syntax is not used. Namely, after interpreting the operators used as the customary prefix operators we can view each Prolog clause as a construct of the form

$$s :- t_1, \ldots, t_n,$$

where s is a term that is neither a variable or a number and each t_i is a term that is not a number.

This syntactic reading respects the first-order logic but has one important disadvantage. Namely, the declarative interpretation of the programs that relied on the use of the predicates is then lost. The ambivalent syntax can be viewed as an attempt to restore the declarative interpretation in the presence of the operators.

4.5 Exercises

Exercise 4.1 Redefine the `len/2` predicate from Figure 3.1 on page 45 so that it can be used both to compute the length of a list, and to build a list of different variables of a specified length, like the `length/2` built-in. *Hint*. Use the `integer/1` built-in which tests whether its argument is an integer.

Exercise 4.2 Suppose we maintain sets as lists. Consider the following two ways of defining the result of adding an element to a set:

```
% add(X, Xs, Ys) :- The set Ys is the result of adding
%                   the element X to the set Ys.

add(X, Xs, Ys) :- member(X, Xs), !, Xs = Ys.
add(X, Xs, [X | Xs]).
```

and

```
add(X, Xs, Xs) :- member(X, Xs), !.
add(X, Xs, [X | Xs]).
```

Find a query for which they yield different answers.

Exercise 4.3 Propose an implementation of a predicate `while(B, S)` which is to simulate the customary `while B do S` statement of imperative programming.

5

Manipulating structures

W E MENTIONED EARLY on that Prolog computations take place over the set of all terms. One of the useful features of Prolog is that it allows us to access the elements of this data by providing various built-ins for inspecting, comparing and decomposing terms. On the other hand, as we shall see, these features compromise the declarative character of the language

Because of the ambivalent syntax of Prolog (discussed in Section 4.1) we shall rather talk about structures instead of terms. These built-ins can be naturally divided into three categories.

5.1 Structure inspection facilities

Here are the most important built-ins belonging to this category.

- `var/1`, which tests whether the structure is a variable:

```
[eclipse 1]: var(X).

X = X
Yes (0.00s cpu)
[eclipse 2]: var(f(X)).

No (0.00s cpu)
```

- `nonvar/1`, which tests whether the structure is not a variable:

  ```
  [eclipse 3]: nonvar(f(X)), nonvar(a).
  ```

  ```
  X = X
  Yes (0.00s cpu)
  ```

- `ground/1`, which tests whether the structure is ground (has no variables):

  ```
  [eclipse 4]: ground(f(a,b,c)).
  ```

  ```
  Yes (0.00s cpu)
  [eclipse 5]: ground(f(a,b,X)).
  ```

  ```
  No (0.00s cpu)
  ```

- `compound/1`, which tests whether the structure is compound:

  ```
  [eclipse 6]: compound(f(a,b,c)).
  ```

  ```
  Yes (0.00s cpu)
  [eclipse 7]: compound(a).
  ```

  ```
  No (0.00s cpu)
  ```

- `number/1`, which tests whether the structure is a number (already mentioned in Section 4.2):

  ```
  [eclipse 8]: number(10), number(-8), number(3.14).
  ```

  ```
  Yes (0.00s cpu)
  ```

- `atom/1`, which tests whether the structure is a non-numeric constant (an *atom* in Prolog's terminology):

  ```
  [eclipse 9]: atom(a).
  ```

  ```
  Yes (0.00s cpu)
  [eclipse 10]: atom(10).
  ```

  ```
  No (0.00s cpu)
  ```

- `atomic/1`, which tests whether the structure is a constant, so an atom or a number:

```
[eclipse 11]: atomic(a), atomic(3.14).
```

```
Yes (0.00s cpu)
```

To see why these built-ins affect the declarative reading of the programs consider a query of the form **A, A**. In the case of pure Prolog its effect is the same as **A**. In fact, the second call of **A** becomes then a test, like in the query `f(X,a) = f(b,Y), f(X,a) = f(b,Y)`. In the presence of the `var/1` built-in things change:

```
[eclipse 12]: var(X), X = 1.
```

```
X = 1
Yes (0.00s cpu)
[eclipse 13]: var(X), X = 1, var(X), X = 1.
```

```
No (0.00s cpu)
```

Also the order of various simple atomic goals now becomes crucial: the query `var(X), X = 1` succeeds but the query `X = 1, var(X)` fails.

5.2 Structure comparison facilities

Next, the following built-ins allows us to compare structures.

- `==/2`, which tests whether two structures are literally identical:

  ```
  [eclipse 14]: f(X) == f(X).
  ```

  ```
  X = X
  Yes (0.00s cpu)
  [eclipse 15]: f(X) == f(Y).
  ```

  ```
  No (0.00s cpu)
  ```

- `\==/2`, which tests whether two structures are not literally identical:

  ```
  [eclipse 16]: f(X) \== f(X).
  ```

  ```
  No (0.00s cpu)
  [eclipse 17]: f(X) \== f(Y).
  ```

  ```
  X = X
  Y = Y
  ```

```
Yes (0.00s cpu)
```

So these two built-ins are used as infix operators. In ECL^{i}PS^e they are defined internally as follows:

```
:- op(700, xfx, [==, \==]).
```

As an example of the use of the built-ins introduced so far consider the following seemingly trivial problem.

Problem Write a Prolog program that tests whether a term is a list.

A natural idea is to mimic the definition of a list:

```
list([]) :- !.
list([_ | Ts]) :- list(Ts).
```

(The cut prevents backtracking in the case of success.) Unfortunately, this program is incorrect. Indeed, the query `list(X)` then succeeds instead of failing:

```
[eclipse 18]: list(X).
```

```
X = []
Yes (0.00s cpu)
```

The obvious correction consists of using in the first clause the ==/2 built-in:

```
list(X) :- X == [], !.
list([_ | Ts]) :- list(Ts).
```

Now, however, the query `list(X)` diverges. The reason is that during its execution a backtracking takes place and then the second clause is repeatedly used. The right remedy turns out to add an appropriate test in the second clause. The resulting program is given in Figure 5.1.

```
% list(X) :- X is a list.

list(X) :- X == [], !.
list([_ | Ts]) :- nonvar(Ts), list(Ts).
```

Fig. 5.1 The LIST program

5.3 Structure decomposition and construction facilities

The built-ins in this category allow us to decompose the structures. To explain their meaning we use the following terminology. Given a structure $f(s_1, \ldots, s_n)$, where $n \geq 0$, we say that f is its *leading symbol*, n is its *arity*, $s_1, \ldots, s_n$ are its *arguments* and s_i is its *ith argument* ($i \in [1..n]$). (So if $n = 0$ the structure has no arguments.) In addition, we call a structure of the form $f(x_1, \ldots, x_n)$, where $n \geq 0$ and $x_1, \ldots, x_n$ are different variables, a *most general structure of arity n*. When $n = 0$ the most general structure is simply a constant.

The following three built-ins are most relevant.

functor/3 The `functor/3` built-in either extracts from a structure the leading symbol and its arity or constructs a most general structure of the given arity with the given function symbol as the leading symbol.

More precisely, consider the query `functor(t, f, n)`. Two cases arise.

- t is a non-variable structure.

    Let `f1` be the leading symbol of `t` and `n1` the arity of `t`. Then the query `functor(t, f, n)` is executed by unifying the pair `(f,n)` with `(f1,n1)`. For example,

    ```
    [eclipse 19]: functor(f(a,b), F, N).


    F = f
    N = 2
    Yes (0.00s cpu)
    [eclipse 20]: functor(c, F, N).


    F = c
    N = 0
    Yes (0.00s cpu)
    ```

    In the presence of the arithmetic operators `functor/3` deals correctly with the infix notation:

    ```
    [eclipse 21]: functor(3*4+5, F, N).


    F = +
    N = 2
    Yes (0.00s cpu)
    ```

Also, `functor/3` allows us to reveal the internal representation of lists:

```
[eclipse 22]: functor([], F, N).

F = []
N = 0
Yes (0.00s cpu)
[eclipse 23]: functor([a | b], F, N).

F = .
N = 2
Yes (0.00s cpu)
```

Indeed, the lists are represented internally using the functor ./2 and the constant []. For example we have:

```
[eclipse 24]: X = .(a, .(b, [])).

X = [a, b]
Yes (0.00s cpu)
```

- t is a variable.

  Then f has to be a non-numeric constant (an atom) and n a natural number. Then the query of functor(t, f, n) is executed by instantiating t to a most general structure of arity n the leading symbol of which is f. For example:

```
[eclipse 25]: functor(T, f, 3).

T = f(_163, _164, _165)
Yes (0.00s cpu)
[eclipse 26]: functor(T, f, 0).

T = f
Yes (0.00s cpu)
[eclipse 27]: functor(T, ., 2).

T = [_162|_163]
Yes (0.00s cpu)
```

All other uses of functor/3 lead to a run-time error.

arg/3 The arg/3 built-in extracts a specific argument from a structure. Consider the query arg(n, t, a). Then n has to be a natural number

and t a compound structure. The query `arg(n, t, a)` is then executed by
unifying the nth argument of t with a. For example:

```
[eclipse 28]: arg(2, f(a, g(a, X), c), A).

X = X
A = g(a, X)
Yes (0.00s cpu)
[eclipse 29]:  arg(2, [a,b,c], A).

A = [b, c]
Yes (0.00s cpu)
```

As an example of the use of these built-ins consider the following problem.

Problem Given a term produce its list of variables (including repetitions).

The desired program is given in Figure 5.2.

This procedure can be applied to an arbitrary structure, for example a
clause:

```
[eclipse 30]: vars(
               app([X|Xs],Ys,[X|Zs]) :- app(Xs,Ys,Zs), List
               ).

X = X
Xs = Xs
Ys = Ys
Zs = Zs
List = [X, Xs, Ys, X, Zs, Xs, Ys, Zs]
Yes (0.00s cpu)
```

Of course, by a minor modification of the above program we can compute
in the same way the list of variables of a term, without repetitions (see
Exercise 5.2).

=../2 The `=../2` built-in (for historic reasons pronounced "univ") either
creates a list which consists of the leading symbol of the structure followed
by its arguments or constructs a structure from a list that starts with a
function symbol and the tail of which is a list of structure arguments.

It is internally defined as an infix operator with the following declaration:

```
% vars(Term, List) :-
%      List is the list of variables of the term Term.


vars(Term, []) :- atomic(Term), !.
vars(Term, [Term]) :- var(Term), !.
vars(Term, List) :-
    compound(Term),
    functor(Term,_,K),
    args(K, Term, List).


% args(K, Term, List) :-
%      List is the list of variables occurring
%      in the first K arguments of the term Term.


args(0, _, []) :- !.
args(K, Term, List) :-
    K > 0,
    K1 is K-1,
    args(K1, Term, L1s),
    arg(K,Term,A),
    vars(A, L2s),
    app(L1s, L2s, List).
```

augmented by the APPEND program of Figure 1.5.

Fig. 5.2 The VARIABLES program

```
:- op(700, xfx, =..).
```

More precisely, consider the query s =.. t. Two cases arise.

- s is a non-variable structure, say $f(s_1, \ldots, s_n)$. Then the query s =.. t is executed by unifying the list $[f, s_1, \ldots, s_n]$ with t. For example:

```
[eclipse 31]: f(a, g(X)) =.. List.
```

```
X = X
List = [f, a, g(X)]
Yes (0.00s cpu)
```

- s is a variable.

  Then t has to be a list, say $[f, s_1, \ldots, s_n]$ the head of which (so f) is a non-numeric constant (an atom). Then the query `s =.. t` is executed by instantiating `s` to the structure $f(s_1, \ldots, s_n)$. For example:

```
[eclipse 32]: T =.. [app, [a,b], [c,d], Zs].
```

```
T = app([a, b], [c, d], Zs)
Zs = Zs
Yes (0.00s cpu)
```

All other uses of `=../2` lead to a run-time error.

So using `=../2` we can construct terms and pass them as arguments. More interestingly, we can construct queries and execute them using the meta-variable facility. This way it is possible to realise higher-order programming in Prolog in the sense that predicates can be passed as arguments. To illustrate this point consider the program `MAP` given in Figure 5.3.

```
% map(P, Xs, Ys) :-
%     The list Ys is the result of applying P
%     elementwise to the list Xs.

map(_, [], []).
map(P, [X | Xs] , [Y | Ys]) :-
    apply(P, [X, Y]),
    map(P, Xs, Ys).

% apply(P, [X1, ..., Xn]) :-
%     Execute the atomic query P(X1, ..., Xn).

apply(P, Xs) :- Query =.. [P|Xs], Query.
```

Fig. 5.3 The `MAP` program

In the last clause `=../2` is used to construct an atomic query. Note the use of the meta-variable `Query`. `MAP` is Prolog's counterpart of a higher-order functional program and it behaves in the expected way. For example, given the clause

```
increment(X, Y) :- Y is X+1.
```

we get

```
[eclipse 33]: map(increment, [1,2,3,4], Ys).

Ys = [2, 3, 4, 5]
Yes (0.00s cpu)
```

5.4 Summary

In this chapter we discussed Prolog built-ins that allow us to manipulate structures. We discussed built-ins that allow us

- to inspect structures:
  - var/1,
  - nonvar/1,
  - ground/1,
  - compound/1,
  - number/1,
  - atom/1,
  - atomic/1,
- to compare structures:
  - ==/2,
  - \==/2,
- to decompose and construct structures:
  - functor/3,
  - arg/3,
  - ../2.

Using these built-ins we can analyse structures and also realise higher-order programming in Prolog.

5.5 Exercises

Exercise 5.1 Write an alternative version of the program VARIABLES from Figure 5.2 using =../2, without any arithmetic operations.

Exercise 5.2 Modify the program VARIABLES from Figure 5.2 to compute the list of variables of a term, without repetitions.

Exercise 5.3 Write a program that implements the substitution operation. The call subs(Input, X, Term, Output) should perform the substitution of the variable X by the term Term in the input term Input. The result should be produced in the last argument.

Part III

Programming with passive constraints

Constraint programming: a primer

6.1 Introduction

C ONSTRAINT PROGRAMMING IS an alternative approach to programming in which the programming process is limited to a generation of requirements (constraints) and a solution of these requirements by means of general or domain specific methods. In the forthcoming chapters we explain how constraint programming is realised in ECL^{i}PS^e.

To this end we shall explain in turn:

- what constraint satisfaction problems and constrained optimisation problems are and how they are solved using constraint programming methods,
- how to generate these problems in ECL^{i}PS^e,
- what support ECL^{i}PS^e provides for general and domain specific methods,
- how to solve constraint satisfaction problems and constrained optimisation problems in ECL^{i}PS^e.

In this chapter we focus on the first topic. Informally, a constraint satisfaction problem consists of a set of constraints, each on a sequence of variables, and the task is to find a solution to it. In turn, a constrained optimisation problem is a constraint satisfaction problem equipped with a cost function and the task is to find an optimal solution w.r.t. the cost function. In the area of constraint programming various methods and techniques were developed to solve both kind of problems and we shall explain briefly their basics.

6.2 Basic concepts

Syntactically, a **constraint** is an atomic formula in some, usually first-order, language. We already encountered in Chapter 3 constraints that involve arithmetic comparison operators, so $x < y$, $x \leq y$, $x = y$, $x \neq y$, $x \geq y$, $x > y$. But several other natural examples exist and we shall discuss them below. Depending on the number of variables used in a constraint we speak about a **unary**, **binary** or **n-ary** constraint. We assume that each constraint has at least one variable.

When discussing the constraints we have in mind their specific **interpretation** determined by the (non-empty) domains of the variables and the meaning assigned to the used function symbols and predicates. For example, if we interpret the variables over the set of integers $\mathcal{Z}$, then $x < y$ determines the set $\{(a, b) \mid a < b, \ a, b \in \mathcal{Z}\}$, since we implicitly interpret $<$ as the 'less than' relation. In turn, if we interpret the variables over the set of reals $\mathcal{R}$, then $x < y$ determines the set $\{(a, b) \mid a < b, \ a, b \in \mathcal{R}\}$.

In general, each interpretation associates with a constraint c a subset of the Cartesian product of the domains of its variables. We refer to such an **interpretation** of a constraint c as a $[c]$. From the context it will be always clear over which domains the variables range and which interpretation of the used function symbols and predicates we have in mind.

An assignment of values to the constraint variables **satisfies a constraint** (is a **solution** to a constraint) if the used sequence of the values belongs to its interpretation. For example, if we interpret the variables over the set of integers, then the assignment $\{(x, -2), (y, 5)\}$ satisfies the constraint $x^2 < y$. We say that a constraint is **satisfiable** if some assignment of values to its variables satisfies it and **unsatisfiable** if no such assignment exists. For example, if we interpret the variables over the set of reals, the constraint $x > x + y$ is satisfiable, whereas if we interpret the variables over the set of natural numbers, it is unsatisfiable.

In turn, a constraint is **solved** if all assignments of values to its variables satisfy it. For example, if we interpret the variables over the set of natural numbers, the constraint $x + y \geq 0$ is solved.

By a **constraint satisfaction problem**, in short a **CSP**, we mean a finite sequence of variables, each ranging over a possibly different domain, and a finite set of constraints, each on a subsequence of the considered variables. The variables used in a CSP are called **decision variables**. We always consider the CSPs in the context of an interpretation. By a **solution to a CSP** we mean an assignment of values to its variables that satisfies each constraint. We say that a CSP is **consistent** (or **feasible**) if it has a solution and **inconsistent** (or **infeasible**) if it does not.

Further, we call a CSP **solved** if each of its constraints is solved. So a CSP is solved if each assignment of values to its variables is a solution. Finally, we say that a CSP is **failed** if one its domains is empty or one of its constraints is unsatisfiable. Clearly, if a CSP is failed then it is inconsistent, but the reverse implication does not hold. In practice it is much easier to check whether a CSP is failed than whether it is inconsistent.

More formally, consider a CSP involving a sequence of variables $X :=$ $x_1, \ldots, x_n$ with respective domains $D_1, \ldots, D_n$, and a finite set $\mathcal{C}$ of constraints, each on a subsequence of X. We write it as $\langle \mathcal{C} \; ; \; x_1 \in D_1, \ldots, x_n \in D_n \rangle$. By a solution to $\langle \mathcal{C} \; ; \; x_1 \in D_1, \ldots, x_n \in D_n \rangle$ we mean an assignment $\{(x_1, d_1), \ldots, (x_n, d_n)\}$, where each d_i is an element of D_i, such that for each constraint $c \in \mathcal{C}$ on the variables $x_{k_1}, \ldots, x_{k_m}$ we have $(d_{k_1}, \ldots, d_{k_m}) \in [c]$, where $[c]$ is the interpretation of c.

Given two CSPs $\langle \mathcal{C} \; ; \; x_1 \in D_1, \ldots, x_n \in D_n \rangle$ and $\langle \mathcal{C}' \; ; \; x_1 \in D_1', \ldots, x_n \in D_n' \rangle$ on the same sequence of variables we say that they are **equivalent** if they have the same set of solutions.

6.3 Example classes of constraints

Let us discuss now the most common classes of constraints we shall deal with. Each of them is uniquely determined by the considered function symbols and predicates. In each case we have a specific interpretation in mind which is clear from the context.

Equality and disequality constraints

This is the simplest meaningful class of constraints. We have no function symbols and just two predicates, equality, '$=$', and disequality, '$\neq$'. The variables are interpreted over an arbitrary domain.

The constraints can be either unary, like $x = x$, or binary, like $x \neq y$. Further, note that the constraint $x = x$ is solved, while the constraint $x \neq x$ is unsatisfiable. In turn, the constraint $x = y$ is satisfiable iff the domains of x and y are not disjoint, and the constraint $x \neq y$ is satisfiable iff either the domains of x and y are disjoint or at least one of them is not a singleton set.

As an example of a CSP involving these constraints take

$$\langle x = y, y \neq z, z \neq u \ ; \ x \in \{a, b, c\}, y \in \{a, b, d\}, z \in \{a, b\}, u \in \{b\}\rangle.$$

It is straightforward to check that $\{(x, b), (y, b), (z, a), (u, b)\}$ is its unique solution.

Boolean constraints

Boolean constraints are formed using specific function symbols called **connectives**. We adopt the unary connective $\neg$ (**negation**) and the binary connectives $\wedge$ (**conjunction**) and $\vee$ (**disjunction**). We also allow two constants, true and false. The resulting terms are called **Boolean expressions**. The binary connectives are written using the infix notation and $\neg$ when applied to a variable is written without the brackets. By a **Boolean constraint** we mean a formula of the form $s = t$, where s, t are Boolean expressions. So the equality symbol '=' is the only predicate in the language. Each Boolean expression s can be viewed as a shorthand for the Boolean constraint $s = $ true.

The variables are interpreted over the set of truth values, identified with $\{0, 1\}$, and are called **Boolean variables**. In turn, the connectives are interpreted using the standard truth tables. This interpretation allows us to interpret each Boolean constraint c on the Boolean variables $x_1, \ldots, x_n$ as a subset of $\{0, 1\}^n$.

For example, the interpretation of the Boolean constraint $(\neg x) \wedge (y \vee z)$, that is $(\neg x) \wedge (y \vee z) = $ true, is the set

$$\{(0, 0, 1), (0, 1, 0), (0, 1, 1)\},$$

where we assume the alphabetic ordering of the variables.

Linear constraints

Next, we define linear constraints. We shall interpret them either over the set of integers or over the set of reals, or over a subset of one of these sets (usually an interval). To start with, we assume a fixed set of **numeric constants** representing either integers or reals.

As in the case of Boolean constraints we introduce the constraints in two steps. By a **linear expression** we mean a term formed in the alphabet that contains

- the assumed numeric constants,
- for each numeric constant r the unary function symbol '$r\cdot$' (representing the multiplication by r),
- two binary function symbols, '$+$' and '$-$', both written in the infix notation.

We also assume that '$+$' and '$-$' are left associative and have the same binding strength.

By a *linear constraint* we mean a formula of the form

$$s \; op \; t,$$

where s and t are linear expressions and $op \in \{<, \leq, =, \neq, \geq, >\}$.

For example, $4 \cdot x + 3 \cdot (y - x + 7)$ is a linear expression and

$$4 \cdot x + 3 \cdot y - x \leq 5 \cdot z + 7 - y$$

is a linear constraint.

When linear constraints are interpreted over the set of reals, it is customary to admit only $\leq, =$ and $\geq$ as the comparison operators.

Arithmetic constraints

Finally, we introduce arithmetic constraints. The only difference between them and linear constraints lies in the use of the multiplication symbol. In the case of linear constraints the multiplication was allowed only if one of its operands (the first one) was a numeric constant. To fit this restriction into the syntax of first-order logic we introduced the unary multiplication symbols '$r\cdot$'. Now we dispense with these unary function symbols and simply allow the multiplication '$\cdot$' as a binary function symbol.

We define the *arithmetic expressions* and *arithmetic constraints* analogously to the linear expressions and linear constraints, but now using the binary multiplication symbol '$\cdot$'. In particular, each linear constraint is an arithmetic constraint.

For example $4 \cdot x + x \cdot y - x + 7$ is an arithmetic expression and

$$4 \cdot x + x \cdot y - x \leq y \cdot (z + 5) - 3 \cdot u$$

is an arithmetic constraint.

6.4 Constraint satisfaction problems: examples

To clarify the introduced concepts and classes of constraints we now discuss some well-known CSPs. Our interest in introducing these examples is twofold.

- We want to clarify the process of formalising a problem as a CSP.

  This process is usually called **modelling**. In general more than one representation of a problem as a CSP exists and the selection of an appropriate representation can have a dramatic impact on the problem solving process.
- In the subsequent chapters we shall explain how the CSPs introduced here are modelled and solved in ECL^{i}PS^e.

6.4.1 Map colouring problems

These are problems that are specified by

- a finite set of *regions*,
- a (smaller) set of *colours*,
- a *neighbour* relation between pairs of regions.

Given a set of regions and of colours and a neighbour relation the problem is to associate a colour with each region so that no two neighbours have the same colour.

To model such a problem as a CSP we simply use disequality constraints. We represent each region i by a variable x_i. The domain of each variable is the set of assumed colours. Then for each pair of regions (i, j) that are neighbours we introduce the constraint $x_i \neq x_j$.

To be more specific suppose that

- there are four regions 1, 2, 3, 4,
- there are three colours, red, yellow, blue,
- The *neighbour* relation consists of the following set of pairs:

$$\{(1,2),(1,3),(1,4),(2,3),(2,4)\},$$

see Figure 6.1.

Then we have four variables x_1, x_2, x_3, x_4, each ranging over the set $\{\text{red}, \text{yellow}, \text{blue}\}$ and the following set of disequality constraints:

$$\{x_1 \neq x_2,\ x_1 \neq x_3,\ x_1 \neq x_4,\ x_2 \neq x_3,\ x_2 \neq x_4\}.$$

This specific problem has six solutions:

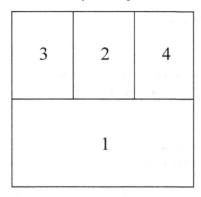

Fig. 6.1 An example map

$\{(x_1, \text{red}), (x_2, \text{yellow}), (x_3, \text{blue}), (x_4, \text{blue})\},$
$\{(x_1, \text{red}), (x_2, \text{blue}), (x_3, \text{yellow}), (x_4, \ \text{yellow})\},$
$\{(x_1, \text{yellow}), (x_2, \text{red}), (x_3, \text{blue}), (x_4, \text{blue})\},$
$\{(x_1, \text{yellow}), (x_2, \text{blue}), (x_3, \text{red}), (x_4, \text{red})\},$
$\{(x_1, \text{blue}), (x_2, \text{red}), (x_3, \text{yellow}), (x_4, \text{yellow})\},$
$\{(x_1, \text{blue}), (x_2, \text{yellow}), (x_3, \text{red}), (x_4, \text{red})\}.$

6.4.2 *SEND + MORE = MONEY* puzzle

This is a classic example of a so-called ***cryptarithmetic problem***. These are mathematical puzzles in which the digits are replaced by letters of the alphabet or other symbols. In the problem under consideration we are asked to replace each letter by a different digit so that the above sum, that is

$$
\begin{array}{r}
SEND \\
+ \ MORE \\
\hline
MONEY
\end{array}
$$

is correct.

The problem can be formulated using linear constraints in a number of different ways. The variables are S, E, N, D, M, O, R, Y. The domain of each variable consists of the integer interval $[0..9]$.

Representation 1 We use the equality constraint

$$
\begin{array}{rcrcrcrcr}
& 1000 \cdot S & + & 100 \cdot E & + & 10 \cdot N & + & D \\
+ & 1000 \cdot M & + & 100 \cdot O & + & 10 \cdot R & + & E \\
= 10000 \cdot M & + & 1000 \cdot O & + & 100 \cdot N & + & 10 \cdot E & + & Y,
\end{array}
$$

two disequality constraints:

$$S \neq 0, \; M \neq 0,$$

and 28 disequality constraints $x \neq y$ for x, y ranging over the set $\{S, E, N, D, M, O, R, Y\}$ with x preceding y in, say, the presented order.

Representation 2 Another natural modelling consists of additionally introducing per column a 'carry' variable ranging over $\{0, 1\}$ and using instead of the above single equality constraint five simpler ones, one for each column:

$$
\begin{aligned}
D + E &= 10 \cdot C_1 + Y, \\
C_1 + N + R &= 10 \cdot C_2 + E, \\
C_2 + E + O &= 10 \cdot C_3 + N, \\
C_3 + S + M &= 10 \cdot C_4 + O, \\
C_4 &= M.
\end{aligned}
$$

Here, $C_1, \ldots, C_4$ are the carry variables.

Representation 3 We replace the 28 disequality constraints $x \neq y$ by a single constraint that stipulates that the variables are pairwise different. Given a sequence of variables $x_1, \ldots, x_n$, where $n \geq 2$, with respective domains $D_1, \ldots, D_n$ we introduce an n-ary `all_different` constraint interpreted as follows:

$$[\texttt{all\_different}(x_1, \ldots, x_n)] := \{(d_1, \ldots, d_n) \mid d_i \neq d_j \text{ for } i \neq j\}.$$

Then we can replace the above 28 disequality constraints by a single constraint

$$\texttt{all\_different}(S, E, N, D, M, O, R, Y).$$

Representation 4 Yet another way to eliminate the above 28 disequality constraints is by following a standard method used in the area of Integer Linear Programming, the objective of which is to find optimal integer solutions to linear constraints over the reals.

For each variable x from $\{S, E, N, D, M, O, R, Y\}$ and a digit d we introduce a $0/1$ variable $is_{x,d}$. The constraint that each variable from $\{S, E, N, D, M, O, R, Y\}$ takes one value is expressed as the set of eight constraints

$$\sum_{d=0}^{9} is_{x,d} = 1,$$

where $x \in \{S, E, N, D, M, O, R, Y\}$. In turn, the **all_different** constraint is expressed as the set of ten constraints

$$\sum_{x \in \{S,E,N,D,M,O,R,Y\}} is_{x,d} \leq 1,$$

where $d \in \{0, 1, \ldots, 9\}$. The 0/1 variables $is_{x,d}$ relate back to the original variables used in the equality constraint(s) via eight constraints

$$\sum_{d=0}^{9} d \cdot is_{x,d} = x,$$

where $x \in \{S, E, N, D, M, O, R, Y\}$.

The disadvantage of this approach is of course that we need to introduce 80 new variables.

The problem under consideration has a unique solution depicted by the following sum:

$$\begin{array}{r} 9567 \\ + \ 1085 \\ \hline 10652 \end{array}$$

That is, the assignment

$$\{(S, 9), (E, 5), (N, 6), (D, 7), (M, 1), (O, 0), (R, 8), (Y, 2)\}$$

is a unique solution of the original CSP and each other discussed representation of the problem has a unique solution, as well.

6.4.3 The n-queens problem

This is probably the most well-known CSP. The problem is to place n queens on the $n \times n$ chess board, where $n \geq 3$, so that they do not attack each other. We discuss two representations of this problem as a CSP.

Representation using 0/1 variables This representation uses n^2 0/1 variables $x_{i,j}$, where $i \in [1..n]$ and $j \in [1..n]$, each of them representing one field of the chess board. The appropriate constraints can then be written using sums of relevant variables.

The following constraints formalise the problem:

- $\sum_{j=1}^{n} x_{i,j} = 1$ for $i \in [1..n]$ (exactly one queen per row),
- $\sum_{j=1}^{n} x_{j,i} = 1$ for $i \in [1..n]$ (exactly one queen per column),

- $x_{i,j} + x_{k,l} \leq 1$ for $i, j, k, l \in [1..n]$ such that $i \neq k$ and $|i - k| = |j - l|$ (at most one queen per diagonal).

The condition $i \neq k$ in the last item ensures that the fields represented by $x_{i,j}$ and $x_{k,l}$ are different.

The obvious disadvantage of this representation is the large number of variables it involves.

Representation using linear constraints A more economic representation of this problem as a CSP uses n variables, $x_1, \ldots, x_n$, each with the domain $[1..n]$. The idea is that x_i denotes the position of the queen placed in the ith column of the chess board.

This representation implies that no two queens are placed in the same column, so we only need to take care of the remaining requirements. They can be formulated as the following disequality constraints for $i \in [1..n]$ and $j \in [1..i - 1]$:

- $x_i \neq x_j$ (at most one queen per row),
- $x_i - x_j \neq i - j$ (at most one queen per SW-NE diagonal),
- $x_i - x_j \neq j - i$ (at most one queen per SE-NW diagonal).

Using the `all_different` constraint introduced in the third representation of the *SEND + MORE = MONEY* problem we can replace the first set of $\frac{n \cdot (n-1)}{2}$ disequalities by a single constraint

$$\texttt{all\_different}(x_1, \ldots, x_n).$$

6.5 Constrained optimisation problems: examples

The general task of constrained optimisation is to find optimal solutions to a set of constraints subject to some cost function *cost*. More precisely, consider a CSP $\mathcal{P} := \langle \mathcal{C} \; ; \; x_1 \in D_1, \ldots, x_n \in D_n \rangle$ together with a function

$$cost : D_1 \times \cdots \times D_n \to \mathcal{R}$$

from the set of all sequences in $D_1 \times \cdots \times D_n$ to the set $\mathcal{R}$ of real numbers. We are interested in finding a solution $\{(x_1, d_1), \ldots, (x_n, d_n)\}$ to $\mathcal{P}$ for which the value $cost(d_1, \ldots, d_n)$ is optimal. In what follows we assume that 'optimal' means 'minimal'. We call then the pair $(\mathcal{P}, cost)$ a **constrained optimisation problem**, in short a **COP**. The area of constrained optimisation is huge and a number of books have been written on this subject. Here we limit ourselves to a presentation of a few simple examples.

6.5.1 The knapsack problem

We are given n objects, each with a volume and a value, and a knapsack of a fixed volume. The problem is to find a collection of the objects with maximal total value that fits in the knapsack. More formally, we have n objects with volumes $a_1, ..., a_n$ and values $b_1, ..., b_n$ and the knapsack volume v. Further, we have n variables, $x_1, ..., x_n$, each with the domain $\{0, 1\}$. The inclusion of the object i in a collection is modelled by setting the value of x_i to 1. The requirement that the collection fits in the knapsack translates to the linear constraint

$$\sum_{i=1}^{n} a_i \cdot x_i \leq v$$

on the variables $x_1, ..., x_n$. We seek a solution to this constraint for which the sum

$$\sum_{i=1}^{n} b_i \cdot x_i$$

is maximal. Since in our setup we seek solutions with a minimal value of the cost function, we use $-\sum_{i=1}^{n} b_i \cdot x_i$ as the cost function.

6.5.2 A coins problem

Consider the following problem.

What is the minimum number of coins that allows one to pay *exactly* any amount smaller than one euro? Recall that there are six different euro cent coins, of denomination 1, 2, 5, 10, 20, 50.

We formulate it as a COP. First, we determine the variables and their domains. Since the question refers to the number of coins, it is natural to adopt the variables that represent the selected amounts of each coin. This brings us to six variables that we denote by $x_1, x_2, x_5, x_{10}, x_{20}, x_{50}$. The idea is that each variable x_i denotes the selected amount of coins of denomination i, so we use $[0..99]$ as the domain for each variable.

Further, we introduce for each $i \in [1..99]$ six variables $x_1^i, x_2^i, x_5^i, x_{10}^i, x_{20}^i, x_{50}^i$ with respectively the same domains as $x_1, x_2, x_5, x_{10}, x_{20}$ and x_{50} to formulate a constraint stating that the amount of i euro cents can be paid exactly using the selected coins. So we have in total 600 variables.

Next, we state the appropriate constraints. For each $i \in [1..99]$ we use the linear constraint

$$x_1^i + 2x_2^i + 5x_5^i + 10x_{10}^i + 20x_{20}^i + 50x_{50}^i = i$$

to state that the amount of i euro cents can be paid using x_1^i coins of 1 euro cent, x_2^i coins of 2 euro cents, x_5^i coins of 5 euro cents, x_{10}^i coins of 10 euro cents, x_{20}^i coins of 20 euro cents and x_{50}^i coins of 50 euro cents.

Additionally, we add the constraints stating that for each $i \in [1..99]$ the amounts x_j^i are respectively smaller than x_j. More precisely, for each $i \in [1..99]$ and $j \in \{1, 2, 5, 10, 20, 50\}$ we use the following constraint:

$$x_j^i \leq x_j.$$

These 594 inequality constraints ensure that each amount of i euro cents can indeed be paid using the collection represented by the x_j variables.

Finally, for each solution to the just formulated CSP the sum

$$x_1 + x_2 + x_5 + x_{10} + x_{20} + x_{50}$$

represents the total amount of coins that we would like to minimise. So it is the appropriate cost function.

6.5.3 A currency design problem

Suppose now that we have the freedom of choosing the values of six coins. What is then the minimum number of coins that allows one to pay exactly any amount smaller than one euro?

To formulate this problem as a COP it suffices to modify the above linear equality constraints but this leads to the arithmetic constraints. Indeed, we just replace each previous linear constraint

$$x_1^i + 2x_2^i + 5x_5^i + 10x_{10}^i + 20x_{20}^i + 50x_{50}^i = i$$

by the arithmetic constraint

$$v_1 \cdot x_1^i + v_2 \cdot x_2^i + v_3 \cdot x_3^i + v_4 \cdot x_4^i + v_5 \cdot x_5^i + v_6 \cdot x_6^i = i,$$

where $v_1, \ldots, v_6$ are the values of the coins. Additionally, we assume that the v_i variables range over $[1..99]$ and are ordered, so stipulate for $i \in [1..5]$ the constraint

$$v_i < v_{i+1}.$$

The rest of the representation is the same.

6.5.4 The facility location problem

This problem is concerned with a choice of a set of facility locations to best serve a given set of customers with a given set of demands.

More precisely, we are given a number of customers and a number of locations for a facility, say a warehouse. There is only one product provided. Each customer i is characterized by

- its demand (in the provided product) dem_i.

In turn, each warehouse location (from now on, just a warehouse) j is characterized by

- its setup cost $scost_j$, and
- its capacity cap_j.

We also have for each warehouse j and each client i the transportation costs $tcost_{i,j}$ of the product from warehouse j to client i, per unit of supplied quantity.

We assume that the total capacity of all the warehouses exceeds (or equals) the total demand from all the customers, i.e.,

$$\sum_j cap_j \geq \sum_i dem_i.$$

Further, we assume that each customer may be served by any set of warehouses. We want to choose a set of warehouses from which the product will be provided to the customers so that

- the demands of all customers are satisfied,
- the *total cost*, which equals the sum of the setup costs of the selected warehouses plus the resulting transportation costs, is minimal.

In Figure 6.2 we illustrate the situation for three warehouses and four customers. With each line connecting a warehouse and a customer a transportation cost is associated.

To formalise this problem as a COP we use two kinds of decision variables. For each warehouse j there is a Boolean variable B_j reflecting whether the warehouse j is open (i.e., chosen) or not. Next, for each warehouse j and customer i there is a **continuous variable** (i.e., a variable ranging over the set of reals) $S_{i,j}$ saying how much of the customer i demand is supplied by the warehouse j.

Then for each warehouse j there is a capacity constraint

$$cap_j \geq \sum_i S_{i,j},$$

and for each customer i there is a demand constraint

$$\sum_j S_{i,j} \geq dem_i.$$

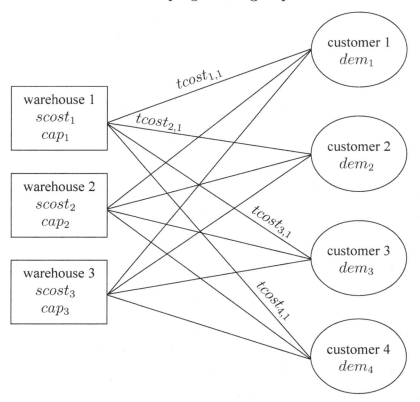

Fig. 6.2 A facility location problem

We also state that the supplies from the warehouses that are not selected equal zero, i.e., for each warehouse j

$$B_j = 0 \rightarrow \forall i : S_{i,j} = 0.$$

Finally, the cost function is the sum of the setup costs plus the transportation costs:

$$\sum_j (B_j \cdot scost_j + \sum_i S_{i,j} \cdot tcost_{i,j}).$$

6.6 Solving CSPs and COPs

The definition of constraint satisfaction problems and constrained optimisation problems is extremely general and it is of course preferable to solve each such problem by domain specific methods. For example, when we deal with systems of linear equations over reals, it is natural to use the methods developed in the area of Linear Algebra and when we deal with systems of linear inequalities over reals, it is preferable to use the methods developed in the area of Linear Programming.

Still, in many situations the constraints used do not adhere to any simple syntax restrictions or are a mixture of several types of constraints. Then it is useful to rely on general methods. Constraint programming developed a collection of such methods. They allow us to solve problems formulated as CSPs and COPs. These methods are based on search. In general two forms of search are used.

6.6.1 Local search

Local search is a generic name for a whole class of search algorithms. Their purpose is to find a solution to a CSP or to a COP by starting with an initial assignment defined on all the variables (called in this context a *state*) and trying to improve its *quality* iteratively, by small (so local) changes, called *moves*. The quality of a state is defined by means of a *cost function*. A simple example of a cost function is the number of constraints violated by the state. Then the quality of a solution is 0.

The basic ingredient of the local search is the notion of a *neighbourhood*, which is a function that assigns to each state s (i.e., an assignment) a set of states, that are called the *neighbours* of s. An execution of a local search algorithm starts in an initial state, obtained by another technique or randomly, and enters a loop in which repeatedly a move is performed from a state to one of its neighbours. The final state is either a solution to the considered CSP (respectively, an optimal solution to a COP) or a 'stop' state. In general the local search is incomplete so a 'stop' state only indicates that no solution has been found so far. Specific forms of local search are obtained by specifying the way the moves are chosen and the way the search is stopped.

6.6.2 Top-down search

In this book we focus on a more common form of search, usually called *top-down search*. This form of search is combined with a *branching* (or *splitting*) strategy. Additionally, a crucial technique for constraint programming of *constraint propagation* is used.

Intuitively, branching allows us to split a given CSP into two or more CSPs the *union* of which is equivalent to the initial CSP. In turn, constraint propagation allows us to transform a given CSP into one that is equivalent but *simpler*. The terms in italic can be made precise. Constraint propagation is alternated with branching. This yields a tree, called a **search tree**, over which a top-down search takes place. The leaves of the tree are CSPs that are either obviously inconsistent (usually with an empty variable domain) or solved. An important aspect of the top-down search is that the search tree is generated 'on the fly'.

An example of a search tree in which we refer explicitly to constraint propagation and branching is depicted in Figure 6.3.

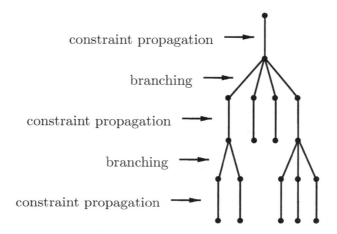

Fig. 6.3 A search tree for a CSP

The standard form of a top-down search is the usual **backtracking search**. It starts at the root of the tree and proceeds by descending to its first descendant. This process continues as long as a node is not a leaf. If a leaf is encountered, the search proceeds by moving back to the closest ancestor node of the leaf that has another descendant or else to the root. If such an ancestor exists, its next descendant is selected. This process continues until the control is back at the root node and all of its descendants have been visited. In Figure 6.4 we depict the backtracking search on a simple tree, where the arrows indicate the order in which the nodes are visited.

The most common form of backtracking search proceeds by ordering the decision variables according to some **variable choice heuristics** and by branching through splitting the domain of a variable. This heuristic may reorder the variable statically, so only once, at the beginning of the search, or dynamically, during the search.

An example of branching is **labelling** that splits a finite domain of a variable into the singleton domains. This corresponds to a systematic ex-

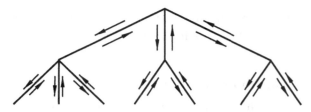

Fig. 6.4 Backtracking search

ploration of all assignments of a value to this variable. The ordering of
the values in each domain is then done according to some **value choice
heuristics**. Another natural form of branching is **bisection** which is appropriate when the domains are intervals or finite sets. In this case the
variable domain is split in two halves by choosing an appropriate mid-point.

This form of backtracking search is usually combined with some form of
constraint propagation that involves removal from the domains of variables
some values that do not participate in any solution. As an example consider
the constraint $x < y$, where the domain of x is $[10..1000]$ and the domain of
y is $[1..50]$. Then the constraint propagation allows us to reduce the domain
of x to $[10..49]$ and the domain of y to $[11..50]$. This domain reduction
can trigger a sequence of further domain reductions concerned with other
constraints in which, if the domain of x or y is further reduced, the constraint
$x < y$ is again selected.

The presence of constraint propagation can be sometimes exploited by
adding to the initial CSP **implied constraints**. These constraints do not
alter the set of solutions but can lead to a smaller search tree. As an example
consider the CSP

$$\langle x^3 + x < 520,\ x^3 + y > 550\ ;\ x \in [1..1000], y \in [1..50] \rangle.$$

If the constraint propagation is available only for linear constraints, when
solving this CSP by backtracking search first a branching will take place. But
in presence of the implied constraint $x < y$ first the constraint propagation
will take place and, as explained above, the domains of x and y will get
reduced to $[10..49]$ and $[11..50]$ before any branching takes place.

The backtracking search is an example of a **complete** search. In this form
of search all possible assignments of values are explored. In the **incomplete
search** one focusses on the most promising assignments selected according
to some heuristics. Various forms of incomplete top-down search can be
described by allocating credit to each value choice, giving more credit to
more promising values. This credit is then available for the search subtree

which remains after choosing that value for that variable. In Section 8.4 we shall discuss in more detail this form of search and program it in Prolog.

6.6.3 Branch and bound search

To solve COPs one takes into account the cost function. The appropriate modification of the backtracking search is called **branch and bound search**. Informally, it can be explained as follows. Suppose that we are interested in finding a solution with the minimal value of the cost function. During the search one maintains the **currently best value** of the cost function in a variable *bound*. This variable is initialised to ∞. Each time a solution with a smaller cost is found, this value is recorded in *bound*.

There are many variations on the branch and bound algorithm. One consideration is what to do after a solution with a new best cost is found. The simplest approach is to restart the computation with the *bound* variable initialised to this new best cost.

A less naive approach is to continue the search for better solutions without restarting. In this case the constraint $cost(x_1, \ldots, x_n) < bound$ is used and each time a solution with a new best cost is found, this cost is dynamically imposed through the constraint $cost(x_1, \ldots, x_n) < bound$. The constraint propagation triggered by this constraint leads to a pruning of the search tree by identifying the nodes under which no solution with a smaller cost can be present.

In Figure 6.5 we depict a possible branch and bound search on the tree already considered in Figure 6.4. The parts of the tree that are ignored during the search are represented using the dotted lines.

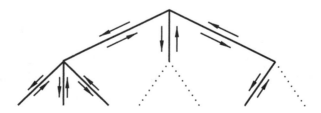

Fig. 6.5 Branch and bound search

Sometimes it is better to give up on the completeness and search for a solution the cost of which is close to the optimum. This can be achieved by imposing each time a tighter bound on the *bound* variable, for example requiring the next solution to be a fixed amount better than the current best. If this fixed amount is, say, 10, then when the branch and bound search terminates, the solution returned is guaranteed to be within 10 of the optimum. Alternatively the improvement can be expressed as a fraction of the current best bound. If the fraction is, say 0.1, and a solution with cost 100 had just been found, then the new bound would be 90. Then, once the branch and bound search terminates, the solution returned is guaranteed to be within 10% off the optimum.

A more radical variant is to exploit the full range of the cost variable from its upper (worst) bound to its lower (best) bound. When a solution is found, this yields a new upper bound on the cost variable. However, the algorithm selects the mid-point between the current upper and lower bounds, and seeks a solution with cost better than this. If there is no solution, the lower bound of the cost is updated, and the new mid-point is selected. Search stops when the upper and lower bounds are sufficiently close. This dichotomic branching approach is only rarely the most efficient.

6.7 From CSPs and COPs to constraint programming

Now that we have explained the basic techniques used to solve constraint satisfaction problems and constrained optimisation problems it is clear how one can try to solve them in any programming language. The distinguishing feature of **constraint programming languages** is that they provide a substantial support for generating and solving CSPs and COPs. First, note that in the traditional programming languages such as C or Java, the variables are varying but *known* entities. So these variables cannot be used to represent the CSP variables that are similar to *unknowns* in the sense of algebra. Hence to represent CSPs one needs to represent the variables differently, for example by means of objects.

In constraint programming languages and systems the representation of the CSP variables and their domains is straightforward thanks to the built-in facilities. As a result the programmer does not need to come up with his/her own way of managing such variables. Additionally, a support is provided for generating constraints. In short, generating CSPs in such languages and systems is considerably simpler than in the traditional programming languages.

Next, the general methods used to solve CSPs and COPs rely on a small number of reasonably well understood sets of techniques that we discussed in the previous section. These techniques, including backtracking and branch and bound search, and various variable and value choice heuristics and other relevant parameters of the search, are often directly available to the programmer.

Finally, several types of CSPs can be solved using specialised, domain specific methods. We already mentioned the examples of linear equations over reals and linear inequalities over reals. In typical constraint programming languages and systems these methods are directly available to the user in the form of **constraint solvers** that can be readily invoked from a program. Additionally, these languages and systems integrate such constraint solvers with the general methods, such as built-in forms of constraint propagation, so that the programmer can rely automatically on both types of methods.

As a result generating and solving of CSPs and COPs in constraint programming languages and systems is considerably simpler than in conventional programming languages. The resulting approach to programming, i.e. **constraint programming**, is radically different from the usual one. In particular, modelling plays an important role, while the programming process is based on a judicious use of the available built-ins.

In the subsequent chapters we shall explain the ECL^iPS^e approach to constraint programming. ECL^iPS^e, as already mentioned, extends Prolog and consequently uses variables as *unknowns*, as in algebra or mathematical logic. This makes it substantially easier to model CPSs and COPs since they use the variables in the same sense. Further, ECL^iPS^e relies on a number of libraries that facilitate the task of the programmer and simplify the task of constraint programming in a dramatic way.

6.8 Summary

The aim of this chapter was to explain the basic principles of constraint programming. To this end we introduced first the concepts of a constraint, constraint satisfaction problem (CSP) and constrained optimisation problem (COP) and illustrated them by means of various examples. We also mentioned the most common classes of constraints considered in practice.

Then we discussed the methods used to solve CSPs and COPs, notably constraint propagation, backtracking search and branch and bound search. We explained how these methods are supported in constraint programming languages. In these languages specialised, domain specific methods are directly available in the form of constraint solvers.

6.9 Exercises

Exercise 6.1 Consider the following puzzle taken from Gardner [1979].

Ten cells numbered $0, \ldots, 9$ inscribe a 10-digit number such that each cell, say i, indicates the total number of occurrences of the digit i in this number. Find this number.

Formulate this problem as a CSP problem.

For your information: the answer is 6210001000.

Exercise 6.2 Consider the following problem:

Find a permutation of numbers $1, \ldots, 10$ such that
- 6 is put on 7th place,
- each number starting from the second one is either bigger by 3 or smaller by 2 than its predecessor.

Formulate this problem as a CSP.

For your information: the only solution is: 3 1 4 2 5 8 6 9 7 10.

Exercise 6.3 A *magic square of order n* is defined to be an $n \times n$ array made out of the integers $1, 2, \ldots, n^2$ arranged so that the sum of every row, column, and the two main diagonals is the same. For example

```
 1 15 24  8 17
23  7 16  5 14
20  4 13 22  6
12 21 10 19  3
 9 18  2 11 25
```

is a magic square of order 5, because each row, column and main diagonal sums up to 65. Formulate the problem of finding a magic square of order n as a CSP.

7

Intermezzo: Iteration in ECL^{i}PS^e

7.1 Introduction

D ECLARATIVE LANGUAGES USE recursion a great deal. Often it is used simply to iterate over a data structure, or an integer range, in which case it makes the program hard to read. An example is the LENGTH program given in Figure 3.1 on page 45:

```
% len(List, N) :- N is the length of the list List.

len([], 0).
len([_ | Ts], N) :- len(Ts, M), N is M+1.
```

It does seem a rather obscure and complicated way of expressing something quite simple. The difficulty is, of course, that declarative programs do not allow the same variable to be reused for different things, so within the pure declarative paradigm, we cannot just walk down the list incrementing a counter.

ECL^{i}PS^e offers a syntax for encoding such iterations in a reasonably natural way. In this chapter we discuss these constructs in a systematic way. In particular we show how they can be used to obtain a non-recursive solution to the classic n-queens problem.

110

7.2 Iterating over lists and integer ranges

The simplest form of iteration is over the members of a list. For the first example we shall iterate over the list [a,b,c], writing each member of the list on a new line using the writeln/1 built-in:

```
[eclipse 1]: ( foreach(El,[a,b,c]) do writeln(El) ).


a
b
c


El = El
Yes (0.00s cpu)
```

The user sees only one variable El, which appears to take at each iteration the value of a different member of the list. However, internally ECL^{i}PS^e turns this iteration into a recursion, so a different variable (El_1, El_2, etc.) is introduced for each member of the list.

A similar iterator, count/3 is used for running a counter over a range of integers:

```
[eclipse 2]: ( count(I,1,4) do writeln(I) ).


1
2
3
4


I = I
Yes (0.00s cpu)
```

The ECL^{i}PS^e iteration construct allows more than one *iterator*, so one can iterate over a list and an integer range simultaneously. Thus we can write out the elements of a list together with a number showing their position in the list as follows:

```
[eclipse 3]: ( foreach(El,[a,b,c]), count(I,1,_)
          do
            writeln(I-El)
          ).


1 - a
```

```
2 - b
3 - c

El = El
I = I
Yes (0.00s cpu)
```

When two or more iterators appear on the *same* level, as in this example, then they all iterate *in step*. In effect there is just one iteration, but at each iteration all the iterators step forward together. In the above example, therefore, at iteration 1, El takes the value a, whilst I takes the value 1. At iteration 2, El takes the value b, whilst I takes the value 2. At the last iteration 3, El takes the value c, whilst I takes the value 3. Because the iteration stops when the end of the list is reached, we do not need to specify a maximum for the integer range in the iterator count(I,1,_).

Later we shall encounter iterators at *different* levels, which is achieved by writing an iteration construct within the query formed by another iteration construct.

Coming back to the current example, with iterators at the same level, we can even use the count iterator to compute the maximum, because it automatically returns the value of I at the last iteration:

```
[eclipse 4]: ( foreach(El,[a,b,c]), count(I,1,Max)
             do
                writeln(I-El)
             ).

El = El
I = I
Max = 3
Yes (0.00s cpu)
1 - a
2 - b
3 - c
```

In the above query Max returns the length of the list. Thus we can find the length of a list by this very construction — we just do not bother to write out the elements:

```
[eclipse 5]: ( foreach(_,[a,b,c]), count(_,1,Length)
             do
                true
```

```
).
```

```
Length = 3
Yes (0.00s cpu)
```

The `foreach/2` iterator walks down the list, and the **count** iterator increments its index at each step. When the end of the list is reached, the iteration stops, and the final value of the counter is returned as the value of the variable **Length**. Curiously, the action taken at each iteration is nothing! The atomic query **true** simply succeeds without doing anything. In particular, we do not use the elements of the list or the counters that are now represented by anonymous variables.

7.3 Iteration specifications in general

An iterator construction has the form

```
( IterationSpecs do Query )
```

where **Query** is any ECL^{i}PS^e query. The iteration specifiers **IterationSpecs** is a comma-separated sequence of iterators, such as

```
foreach(El,List), count(I,1,Length)
```

in the example queries above.

In this section we shall go through the different iterators, exploring how they can be used to process lists, ranges, compound terms (structures), and arrays. We shall also see how to pass arguments into an iteration.

7.3.1 Constructing lists

We have seen how the iterator **foreach** allows us to walk down a list. It can also be used to construct a list. To see how let us construct a list of increasing integers, starting at 1. We shall give the length of the list as, say, 4:

```
[eclipse 6]: ( foreach(El,List), count(I,1,4) do El = I ).
```

```
El = El
List = [1, 2, 3, 4]
I = I
Yes (0.00s cpu)
```

Thus to construct a list of given length we can use the very same code we used for measuring the length of a list, except that this time we *input* the length, and *output* the list.

Notice that the variables El and I are not instantiated on completion of the iteration. Their scope is local to the iteration construct, and even local to each iteration. This means that we can construct a list of *different* variables by simply replacing El = I in the above by **true**. To make clear these are different variables, it is necessary to set the ECL^{i}PS^e 'output_mode' to output the *internal* variable names.[1] With the new output mode the behaviour is as follows:

```
[eclipse 7]: ( foreach(El,List), count(I,1,4) do true ).
```

```
** Warning: Singleton local variable El in do-loop
            (not used in loop body)
** Warning: Singleton local variable I in do-loop
            (not used in loop body)
El = El_80
List = [El_386, El_390, El_394, El_398]
I = I_100
Yes (0.00s cpu)
```

As usual we can eliminate the warnings by using anonymous variables, but this has no effect on the output itself:

```
[eclipse 8]: ( foreach(_,List), count(_,1,4) do true ).
```

```
List = [_339, _341, _343, _345]
Yes (0.00s cpu)
```

Now we are finally prepared to return to the **LENGTH** program discussed in the introduction to this chapter. Because we can use the iterators both for input and output, we could use exactly these iterators to implement the len/2 predicate which works in both directions — to compute the length of a list, and to build a list of different variables of a specified length. The resulting program is given in Figure 7.1.

We now have:

```
[eclipse 9]: len([a,b,c], N).
```

```
N = 3
```

[1] To set the output mode one can use set_flag(output_mode,"VmQP").

```
% len(List, N) :-
%     N is the length of the list List
%     or List is a list of variables of length N.


len(List, N) :-
    ( foreach(_,List), count(_,1,N) do true ).
```

Fig. 7.1 A non-recursive LENGTH program

Yes (0.00s cpu)
[eclipse 10]: len(Ls, 4).

Ls = [_159, _161, _163, _165]
Yes (0.00s cpu)

Finally, in case the maximum is an input (integer or expression), the iterator for/3 can be used instead of count/3, with the same meaning:

[eclipse 11]: (for(I,1,5) do write(I), write(' ')).

I = I
Yes (0.00s cpu)
1 2 3 4 5

7.3.2 Passing arguments into and out of iterations

Given an input list of integers, we can output a list of their successors as follows:

```
[eclipse 12]: ( foreach(In,[1,2,3,4]),
                foreach(Out,OutList)
             do
                Out is In+1
             ).
```

In = In
Out = Out
OutList = [2, 3, 4, 5]
Yes (0.00s cpu)

The reader should compare it with the MAP program from Figure 5.3 and query No. 31 from page 84. Just as In and Out in the above query have scope local to a single iteration, so we can add other local variables in the body of the query. For example, we can input a list of characters and output a list of their ASCII successors as follows:

```
[eclipse 13]: ( foreach(In,[a,b,c]),
               foreach(Out,OutList)
            do
              char_code(In,InCode),
              OutCode is InCode+1,
              char_code(Out,OutCode)
            ).
```

```
In = In
Out = Out
OutList = [b, c, d]
InCode = InCode
OutCode = OutCode
Yes (0.00s cpu)
```

(The char_code/2 built-in provides a bi-directional conversion between the characters and the ASCII codes.) Each variable occurring in a query inside the iteration has local scope.

It is straightforward to pass a value, such as 5, into an iteration, as follows:

```
[eclipse 14]: ( foreach(In,[1,2,3]),
               foreach(Out,OutList)
            do
              Out is In+5
            ).
```

```
In = In
Out = Out
OutList = [6,7,8]
Yes (0.00s cpu)
```

However, we cannot simply use a variable in place of the 5 in the above query, because ECL^{i}PS^e treats any variable in the body of an iteration construct as local, even if a variable with the same name also occurs outside the iteration. For example the following behaviour is not really what we want:

```
[eclipse 15]: Var = 5,
              ( foreach(In,[1,2,3]),
                foreach(Out,OutList)
              do
                Out is In+Var
              ).
```

```
*** Warning: Singleton local variable Var in do-loop,
             maybe param(Var) missing?
instantiation fault in +(1, Var_487, Out_486) in module eclipse
Abort
```

To pass a (variable) argument into an iteration an extra iterator is used. It is simply called **param**. We make the scope of **Var** global by passing it in as a parameter, thus:

```
[eclipse 16]: Var = 5,
              ( foreach(In,[1,2,3]),
                foreach(Out,OutList),
                param(Var)
              do
                Out is In+Var
              ).
```

```
Var = 5
In = In
Out = Out
OutList = [6, 7, 8]
Yes (0.00s cpu)
```

We can now build a single clause program where the number to be added to each element is supplied as an argument:

```
add_const(Increment, InList, OutList) :-
   ( foreach(In,InList),
     foreach(Out,OutList),
     param(Increment)
   do
     Out is In+Increment
   ).
```

Any number of parameters can be passed into an iteration. For example we can increment positive elements by one amount and decrement negative elements by a different amount. The resulting program is given in Figure 7.2. Note that here **param** takes two arguments.

```
add_const(Increment, Decrement, InList, OutList) :-
    ( foreach(In,InList),
      foreach(Out,OutList),
      param(Increment,Decrement)
    do
      ( In >= 0 ->
        Out is In+Increment
      ;
        Out is In-Decrement
      )
    ).
```

Fig. 7.2 An INCREMENT/DECREMENT program

We have then for example:

```
[eclipse 17]: add_const(3, 5, [2, -3, 5, -2, 4], OutList).

OutList = [5, -8, 8, -7, 7]
Yes (0.00s cpu)
```

The **param** iterator can also be used to thread the initial value of a variable into the loop. Here is a simple example. Consider the clause

```
inc(N, Input, Output) :-
    ( foreach(In,Input),
      foreach(N:Out,Output),
      param(N)
    do
      Out is In+1
    ).
```

Then we have:

```
[eclipse 18]: inc(3, [4,5,6,7], Output).

Output = [3 : 5, 3 : 6, 3 : 7, 3 : 8]
Yes (0.00s cpu)
```

We shall see this use of `param` in Section 8.4. Without `param(N)` we would get the following behaviour (and a 'Singleton variables' warning during the compilation time):

```
[eclipse 19]: inc(3, [4,5,6,7], Output).

Output = [N : 5, N : 6, N : 7, N : 8]
Yes (0.00s cpu)
```

7.3.3 Iterations within iterations

Let us multiply now all the numbers in one range, say 1..3, by all the numbers in another range, say 5..9. We can do this using an iteration in the body of an outer iteration, thus:

```
[eclipse 20]: ( for(I,1,3)
               do
                 ( for(J,5,9),
                   param(I)
                 do
                   K is I*J,
                   write(K), write(' ')
                 )
               ).

I = I
J = J
K = K
Yes (0.00s cpu)
5 6 7 8 9 10 12 14 16 18 15 18 21 24 27
```

Notice the use of the `param(I)` to pass the argument `I` into the inner iteration.

Because of the need to pass in parameters embedded iterations can be complicated to write. Therefore a facility is provided to iterate over multiple ranges using a single iterator `multifor/3`. The same example as above can be written:

```
[eclipse 21]: ( multifor([I,J],[1,5],[3,9])
               do
                 K is I*J,
                 write(K), write(' ')
```

```
             ).

I = I
J = J
K = K
Yes (0.00s cpu)
5 6 7 8 9 10 12 14 16 18 15 18 21 24 27
```

7.3.4 Iterating over structures

For applications where the number of components is fixed, it is usually more efficient to use compound terms rather than lists to hold the data. Thus instead of a list of variables [X,Y,Z], we have a term such as p(X,Y,Z). To iterate over the arguments of a term, the appropriate iterator is foreacharg/2:

```
[eclipse 22]: ( foreacharg(Arg,p(a,b,c)) do writeln(Arg) ).

Arg = Arg
Yes (0.00s cpu)
a
b
c
```

The efficiency comes from being able to access components directly from their location in the structure. In the following example we fill a structure with values, and then access the third component:

```
[eclipse 23]:   functor(Struct,p,3),
                ( foreach(El, [val1,val2,val3]),
                  foreacharg(El, Struct)
                do
                  true
                ),
                arg(3, Struct, X).

Struct = p(val1, val2, val3)
El = El
X = val3
Yes (0.00s cpu)
```

7.4 Arrays and iterations

In ECL^{i}PS^e *arrays* are structures with the specific functor []. To create them and specify their, possibly multi-dimensional, size, the built-in dim/2 is used. For example, to create a one-dimensional array Array of size 3 we write:

```
[eclipse 24]: dim(Array,[3]).
```

```
Array = [](_162, _163, _164)
Yes (0.00s cpu)
```

In turn, the query dim(Array,[3,2]) creates a two-dimensional array Array of size 3 by 2:

```
[eclipse 25]: dim(Array,[3,2]).
```

```
Array = []([](_174, _175), [](_171, _172), [](_168, _169))
Yes (0.00s cpu)
```

To assign a value to an array component or to access the value of an array component one can use the ECL^{i}PS^e subscript/3 built-in:

```
[eclipse 26]: dim(Array,[3,2]), subscript(Array,[1,2],5).
```

```
Array = []([](_263, 5), [](_260, _261), [](_257, _258))
Yes (0.00s cpu)
```

```
[eclipse 27]: dim(Array,[3]), subscript(Array,[2],a),
              subscript(Array,[2], X).
```

```
Array = [](_287, a, _289)
X = a
Yes (0.00s cpu)
```

The components of an array can also be accessed using the customary subscript notation. For example:

```
[eclipse 28]: dim(Array,[3,2]), subscript(Array,[1,2],5),
              X is Array[1,2] - 2, Y = f(Array[1,2]).
```

```
Array = []([](_444, 5), [](_441, _442), [](_438, _439))
X = 3
Y = f([]([](_444, 5), [](_441, _442), [](_438, _439))[1, 2])
```

```
Yes (0.00s cpu)
```

Note that the value of Y is not f(5) since the argument of f(Array[1,2])
is not evaluated. To assign f(5) to Y we would need to explicitly evaluate f(Array[1,2]) using Z is f(Array[1,2]), Y = f(Z) instead of Y =
f(Array[1,2]).

In the context of arrays the is/2 evaluator is extended to allow us to
access array elements or to transform (a part of) a row or a column into a
list:

```
[eclipse 29]: A = [][([](1, 2),
                      [](3, 4),
                      [](5, X)),
               El is A[3,2],
               Row is A[1, 1..2],
               Col is A[2..3, 2].


A = [][([](1, 2), [](3, 4), [](5, X))
X = X
El = X
Row = [1, 2]
Col = [4, X]
Yes (0.00s cpu)
```

We can also use it to transform a subarray into a list of lists:

```
[eclipse 30]: A = [][([](1, 2),
                      [](3, 4),
                      [](5, X)),
               Sub is A[2..3, 1..2].


A = [][([](1, 2), [](3, 4), [](5, X))
X = X
Sub = [[3, 4], [5, X]]
Yes (0.00s cpu)
```

With arrays we can use the more general iterator foreachelem/2 which
iterates over all the elements of a, possibly multi-dimensional, array. The
query No. 23 from the previous subsection can be rewritten using arrays as:

```
[eclipse 31]: dim(Array,[3]),
              ( foreach(El, [val1,val2,val3]),
                foreachelem(El, Array)
```

```
        do
          true
        ),
        X is Array[3].
```

```
Array = [](val1, val2, val3)
El = El
X = val3
Yes (0.00s cpu)
```

However, we can now also build and access embedded components:

```
[eclipse 32]: dim(Array,[3,2]),
              ( foreach(El, [el11,el12,el21,el22,el31,el32]),
                foreachelem(El, Array)
              do
                true
              ),
              X is Array[2,2].
```

```
Array = [](](el11, el12), [](el21, el22), [](el31, el32))
El = El
X = el22
Yes (0.00s cpu)
```

A useful variant of `foreachelem/2`, with one more argument, additionally returns the index of each component. This allows us, for example, to transpose a matrix quite easily. The program is given in Figure 7.3. It makes use of the fact that the `dim/2` built-in also allows us to retrieve the sizes of a given array. Using this program matrices of arbitrary sizes can be transposed.

We can use this program on any 2 dimensional matrix:

```
[eclipse 33]: Matrix = [](](el11, el12),
                           [](el21, el22),
                           [](el31, el32)),
              transpose(Matrix,Transpose).
```

```
Matrix = [](](el11, el12), [](el21, el22), [](el31, el32))
Transpose = [](](el11, el21, el31), [](el12, el22, el32))
Yes (0.00s cpu)
```

```
% transpose(Matrix, Transpose) :-
%     Transpose is a transpose of the matrix Matrix.

transpose(Matrix, Transpose) :-
    dim(Matrix,[R,C]),
    dim(Transpose,[C,R]),
    ( foreachelem(El,Matrix,[I,J]),
      param(Transpose)
    do
      subscript(Transpose,[J,I],El)
    ).
```

Fig. 7.3 The TRANSPOSE program

7.5 fromto/4: the most general iterator

The iterators introduced so far iterated over single components of the data structure dealing with one element of the list/range/structure at a time. In ECL^{i}PS^e a more general form of iterator is provided that allows us to organise more complex forms of iteration and even replace *all* recursion by iteration. This iterator, fromto/4, has four arguments:

fromto(First,In,Out,Last).

This iterator works by starting at the first iteration with In = First. The first iteration computes a value for Out. Now this value is threaded at the second iteration into In. So at the second iteration the value of In is the value taken by Out at the first iteration. Subsequently at each iteration the value of Out is threaded into the value of In at the next iteration. The iteration stops when Out = Last. The control flow is informally depicted in Figure 7.4.

fromto(First, In,   Out,   Last)

Fig. 7.4 The control flow in fromto/4

A simple example is iteration down a list:

```
[eclipse 34]: ( fromto([a,b,c],[Head | Tail],Tail,[])
                do
```

```
                     writeln(Head)
               ).
a
b
c

Head = Head
Tail = Tail
Yes (0.00s cpu)
```

The reader may note that this is a possible implementation of the **foreach/2** iterator. Indeed, all the other iterators can be implemented using **fromto/4**. Our informal description of the behaviour of **fromto** is highly procedural. However, the behaviour of the **fromto/4** construct is more powerful than a procedural description might suggest. In fact, this same construct can be used to construct a value of **First** backwards from the value of **Last**. In the following two examples we show **fromto/4** using

- its *first* argument as the full list,
- its *last* argument as the full list.

In both of them **fromto/4** and **foreach/2** iterate in step.

```
[eclipse 35]: ( fromto([a,b,c],[Head | Tail],Tail,[]),
                foreach(El,List)
           do
             El = Head
           ).

Head = Head
Tail = Tail
El = El
List = [a, b, c]
Yes (0.00s cpu)

[eclipse 36]: ( fromto([],Tail,[Head | Tail],[a,b,c]),
                foreach(El,List)
           do
             El = Head
           ).

Tail = Tail
```

```
Head = Head
El = El
List = [c, b, a]
Yes (0.00s cpu)
```

The second query constructs the list [c,b,a] by putting one at a time an element, being a new intermediate variable, on the front of an initially empty list. The actual values of the list elements are unknown until the iteration terminates, at which point all the intermediate variables, as well as the output list List, become fully instantiated.

So using the fromto/4 iterator we can reverse a list in a simple and elegant way. The program is given in Figure 7.5.

```
% rev(List, Reverse) :-
%     Reverse is a reverse of the list List or
%     List is a reverse of the list Reverse.

rev(List, Reverse) :-
    ( fromto([],Tail,[Head | Tail],Reverse),
      foreach(El,List) do El = Head ).
```

Fig. 7.5 A non-recursive REVERSE program

It can be used in both directions:

[eclipse 37]: rev([a,b,c], Reverse), rev(List, Reverse).

```
Reverse = [c, b, a]
List = [a, b, c]
Yes (0.00s cpu)
```

The fromto/4 iterator can also be used to iterate down the lists in cases where more than one element needs to be 'visible' at each iteration. Let us use this, first, to write a non-recursive version of the program ORDERED from Figure 3.3 on page 48 that checks whether a list is an ≤-ordered list of numbers. The program is given in Figure 7.6.

Here the iterator

fromto(List,[This,Next | Rest],[Next | Rest],[_])

iterates down a non-empty list and at each iteration returns the tail of the remaining list.

```
% ordered(Xs) :- Xs is an =<-ordered list of numbers.

ordered(List) :-
    ( List = [] ->
      true
    ;
      ( fromto(List,[This,Next | Rest],[Next | Rest],[_])
      do
        This =< Next
      )
    ).
```

Fig. 7.6 A non-recursive ORDERED program

The previous iterators have another limitation that all the different iterators in a single iteration must have the same number of components. Thus
the output list/range/structure must have the same number of components
as the input. This makes it impossible to use the previous iterators to filter
a list, for example, constructing a list of only those elements that pass a
test. To take an input list of integers and output a list of only the positive
integers it is therefore necessary to use the **fromto/4** iterator, thus:

```
[eclipse 38]: ( foreach(El,[2,-3,5,-2,4]),
               fromto([],This,Next,PosList)
           do
               ( El >= 0 -> Next = [El | This] ; Next = This )
           ).
```

```
El = El
This = This
Next = Next
PosList = [4, 5, 2]
Yes (0.00s cpu)
```

The output list is in the reverse order from the input list, because each new
positive integer is added in front of the previous ones. To have the output
come in the same order as the input, the following iteration is required:

```
[eclipse 39]: ( foreach(El,[2,-3,5,-2,4]),
               fromto(PosList,This,Next,[])
```

```
             do
               ( El >= 0 -> This = [El | Next] ; This = Next )
             ).


El = El
PosList = [2, 5, 4]
This = This
Next = Next
Yes (0.00s cpu)
```

The `fromto/4` iterator is sometimes just used to hold a particular value, such as the chosen one. Say, we have a list of items with names and values, and we want the name of the cheapest item:

```
[eclipse 40]: ( foreach(El,[a:3,b:6,c:2,d:4]),
                fromto(none:100,Old,New,Name:_)
             do
               El = _:ElVal,
               Old = _:OldVal,
               ( ElVal < OldVal -> New = El ; New = Old )
             ).


Old = Old
New = New
Name = c
ElVal = ElVal
OldVal = OldVal
Yes (0.00s cpu)
```

Finally, the `fromto/4` iterator is often used to check a stopping condition. Let us copy one list into another until we reach a perfect square (i.e., a square of an integer):[2]

```
[eclipse 41]: ( fromto([3,5,3,4,6,10],[In | Rest],Rest,_),
                foreach(In,OutList),
                fromto(go,_,Next,stop)
             do
```

---

[2] Here is one way to write `perfect_square/1` in ECL^{i}PS^e:
`perfect_square(In) :- Sqrt is fix(round(sqrt(In))), In =:= Sqrt*Sqrt.`
The `sqrt/1` built-in computes the positive square root of its argument (e.g., `X` is `sqrt(9.61)` assigns `3.1` to `X`), `round/1` rounds a real or integer number to the nearest integral value of the same type (e.g., `2.3` to `2.0`, `3` to `3` and `2.6` to `3.0`) while `fix/1` converts any number to an integer, rounding towards 0 (e.g., `6.8` to `6`, `6.0` to `6` and `-7.9` to `-7`).

```
( perfect_square(In) ->
  Next = stop
;
  Next = go
)
).
```

```
In = In
Rest = Rest
OutList = [3, 5, 3, 4]
Next = Next
Yes (0.00s cpu)
```

In this example the first `fromto/4` iterator goes through the input list, while the second `fromto/4` iterator checks the stopping condition at each iteration. This enables the iterations to stop before the input list has been exhausted.

7.6 The *n*-queens problem

As the final example of an ECL^{i}PS^e program that shows the use of iterators we provide a non-recursive solution to the *n*-queens problem introduced in Subsection 6.4.3. Recall that the problem calls for placing *n* queens on the $n \times n$ chess board, where $n \geq 3$, so that they do not attack each other.

A natural way of encoding the program in ECL^{i}PS^e using iterators is given in Figure 7.7.

In this program the `select_val/3` predicate is used to generate upon demand successive integer values in the range `[1..Number]`. For each column J these values (held in the variable `Qj`) are tentatively assigned to the subscripted variable `QueenStruct[J]`, using the call

```
subscript(QueenStruct,[J],Qj),
```

upon which a check is made that the so placed queen does not come under attack by the queens already placed in the previous columns.

The solution is generated as an array, for example:

```
[eclipse 43]: queens(QueenStruct, 8).
```

```
QueenStruct = [](1, 5, 8, 6, 3, 7, 2, 4)
Yes (0.02s cpu, solution 1, maybe more) ?
```

This solution corresponds to Figure 7.8.

```
% queens(QueenStruct, Number) :- The array QueenStruct
%      is a solution to the Number-queens problem.

queens(QueenStruct, Number) :-
    dim(QueenStruct,[Number]),
    ( for(J,1,Number),
      param(QueenStruct,Number)
    do
      select_val(1, Number, Qj),
      subscript(QueenStruct,[J],Qj),
      ( for(I,1,J-1),
        param(J,Qj,QueenStruct)
      do
        QueenStruct[I] =\= Qj,
        QueenStruct[I]-Qj =\= I-J,
        QueenStruct[I]-Qj =\= J-I
      )
    ).
```

augmented by the SELECT program of Figure 3.2.

Fig. 7.7 The QUEENS program

7.7 Summary

Iterators are typically used to iterate over data structures. They can also be used as an alternative for recursion. In many situations the resulting programs are simpler.

We introduced the iteration construct

```
( IterationSpecs do Query )
```

and the different iterators which can be used within the sequence of the iterator specifiers IterationSpecs. In the process we also introduced the arrays that are declared in ECL^{i}PS^e using the dim/2 built-in. The subscript/3 built-in allows us to assign a value to an array component or to test its value.

We discussed in turn the following iterators:[3]

- For iterating over lists:
  foreach(El,List) do Query(El).

  Iterate Query(El) over each element El of the list List.

---

[3] We also list here the most general versions of the discussed constructs.

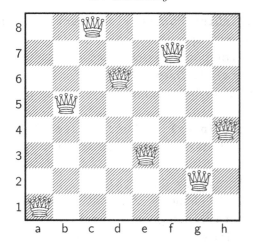

Fig. 7.8 One of 92 solutions to the 8-queens problem

- For iterating over an integer range:

  `count(I,MinExpr,Max) do Query(I).`

    Iterate `Query(I)` with `I` increasing at each iteration starting from
    `MinExpr`. `Max` can be a number, in which case iteration stops when
    `I = Max`, or it can be a variable, in which case it returns the value of
    `I` when iteration is ended by another iterator.

  `for(I,MinExpr,MaxExpr) do Query(I).`

    Similar to `count` above, except `MaxExpr` must be an integer expression.

  `for(I,MinExpr,MaxExpr,Increment) do Query(I).`

    Iterate `Query(I)` with `I` ranging from `MinExpr` to `MaxExpr`
    in increments of `Increment`.

- For passing arguments or variables into an iteration:

  ```
  ( Iterator_1,
    ...,
    Iterator_n,
    param(Argument1,...,Variable,...)
  do
    Query(..., Argument1, ..., Variable, ...).
  ).
  ```

- For iterating over one or more integer ranges:

  `multifor(List,MinList,MaxList) do Query(List).`

    Iterate `Query(List)` with `List` ranging over all combinations of
    integers from `MinList` to `MaxList`.

```
multifor(List,MinList,MaxList,IncrementList) do Query(List).
```
   As above, but with specified increments.

- For iterating over compound terms, especially arrays:
```
foreacharg(X,Term) do Query(X).
```
   Iterate `Query(X)` with X ranging over all the arguments of the structure
   `Term`.
```
foreacharg(X,Term,Index) do Query(X,Index).
```
   As before, with `Index` recording the argument position of X in the
   term.
```
foreachelem(X,Array) do Query(X).
```
   Iterate over all the elements of a multi-dimensional array.
```
foreachelem(X,Array,Index) do Query(X,Index).
```
   As before, but `Index` is set to the multi-dimensional index of the
   element.
```
foreachelem(Array,Index) do Query(Index).
```
   As before, but only use the index.

- The most general iterator:
```
fromto(First,In,Out,Last) do Query(In,Out).
```
   Iterate `Query(In,Out)` starting with `In = First`, until `Out = Last`.

7.8 Exercises

Exercise 7.1 Count the number of non-variable elements in a list without
using recursion.

Exercise 7.2 Count the number of non-variable elements in an array without using recursion.

Exercise 7.3 Write a non-recursive version of the the `select_val/3` predicate from Figure 3.2 on page 46.

Exercise 7.4 Suggest an implementation of the

```
( count(I,K,L) do Body )
```

iterator using the `fromto/4` iterator.

8

Top-down search with passive constraints

8.1 Introduction

I N THIS CHAPTER we discuss how to solve finite CSPs in Prolog by means of top-down search. In ***top-down search*** one repeatedly tries to assign a value to each decision variable in turn. During the search process the decision variables and the values used can be reordered statically or dynamically. Also, during the search process an assignment of a value to a variable can be undone through backtracking. Further, the search can be ***complete*** or ***incomplete*** depending on whether all possible assignments are explored during the search. In what follows we discuss how these options can be implemented in Prolog. Then we shall discuss the facilities offered by ECL^{i}PS^e that allow us to count the number of backtracks, the most widely used measure of efficiency concerned with top-down search.

Prolog supports only passive constraints, in the sense of Section 3.4. In other words, the constraints can be used only as *tests*. This limitation significantly affects the search process. First, the constraints can be invoked only when all their variables are fully instantiated. As a result a natural encoding of a problem has to be sometimes rewritten to avoid run-time errors. Secondly, some obvious inferences that could reduce the search space have to be implemented in an ad hoc way, even though in many situations,

133

for example in the case of Boolean constraints, each time the same principle could be invoked. In the subsequent chapters we shall gradually relax these limitations, first by allowing, in the next chapter, passive constraints without the risk of run-time errors, and second, starting with Chapter 10, by allowing active constraints.

8.2 Solving CSPs using Prolog

The most natural way to solve a finite CSP in Prolog is to use a program that has the following shape:

```
solve(List):-
    declareDomains(List),
    search(List),
    testConstraints(List).
```

Here `List` is a list of the CSP variables. The first atomic goal, `declareDomains(List)` sets up the information about the domains of the variables from `List`, while the atomic goal `search(List)` launches the appropriately chosen search process. Often the information about the domains is put directly into the atomic goal `search(List)`. Finally, the atomic goal `testConstraints(List)` tests whether the generated variable instantiations satisfy the constraints of the considered CSP.

This approach is usually called 'generate and test' and is obviously extremely inefficient. The reason is that during the search process all possible variable instantiations are generated and their number is typically huge. For example, for the *SEND + MORE = MONEY* problem formalised using eight decision variables `S,E,N,D,M,O,R,Y` the corresponding search tree has 10^8 leaves and such an approach does not generate any solution in a reasonable amount of time.

A better approach is to try to test the constraints as soon as possible. For example, in the case of the *SEND + MORE = MONEY* problem it is obviously better to test the constraint `S =\= E` as soon as the values for `S` and `E` are generated, instead of only after the values for all decision variables have been generated. Indeed, the combinations of values with `S` and `E` equal are not considered then.

In general such an approach requires an appropriate interleaving of the execution of the atomic goals `search(List)` and `testConstraints(List)` and is not straightforward to achieve in a generic way. The `suspend` library that will be discussed in the next chapter automatically ensures such an interleaved execution.

But we are running ahead of ourselves. In this chapter we focus solely on the search process encoded in the **search/1** procedure. Later, in Chapter 11, we shall see how this search process can be naturally combined with constraint propagation.

8.3 Backtracking search in Prolog

We already discussed backtracking search in Section 6.6. Now we explain how to program it in Prolog. In what follows we focus on labelling as the branching method. Recall that labelling splits a finite domain of a variable into singletons. This does not yet uniquely define the resulting search procedure since we are still faced with the choice of the order in which the variables are labelled and the choice in which the values in the variable domains are selected. Let us discuss now the consequences of both choices.

8.3.1 The variable ordering

It is perhaps surprising, but the order of the variables can have quite a dramatic effect on the size of the search tree, even though it cannot change the number of leaves. Let us take a very simple tree as an example for this discussion. We have just two variables, X and Y. Suppose X has two possible values, and Y has four. Assuming there are no constraints on the values of X and Y, we can draw a complete search tree that finds all the possible pairs of values for X and Y. In Figure 8.1, we order the variable X before Y. However, if we label Y before X, we get the tree in Figure 8.2.

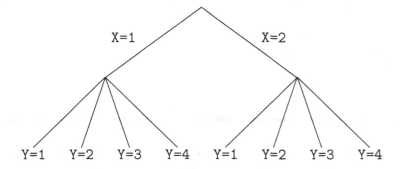

Fig. 8.1 A full search tree with two variables

Note that both trees have eight leaves corresponding to the eight possible pairs of values for X and Y but have different number of internal nodes. The

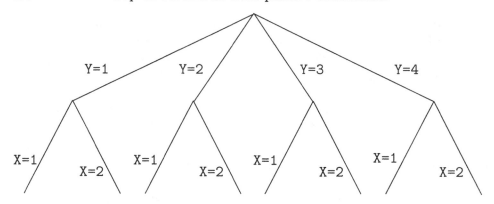

Fig. 8.2 The search tree with a reversed variable ordering

second tree has more internal nodes, so it is harder to search. A way to keep the number of internal nodes as small as possible is to label earlier the variables with fewer choices. If we had four variables with respectively one, two, three and four alternative values, then by ordering the variables with the smallest domains first the number of internal nodes in the tree is $1 + (1 \times 2) + (1 \times 2 \times 3) = 9$. However, the worst ordering gives $4 + (4 \times 3) + (4 \times 3 \times 2) = 40$ internal nodes.

The real payoff from a better variable ordering comes when there are constraints to be satisfied. To keep the example very simple, we will just have one constraint, X + Y =:= 6. The program invoking this search is shown in Figure 8.3 and the search tree explored by this program is depicted in Figure 8.4.

```
search(X,Y) :-
    member(X, [1,2]),
    member(Y, [1,2,3,4]),
    X+Y =:= 6.
```

Fig. 8.3 A two variable problem

The corresponding search behaviour, depth-first search with backtracking, is automatically provided by the underlying Prolog computation model and its implementation. The search tree has 11 nodes and all of them have to be visited to reach the solution at the last leaf of the tree. Now, if the variables are reordered, 13 nodes have to be visited to reach the solution. This is shown in Figure 8.5.

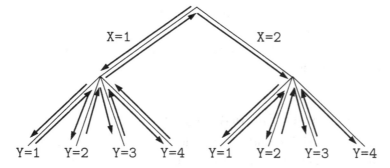

Fig. 8.4 Searching a two variable tree

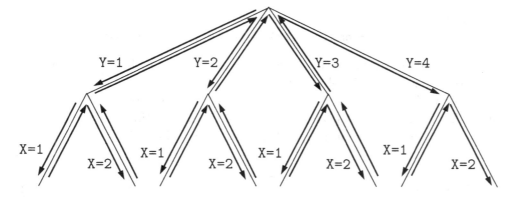

Fig. 8.5 Searching another two variable tree

We shall see in Chapter 11 that with active constraints the variable ordering can have a tremendous influence on the number of search steps needed to find a solution, or to prove that none exists.

8.3.2 The value ordering

If we could always choose the right value for each variable, then search would be unnecessary: we would find a solution first time whenever there was one. Would that life were so simple!

A surprising fact about different value orderings is that they do not affect the size of the search tree. In fact, if there is no solution, then the same number of search nodes needs to be explored whatever value ordering is chosen. This remains true whatever the constraints are.

Where value orderings become important is for incomplete search. Most practical problems have search trees so large that they cannot be explored completely, and so value orderings are very important in practice. If the program is only going to explore part of the search tree, it must explore the part where there is most likely to be a good solution. We shall return to this matter in the next section.

8.3.3 Variable and value ordering in Prolog

Controlling the variable and value ordering is very easy in Prolog. Assume the variables are kept in a list, and each variable is paired with its domain, thus [X-[1,2],Y-[1,2,3,4]]. A naive labelling procedure simply tries the values and variables in the order they appear:

```
naive_search(List) :-
    ( foreach(Var-Domain,List) do member(Var, Domain) ).
```

The variable order and the value order are built into this search routine. The following generic labelling procedure enables the programmer to choose the next variable and the next value freely. As will be shown in Chapter 11, in ECL^{i}PS^e these choices can be supported by information which is gleaned during search. This generic search procedure can be written as in Figure 8.6.

```
% search(List) :-
%      Assign values from the variable domains
%      to all the Var-Domain pairs in List.

search(List) :-
    ( fromto(List, Vars, Rest, [])
    do
      choose_var(Vars, Var-Domain, Rest),
      choose_val(Domain, Val),
      Var = Val
    ).
```

Fig. 8.6 Generic search in ECL^{i}PS^e

To complete this labelling procedure we then write specific procedures for choose_var/3 and choose_val/2. For example, the behaviour of the naive_search/1 procedure defined above is reproduced by encoding the choose_var/3 and choose_val/2 predicates as in Figure 8.7.

```
% choose_var(List, Var, Rest) :-
%     Var is a member of List and
%     Rest contains all the other members.

choose_var(List, Var, Rest) :- List = [Var | Rest].

% choose_val(Domain, Val) :- Val is a member of Domain.

choose_val(Domain, Val) :- member(Val, Domain).
```

Fig. 8.7 Naive variable and value choice

An important point to note is that choose_var/3 does not introduce any choice points, because only one variable ordering is needed to carry out a complete search. However choose_val/2 does introduce choice points: in fact the search tree is completely defined by the set of value choices at each node of the search tree.

8.4 Incomplete search

In this section we shall assume that using some heuristics the domains of the variables have already been ordered so that the 'better' values appear earlier. Then it is natural to ensure that an incomplete search will try values appearing earlier in the variable domains.

The simplest form of incomplete search is to try only a limited number of alternatives for each variable. This can be achieved by selecting a limited number of domain values, and choosing only from those, as shown in the program in Figure 8.8. For this purpose we specify a maximum number N of values to be considered in each domain, and ensure that on backtracking the search only tries at most the first N values from each domain. This is done by using the select_best/3 procedure which selects the appropriate values in each domain. The atomic query select_best(N, Domain, BestList) succeeds only once and leaves no choice points. Consequently, if N = 1, then no backtracking arises. The resulting search method is called then *greedy search*.

The extra argument N in choose_val/3 must be passed into the generic search procedure from Figure 8.6 as a parameter.

Recall from Section 6.6 that the most general method of limiting the search is obtained by allocating credit to each value choice, giving more

```
% choose_val(N, Domain, Val) :-
%      Val is one of the N "best" values in Domain.

choose_val(N, Domain, Val) :-
    select_best(N, Domain, BestList),
    member(Val, BestList).

select_best(N, Domain, BestList) :-
    ( N >= length(Domain) ->
      BestList = Domain
    ;
      length(BestList, N),
      append(BestList, _, Domain)
    ).
```

Fig. 8.8 Selecting only the N best values

credit to values which seem more likely to be a good choice. This credit is then available for the search subtree which remains after choosing that value for that variable. To program this procedure we modify accordingly the generic search procedure from Figure 8.6. The resulting generic credit search procedure is shown in Figure 8.9.

The difference between this generic search procedure and the one from Figure 8.6 is that during the iteration down the variable list the credit is being maintained. The initial credit equals Credit and in each loop iteration is reduced from the current credit CurCredit to the new credit NewCredit. This reduction takes place during the value selection to the variable Var, in the call choose_val(Domain, Val, CurCredit, NewCredit). The new credit NewCredit is then available for the remainder of the search concerned with the list Rest.

This search/2 procedure needs to be completed by choosing the choose_var/3 procedure and the share_credit/3 procedure that manages the credit allocation. As an example of the latter let us encode the program in Figure 8.8 as a credit allocation procedure. The corresponding share_credit/3 procedure is shown in Figure 8.10.

In this program the iteration is controlled by the amount of credit left. The initial credit equals N and in each loop iteration is reduced from the current credit CurCredit to the new credit NewCredit by 1, or to 0 if no

```
% search(List, Credit) :-
%     Search for solutions with a given Credit.


search(List, Credit) :-
    ( fromto(List, Vars, Rest, []),
      fromto(Credit, CurCredit, NewCredit, _)
    do
      choose_var(Vars, Var-Domain, Rest),
      choose_val(Domain, Val, CurCredit, NewCredit),
      Var = Val
    ).


choose_val(Domain, Val, CurCredit, NewCredit) :-
    share_credit(Domain, CurCredit, DomCredList),
    member(Val-NewCredit, DomCredList).
```

Fig. 8.9 Generic credit search

elements are left. The initial credit N is used to select the first N elements of the domain Domain (or all the elements if the domain has fewer than N elements). During the iteration the list DomCredList is built by assigning to each selected element in turn the same, initial, credit N. The latter is achieved by using the param(N) iterator.

We have then for example:

```
[eclipse 1]: share_credit([1,2,3,4,5,6,7,8,9], 5, DomCredList).

DomCredList = [1 - 5, 2 - 5, 3 - 5, 4 - 5, 5 - 5]
Yes (0.00s cpu)
[eclipse 2]: share_credit([1,2,3,4], 5, DomCredList).

DomCredList = [1 - 5, 2 - 5, 3 - 5, 4 - 5]
Yes (0.00s cpu)
```

Because we keep allocating to the selected elements the same, initial, credit, in the original search/2 procedure from Figure 8.9 the current credit CurCredit remains equal to the initial credit Credit, which ensures the correct operation of each call
share_credit(Domain, CurCredit, DomCredList).
In particular the query

```
% share_credit(Domain, N, DomCredList) :-
%     Admit only the first N values.

share_credit(Domain, N, DomCredList) :-
    ( fromto(N, CurCredit, NewCredit, 0),
      fromto(Domain, [Val|Tail], Tail, _),
      foreach(Val-N, DomCredList),
      param(N)
    do
      ( Tail = [] ->
        NewCredit is 0
      ;
        NewCredit is CurCredit - 1
      )
    ).
```

Fig. 8.10 Admit the best N values

search([X-[1,2,3,4,5,6,7,8,9], Y-[1,2,3,4], Z-[1,2,3,4]], 5)

generates 80 solutions for (X,Y,Z), since with the above share_credit/3 procedure the admissible values are 1,2,3,4,5 for X and 1,2,3,4 for Y and for Z.

We used this example of credit allocation because it is familiar to the reader, but it is not a very natural use of credit-based search. A more natural example of credit allocation is to allocate half the credit to the first value in the domain, half of the remaining credit to the second value and so on. When only one unit of credit remains, it is allocated to the next element in the domain and no more alternatives are explored for this variable. This focusses the search effort on the most promising part of the search tree. The code is shown in Figure 8.11.

The expression fix(ceiling(CurCredit/2)), which appears in the code, returns the smallest integer greater than or equal to CurCredit/2. In this program the iteration is also controlled by the amount of credit left. However, in contrast to the share_credit/3 procedure of Figure 8.10, in each loop iteration the current credit can now be reduced by a larger amount than 1. Also, the allocated credit is now diminishing. As a result the iteration can terminate without retaining in DomCredList all domain values even if the domain Domain has fewer elements than the initial credit N.

```
% share_credit(Domain, N, DomCredList) :-
%     Allocate credit N by binary chop.

share_credit(Domain, N, DomCredList) :-
    ( fromto(N, CurCredit, NewCredit, 0),
      fromto(Domain, [Val|Tail], Tail, _),
      foreach(Val-Credit, DomCredList)
    do
      ( Tail = [] ->
        Credit is CurCredit
      ;
        Credit is fix(ceiling(CurCredit/2))
      ),
      NewCredit is CurCredit - Credit
    ).
```

Fig. 8.11 Allocating half remaining credit to next best value

For example, we have:

```
[eclipse 3]: share_credit([1,2,3,4,5,6,7,8,9],
                          5, DomCredList).

DomCredList = [1 - 3, 2 - 1, 3 - 1]
Yes (0.00s cpu)

[eclipse 4]: share_credit([1,2,3,4,5,6,7,8,9],
                          1000, DomCredList).

DomCredList = [1 - 500, 2 - 250, 3 - 125, 4 - 63,
               5 - 31,  6 - 16,  7 - 8,   8 - 4, 9 - 3]
Yes (0.00s cpu)
```

As a result, with the above **share_credit/3** procedure the query

```
search([X-[1,2,3,4,5,6,7,8,9], Y-[1,2,3,4], Z-[1,2,3,4]], 5)
```

now generates only five solutions for (X,Y,Z).

To further clarify this form of credit allocation consider the query

```
search([X-[1,2,3], Y-[1,2,3], Z-[1,2,3]], 8)
```

that produces eight solutions for (X,Y,Z):

$$(1,1,1), \ (1,1,2), \ (1,2,1), \ (1,3,1),$$
$$(2,1,1), \ (2,2,1), \ (3,1,1), \ (3,2,1),$$

These solutions correspond to the explored leaves in the search tree depicted in Figure 8.12. The explored part of the tree is put in bold.

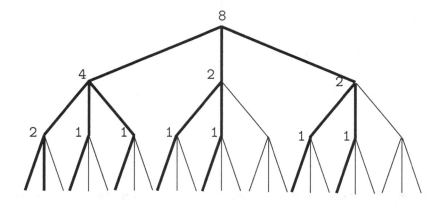

Fig. 8.12 Credit based search with initial credit 8

The total credit allocated to all the values at a search node is equal to the available credit N. Hence it follows that the total credit allocated throughout the search tree is equal to the initial input credit at the top of the search tree. Consequently, this form of credit sharing gives the programmer precise control over the maximum number of nodes explored.

Another way to use credit is as a measure of distance from the preferred left-hand branch of the search tree. This approach has been called *limited discrepancy search*. The same amount of credit is allocated to the first value as was input to the search node. An amount of credit one less than the input is allocated to the second value; one less again to the third value; and so on. The total credit allocated to alternative values, in this case, exceeds the input credit. This share_credit/3 procedure is shown in Figure 8.13.

So, as in the case of the share_credit/3 procedure from Figure 8.10 on page 142, the same elements are selected. However, instead of the same credit, N, now the diminishing credit, CurCredit, is allocated to these elements.

For example we now have:

```
[eclipse 5]: share_credit([1,2,3,4,5,6,7,8,9],
                          5, DomCredList).
```

```
% share_credit(Domain, N, DomCredList) :-
%    Allocate credit N by discrepancy.

share_credit(Domain, N, DomCredList) :-
   ( fromto(N, CurrCredit, NewCredit, -1),
     fromto(Domain, [Val|Tail], Tail, _),
     foreach(Val-CurrCredit, DomCredList)
   do
     ( Tail = [] ->
       NewCredit is -1
     ;
       NewCredit is CurrCredit-1
     )
   ).
```

Fig. 8.13 Limited discrepancy credit allocation

```
DomCredList = [1 - 5, 2 - 4, 3 - 3, 4 - 2, 5 - 1, 6 - 0]
Yes (0.00s cpu)

[eclipse 6]: share_credit([1,2,3,4], 5, DomCredList).

DomCredList = [1 - 5, 2 - 4, 3 - 3, 4 - 2]
Yes (0.00s cpu)
```

Because of this difference the query

```
search([X-[1,2,3,4,5,6,7,8,9], Y-[1,2,3,4], Z-[1,2,3,4]], 4).
```

generates now 33 solutions for (X,Y,Z).

To further clarify the limited discrepancy credit allocation assume the initial credit of 1 and consider the query

```
search([X-[1,2], Y-[1,2], Z-[1,2], U-[1,2], V-[1,2]], 1).
```

It produces six solutions for (X,Y,Z,U,V):

$$(1,1,1,1,1), \ (1,1,1,1,2), \ (1,1,1,2,1),$$
$$(1,1,2,1,1), \ (1,2,1,1,1), \ (2,1,1,1,1).$$

These solutions correspond to the explored leaves in the search tree depicted in Figure 8.14. The explored part of the tree is put in bold.

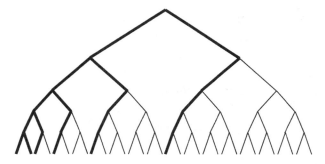

Fig. 8.14 Limited discrepancy search tree

To complete the introduction to incomplete search we should mention bounded backtrack search, and time limited search. These approaches do not attempt to spread the search around the search tree. They explore the tree strictly depth first and left-to-right, but simply stop search when a certain limit is reached. Both are supported by the built-in `search/6` predicate in ECL^{i}PS^e, which we will discuss in Chapter 11.

8.5 Non-logical variables

Occasionally one needs to resort to counting on the system level, for example to compute the number of successful computations, nodes in a computation tree, the number of times a query succeeds, etc. To deal with such matters ECL^{i}PS^e offers ***non-logical variables***. In general, non-logical variables are atoms (so start with a lower case letter), which distinguishes them from the customary ECL^{i}PS^e variables.

ECL^{i}PS^e provides four built-ins that allow us to manipulate non-logical variables:

- `setval/2`,
- `incval/1`,
- `decval/1`,
- `getval/2`.

`setval/2` assigns a value to a non-logical variable. In turn, `incval/1` increments the value of the non-logical variable by 1, while `decval/1` decrements the value of the non-logical variable by 1. In both cases the current value of the variable has to be an integer. Otherwise a run-time error arises.

Finally, `getval/2` either assigns the value of a non-logical variable to a logical variable (this is the only way the values of non-logical variables can be accessed) or tests whether a non-logical variable has a given value.

Thus we have for example:

```
[eclipse 7]: N is 3, setval(count,N),
             incval(count), getval(count, M).
```

```
N = 3
M = 4
Yes (0.00s cpu)
```

```
[eclipse 8]: setval(step,a), getval(step,a).
```

```
Yes (0.00s cpu)
[eclipse 9]: setval(step,a), getval(step,b).
```

```
No (0.00s cpu)
```

The usefulness of non-logical variables stems from the fact that their values persist through backtracking. For example we have:

```
[eclipse 10]: setval(count,0),
              ( incval(count), fail
              ;
                true
              ),
              getval(count, N).
```

```
N = 1
Yes (0.00s cpu)
```

As a slightly less trivial example let us count now the number of times a query succeeds. The appropriate program is given in Figure 8.15.

It is useful to see that the execution of the query succeed(Q, N) does not instantiate any of the variables of the query Q. We have for example:

```
[eclipse 11]: succeed(X = a; X = b; X = c, N).
```

```
X = X
N = 3
Yes (0.00s cpu)
```

```
% succeed(Q, N) :-
%     N is the number of times the query Q succeeds.

succeed(Q, N) :-
    ( setval(count,0),
      Q,
      incval(count),
      fail
    ;
      true
    ),
    getval(count,N).
```

Fig. 8.15 Counting the number of successes

Of course, if the query Q diverges or succeeds infinitely often, the query succeed(Q, N) diverges.

Finally, non-logical variables persist across the clauses. To clarify this point and to show usefulness of this feature consider the problem of checking whether a query succeeds exactly once. To this end we could run the query succeed(Q, 1). This way, however, we let the computation continue after it is clear that more than one solution exists. Moreover, this query can diverge.

A better solution is to use the program given in Figure 8.16 and run the query one(Q). During the execution of this query the non-logical variable x is introduced and modified during the execution of the atomic query not(twice(Q)) but is tested, using getval(x,1), only upon termination of this query. The execution of the query one(Q) does not instantiate any of the variables of the query Q.

The non-logical variables are ideal for simple programs but for large programs there is a risk of the same non-logical variable name being used for different purposes, and therefore being updated by different procedures. So the fact that these variables persist across the clauses can lead to erroneous outcomes. For example, if count is modified during the execution of the query Q, then the count reported by the call succeed(Q, N) can be wrong, for example:

[eclipse 12]: succeed(setval(count,7), N).

```
% one(Q) :- The query Q succeeds exactly once.

one(Q) :-
    not(twice(Q)),    % The query Q succeeds at most once.
    getval(x,1).      % The query Q succeeds at least once.

% twice(Q) :- The query Q succeeds at least twice.

twice(Q) :-
    setval(x,0),
    Q,
    incval(x),
    getval(x,2), !.
```

Fig. 8.16 Checking that a query succeeds exactly once

```
N = 8
Yes (0.00s cpu)
```

To avoid variable clashes of this kind, ECL^{i}PS^e offers a special global variable called a **shelf** whose name is automatically generated by the system. Each shelf has a different name and so clashes are avoided. As our intention is to focus on the basic concepts of ECL^{i}PS^e we do not pursue this topic further.

8.6 Counting the number of backtracks

We now use the non-logical variables to count the number of backtracks, which is the most widely used measure of search effort required to find a solution, or to find all solutions. However, this can be done in alternative ways which we illustrate with the following simple example:

```
[eclipse 13]: member(X, [1,2]), member(Y, [1,2]), X+Y =:= 3.

X = 1
Y = 2
Yes (0.00s cpu, solution 1, maybe more) ? ;

X = 2
Y = 1
```

```
Yes (0.00s cpu, solution 2, maybe more) ? ;

No (0.00s cpu)
```

The search behaviour associated with this query is illustrated in Figure 8.17.

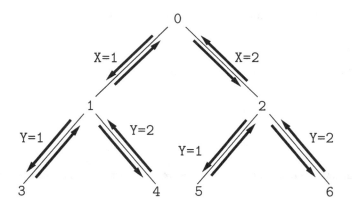

Fig. 8.17 Search and backtracking

The number of upward arrows in this figure is six, and this is one measure of the number of backtracks. The backtracking measure that is most often used, however, only counts four backtracks in this search behaviour.

The reason is that when a failure lower in the search tree causes backtracking to a point several levels higher in the tree, this is usually counted as a single backtrack. Consequently the upward arrows from node 4 to node 0 only count as a single backtrack. Similarly, the final failure at node 6 which completes the search is only counted as a single backtrack.

To count backtracks according to these two measures, we augment our generic search procedure from Figure 8.6 with three atomic goals: to initialise the backtrack count, to count backtracks, and to retrieve the final count. The augmented generic search procedure is shown in Figure 8.18.

The backtrack information is recorded in non-logical variables and is maintained through backtracking. The implementation of the backtracking predicates that includes each backtrack step (yielding a total of six backtracks in the previous toy search example) is shown in Figure 8.19. In this case we simply increment the **backtracks** variable on backtracking. The predicate **count_backtracks** is implemented using the auxiliary predicate **on_backtracking** that takes a query as an argument and calls it on backtracking. Subsequently it fails so that backtracking continues.

```
% search(List, Backtracks) :-
%     Find a solution and count the number of backtracks.

search(List, Backtracks) :-
    init_backtracks,
    ( fromto(List, Vars, Rest,[])
    do
      choose_var(Vars, Var-Domain, Rest),
      choose_val(Domain, Val),
      Var = Val,
      count_backtracks
    ),
    get_backtracks(Backtracks).
```

Fig. 8.18 Generic search with backtrack count

```
init_backtracks :-
    setval(backtracks,0).

get_backtracks(B) :-
    getval(backtracks,B).

count_backtracks :-
    on_backtracking(incval(backtracks)).

on_backtracking(_).    % Until a failure happens do nothing.
                       % The second clause is entered
on_backtracking(Q) :-  % on backtracking.
    once(Q)            % Query Q is called, but only once.
    fail.              % Backtracking continues afterwards.
```

Fig. 8.19 Predicates implementing backtrack counting

The implementation of the **count_backtracks** predicate that counts an uninterrupted sequence of backtracking steps as one backtrack (the 'clever' **count_backtracks**) is more complicated. We provide in Figure 8.20 two implementations. The first one uses the **on_backtracking** predicate and is

more clear, though less efficient. The second one implements the counting
process directly.

```
% First implementation

count_backtracks :-
    setval(single_step,true).
count_backtracks :-
    on_backtracking(clever_count).

clever_count :-
    ( getval(single_step,true) ->
      incval(backtracks)
    ;
      true
    ),
    setval(single_step, false).

% Second implementation

count_backtracks :-
    setval(single_step,true).
count_backtracks :-
    getval(single_step,true),
    incval(backtracks),
    setval(single_step,false).
```

Fig. 8.20 Two implementations of 'clever' count_backtracks

In Chapter 11 we shall use the implementation of the backtrack counting
based on the 'clever' count_backtracks predicate to assess various ways
of implementing search. In the presence of ECL^{i}PS^e libraries that support
constraint programming the number of backtracks differs from the case of
Prolog programs. The reason is that the size of the search trees is then
different due to the constraint propagation process that we shall discuss
extensively in Chapter 10.

8.7 Summary

In this chapter we discussed how finite CSPs can be solved in Prolog by means of top-down search. This brought us to a discussion of complete and incomplete forms of top-down search. For the complete top-down search we discussed the impact of the variable ordering and the value ordering. For the incomplete top-down search we focussed on the implementations of various forms of credit-based search, including the limited discrepancy search.

We also discussed ECL^{i}PS^e facilities that allow us to count the number of backtracks. They consist of non-logical variables and the following four built-ins using which we can manipulate them:

- setval/2,
- incval/1,
- decval/1,
- getval/2.

The distinguishing feature of non-logical variables is that their values persist through backtracking.

8.8 Exercises

Exercise 8.1 Count the number of variable elements in an array without using recursion or the fromto/4 built-in, but using the non-logical variables instead.

Exercise 8.2 Write a predicate all_solutions(Query, List) that returns all the solutions to a query as a list. For example if p/2 is defined by:

```
p(a,Y) :- q(Y).
p(b,Y) :- r(Y).
q(1).
q(2).
r(1).
```

then the query all_solutions(p(X,Y), List) should return

```
List = [p(a, 1), p(a, 2), p(b, 1)].
```

Hint. Use the non-logical variables.

Exercise 8.3 The `naive_search/1` predicate from page 138 can be alternatively defined by

```
naive_search1(Vars, Vals) :-
    ( foreach(V,Vars), param(Vals) do member(V,Vals) ).
```

It searches for all possible assignments of the values to the variables. For example the query `naive_search1([X,Y,Z], [1,2])` returns
X=1, Y=1, Z=1
and then the following on backtracking
X=1, Y=1, Z=2,
X=1, Y=2, Z=1,
X=1, Y=2, Z=2,
etc.

Modify `naive_search1/2` to a predicate `naive_search2/2` that displays its search tree using the names `v1`, `v2`, `v3` and so on for the variables. For example the query `naive_search2([X,Y,Z], [1,2]), fail` should produce the following output:

```
v0 = 1 v1 = 1 v2 = 1
               v2 = 2
       v1 = 2 v2 = 1
               v2 = 2
v0 = 2 v1 = 1 v2 = 1
               v2 = 2
       v1 = 2 v2 = 1
               v2 = 2
```

Hint. Use the non-logical variables and the **on_backtracking/1** predicate defined in Figure 8.19 on page 151.

9

The suspend *library*

9.1 Introduction

I N THIS CHAPTER we introduce the first ECL^{i}PS^e library, called suspend. It allows us to implement constraints. This library lacks the important facility of *constraint propagation* (briefly mentioned in Chapter 6) and consequently is of little use for solving computationally intensive problems. On the other hand, it is used to implement all the other, more sophisticated, constraint solvers in ECL^{i}PS^e and is an excellent pedagogical tool for introducing constraints in the context of ECL^{i}PS^e.

The suspend library still supports only passive constraints and as a result is only the first step towards realising constraint programming. It improves upon the computation model of Prolog by automatically preventing the occurrence of run-time errors for arithmetic constraints, by delaying them until all their variables are fully instantiated. This modified computation mechanism is provided for a larger class of constraints that also includes Boolean constraints. As we shall see, this leads to a more flexible programming style in the presence of constraints.

In particular, using the suspend library we can easily generate CSPs and solve them in a natural way. How this is done is the topic of the current chapter.

9.2 Solving CSPs and COPs using ECL^{i}PS^e

Let us begin by explaining how CSPs are solved in presence of ECL^{i}PS^e libraries. Each such ECL^{i}PS^e program has the following shape:

```
:- lib(my_library).

solve(List):-
    declareDomains(List),
    generateConstraints(List),
    search(List).
```

The first line loads the appropriate library, here `my_library`. Next, `List` is a list of the CSP variables. The atomic goal `declareDomains(List)` generates the domains of the variables from `List` and the atomic goal `generateConstraints(List)` generates the desired constraints. Finally, the atomic goal `search(List)` launches the appropriately chosen search process that results in solving the generated CSP (or establishing its inconsistency).

So we use here a different approach than in Chapter 8 where we discussed how to solve CSPs using Prolog. Indeed, the constraints are now generated first and only then the search is launched. This difference is fundamental and in the presence of appropriate libraries supporting constraint processing it can lead to substantial gains in computing time.

To solve a COP we also need to generate the cost function. This is often done together with the generation of constraints. So conceptually we use then an ECL^{i}PS^e program that looks as follows:

```
:- lib(my_library).

solve(List):-
    declareDomains(List),
    generateConstraints_and_Cost(List, Cost),
    search(List, Cost).
```

The ECL^{i}PS^e system provides a collection of libraries that can be used to generate and solve CSPs and COPs. Each such library offers the user a set of built-ins that deal with specific constraints (for example linear constraints) and specific methods used to solve them (for example branch and bound).

In ECL^{i}PS^e each library, say `my_library`, can be accessed in three different ways.

- By prefixing an atomic query with its name, for example

`suspend:(2 < Y+1).`

This is in particular needed when a reference is made to a predicate, like <, that is already present in Prolog or in another library;
- By loading it by means of the query `lib(my_library)`;
- By loading it using the declaration

`:- lib(my_library).`

at the beginning of the program.

9.3 Introducing the suspend library

Let us focus now on the **suspend** library. To properly understand its usefulness let us return to the Prolog approach to arithmetic discussed in Chapter 3. As already mentioned, its drawback is that when certain atomic goals are not sufficiently instantiated a run-time error arises. One example of this is

```
[eclipse 1]: 2 < Y+1, Y = 3.
instantiation fault in +(Y, 1, _173)
Abort
```

This makes it difficult to generate CSPs in Prolog. The **suspend** library allows us to overcome this difficulty by enabling certain atomic goals to be *delayed* until the variables have become sufficiently instantiated for its evaluation to go ahead. So using the **suspend** library we can suspend the relevant query in the above example until it is ready for evaluation:

```
[eclipse 2]: suspend:(2 < Y+1), Y = 3.

Y = 3
Yes (0.00s cpu)
```

So in the presence of the **suspend** library a more complex computation mechanism is used than in Prolog. In Prolog in each query the leftmost atomic goal is selected. Now in each query the leftmost atomic goal that is either non-arithmetic (that is, does not involve an arithmetic comparison predicate) or ground is selected. We can make explicit how the Prolog selection rule is changed to handle delayed queries by writing a meta-interpreter that does it.

We start by revising the META_INTERPRETER program from Figure 4.4 on page 72 as follows:

```
solve(true) :- !.
solve((A,B)) :- !, solve(A), solve(B).
solve(H) :- rule(H, Body), solve(Body).

rule(A, B) :-
    functor(A,F,N),
    is_dynamic(F/N),
    clause(A, B).
rule(A, true) :- A.
```

The definition has been changed to use rule/2 instead of clause/2. The is_dynamic(F/N) built-in tests whether the predicate F/N has been declared as dynamic (see page 70). We obtain this way a meta-interpreter for programs that use built-ins, for example the comparison predicates. As in the programs SOLVE and SOLVE2 from Figures 4.4 and 4.5 the handling of built-ins is just shifted to the 'system level'.

The above meta-interpreter always chooses the leftmost atomic goal to solve next. The modified meta-interpreter is given in Figure 9.1. Naturally, the suspend library is not really implemented in this way.

To enable an atomic goal to be delayed (in case it is arithmetic and not ground) we introduce two extra arguments to pass the delayed goals through each call. Further, the new meta-interpreter has an extra clause that delays, through a call of the postpone/1 predicate, an atomic goal if it is not ready to be solved immediately. This is a non-ground atomic goal of the form suspend:A. Such a goal is added to the currently delayed goal.

In the last clause for solve/3, after unifying the atomic goal H with the head of a program clause, the meta-interpreter tries to solve the current delayed goal, SuspIn, before solving the body Body. This is done in the same way as solving the input query, using the call solve(SuspIn, true, Susp2).

Finally, to handle suspend-qualified atomic goals a new rule is added to the definition of rule/2. This clause is needed only when the suspend library is not available or is not loaded.

This meta-interpreter now delays non-ground suspend-qualified goals as required:

```
[eclipse 3]: solve((2 < Y + 1, Y = 3), true, SuspOut).
instantiation fault in +(Y, 1, _254)
```

```
solve(true, Susp, Susp) :- !.
solve((A,B), SuspIn, SuspOut) :- !,
    solve(A, SuspIn, Susp2),
    solve(B, Susp2, SuspOut).
solve(A, Susp, (A,Susp)) :-
    postpone(A), !.
solve(H, SuspIn, SuspOut) :-
    rule(H, Body),
    solve(SuspIn, true, Susp2),
    solve(Body, Susp2, SuspOut).

rule(A, B) :-
    functor(A,F,N),
    is_dynamic(F/N),
    clause(A, B).
rule(suspend:A, true) :- !, A.
rule(A, true)  :- A.

postpone(suspend:A)  :- not ground(A).
```

Fig. 9.1 The META_INTERPRETER program for the suspend library

Abort

```
[eclipse 4]: solve((suspend:(2 < Y + 1),Y = 3), true, SuspOut).
Y = 3
SuspOut = true
Yes (0.00s cpu)
```

In general, a query solve(A, SuspIn, SuspOut) succeeds if the query A succeeds using the new selection rule of the atomic goals. The current delayed goal is SuspIn and upon termination the new delayed goal is SuspOut.

The dynamic reordering of the atomic goals made provided through the suspend library is more powerful than one might expect. A striking example will be provided at the end of Subsection 9.4.2.

9.4 Core constraints

ECL^{i}PS^e supports a number of **core constraints** that are available in all the constraint solvers where they make sense. These constraints comprise:

- **Boolean constraints** which are the Boolean connectives `neg/1`, `and/2`, `or/2` and `=>/2` ('implies'), the last three of which can also be written in the infix form,
- **arithmetic constraints** which are built using the arithmetic comparison predicates and the operations considered in Section 3.2,
- variable declarations (numeric ranges and numeric type declarations): they are viewed as unary constraints, and
- so-called 'reified' constraints.

The programmer can use these constraints freely to model the problem, and then select which constraint solver(s) to send them to, when experimenting with algorithms for solving the problem. In particular, these constraints are available in the **suspend** library.

9.4.1 Boolean constraints

In ECL^{i}PS^e the Boolean constants are represented as 0 for **false** and 1 for **true**. Thus negation can be implemented as subtraction from 1, conjunction can be implemented as minimum, and so on.

Let us illustrate the **suspend** behaviour on disjunction **or**:

```
[eclipse 5]: suspend:(X or Y), X = 0.

X = 0
Y = Y

Delayed goals:
        suspend : (0 or Y)
Yes (0.00s cpu)
```

So the atomic goal X **or** Y got only partially instantiated – X got instantiated to 1 – and the resulting atomic goal, 0 **or** Y, got *delayed*, so suspended. This clarifies the displayed information.

This behaviour is not very powerful. The implementation of **or** in the **suspend** library has failed to infer that Y must take the value 1. In general, the delayed query is selected only once all its variables are instantiated. This can lead to a success:

```
[eclipse 6]: suspend:(X or Y), X = 0, Y = 1.
```

```
X = 0
Y = 1
Yes (0.00s cpu)
```

or to a failure:

```
[eclipse 7]: suspend:(X or Y), X = 0, Y = 0.
```

```
No (0.00s cpu)
```

The same holds for all the core constraints: nothing is done until the query is completely instantiated (i.e. becomes ground).

To implement Boolean constraints in Prolog we need to follow a different approach and list the true facts. For example the **or** constraint would be defined by three facts:

```
1 or 1.
1 or 0.
0 or 1.
```

Then the query X or Y, X = 0, Y = 1 succeeds as well, but, in contrast to the approach based on the **suspend** library, the computation now involves backtracking.

In general, if a core constraint becomes fully instantiated it is either deleted (when it succeeds) or it causes a failure (when it fails) which can trigger backtracking, as in the case of customary Prolog computations.

9.4.2 Arithmetic constraints

The six arithmetic comparison predicates introduced in Section 3.3 are available as core constraints. Consequently, in the presence of the **suspend** library they can be used to model CSPs. So as before these predicates can be used for testing:

```
[eclipse 8]: suspend:(1+2 =:= 3).
```

```
Yes (0.00s cpu)
[eclipse 9]: suspend:(1+2 > 2+3).
```

```
No (0.00s cpu)
```

but also for generating constraints in the form of delayed (atomic) goals:

```
[eclipse 10]: suspend:(2+4 > Y), suspend:(Y > 2).
```

Y = Y

```
Delayed goals:
        suspend : (2 + 4 > Y)
        suspend : (Y > 2)
Yes (0.00s cpu)
```

and for solving them through an instantiation:

```
[eclipse 11]: suspend:(2+4 > Y), suspend:(Y > 2), Y = 5.
```

Y = 5
Yes (0.00s cpu)

In particular, thanks to this delay mechanism we can first generate constraints and then solve them by a systematic generation of the candidates values for the relevant variables.

Once the **suspend** library is loaded, these arithmetic constraints can be written in a more compact way, using the $ prefix (though the equality and disequality are written differently). So we have six arithmetic comparison constraints:

- 'less than', written as $<,
- 'less than or equal', written as $=<,
- 'equality', written as $=,
- 'disequality', written as $\=,
- 'greater than or equal', written as $>=,
- 'greater than', written as $>.

In contrast to the corresponding original arithmetic comparison predicates,

$$<, =<, =:=, =\=, =\=,>=, >,$$

they can be used in queries with variables, like in

```
[eclipse 12]: 1 + 2 $= Y.
```

Y = Y

```
Delayed goals:
        suspend : (1 + 2 =:= Y)
```

```
Yes (0.00s cpu)
```

This shows that once the **suspend** library is loaded 1 + 2 $= Y is indeed a shorthand for **suspend:** (1 + 2 =:= Y). So, as long as only the **suspend** library is loaded in ECL^{i}PS^e, there is no need to explicitly module qualify each constraint that refers to an arithmetic comparison predicate.

The following example should clarify the difference between =/2, $=/2, and =:=/2:

```
[eclipse 13]: X = 1 + 2.

X = 1 + 2
Yes (0.00s cpu)
[eclipse 14]: X $= 1 + 2.

X = X

Delayed goals:
        suspend : (X =:= 1 + 2)
Yes (0.00s cpu)
[eclipse 15]: X =:= 1 + 2.
instantiation fault in X =:= 3 in module eclipse
Abort
```

In particular, the query X $= 1 + 2 is delayed, while its Prolog counterpart X =:= 1 + 2, as already explained in Section 3.3, yields a run-time error.

A non-trivial example showing that the **suspend** library allows us to solve more queries than Prolog is the following one. Let us modify the QUICKSORT program of Figure 3.4 in Section 3.3 by treating the arithmetic comparison operators as constraints, so by using the following modified definition of the part/4 predicate:

```
part(_, [], [], []).
part(X, [Y|Xs], [Y|Ls], Bs) :- X $> Y, part(X, Xs, Ls, Bs).
part(X, [Y|Xs], Ls, [Y|Bs]) :- X $=< Y, part(X, Xs, Ls, Bs).
```

Then we can successfully run queries such as:

```
[eclipse 16]: qs([3.14, Y, 1, 5.5], [T, 2, U, Z]).

Y = 2
T = 1
U = 3.14
```

```
Z = 5.5
Yes (0.00s cpu, solution 1, maybe more) ? ;

No (0.00s cpu)
```

The same behaviour holds for all the considered modifications of QUICKSORT.

9.4.3 Variable declarations

As already mentioned, specific variable declarations are available in the **suspend** library. Variable declarations will be important in the next chapter in which we study two ECL^{i}PS^e libraries that allow us to automatically reduce variable domains. In contrast, variable declarations are hardly relevant in the **suspend** library and the atomic goal declareDomains(List) could equally well be deleted from the definition of the solve/1 predicate on page 156.

Indeed, suspending a variable declaration until the variable is instantiated does not seem to be common sense. However, it does illustrate the fact that in ECL^{i}PS^e a variable declaration is simply a unary constraint on the variable, in principle no different from any other constraints. Also, the presence of variable declarations allows us to write programs that we can execute using both the **suspend** library and subsequent, more powerful libraries.

In the **suspend** library two types of variable declaration are provided. The first one is a *range* declaration. An example is

```
[eclipse 17]: suspend:(X :: 1..9).

X = X

Delayed goals:
        suspend : (X :: 1 .. 9)
Yes (0.00s cpu)
```

This query generates a declaration of the variable X by stipulating that it ranges over the integer interval [1..9]. The ECL^{i}PS^e prompt confirms that this variable declaration is interpreted as a unary constraint. Once the **suspend** library is loaded, we can simply write X :: 1..9 instead of suspend:(X :: 1..9) and similarly with all other declarations here discussed. From now on we assume that the **suspend** library is loaded.

To abbreviate multiple declarations with the same domain a list notation can be used:

```
[S,E,N,D,M,O,R,Y] :: 0..9.
```

The domain bounds can be parameters that will be instantiated at the run-time, as in the following example:

```
declare(M, N, List):- List :: M..N.
```

Then the query `declare(0, 9, [S,E,N,D,M,O,R,Y])` achieves the effect of the above declaration.

When handled by the **suspend** library the range is only used as a test whether the variable becomes correctly instantiated:

```
[eclipse 18]: X :: 1..9, X = 5.
```

```
X = 5
Yes (0.00s cpu)
[eclipse 19]: X :: 1..9, X = 0.
```

```
No (0.00s cpu)
```

Finally, by using '`$::`' instead of '`::`' we can declare variables ranging over a real interval:

```
[eclipse 20]: X :: 1..9, X = 2.5.
```

```
No (0.00s cpu)
[eclipse 21]: X $:: 1..9, X = 2.5.
```

```
X = 2.5
Yes (0.00s cpu)
```

The same can be achieved by using reals as bounds.

The second form of a variable declaration in the **suspend** library is provided by the **integers/1** and **reals/1** constraints. An example is

```
integers(X)
```

which declares the variable X ranging over the set of integers. Such declarations can be viewed as a form of type declarations. As before, multiple declarations can be written using the list notation. The following sample queries illustrate the use of these two forms of variable declarations:

```
[eclipse 22]: integers([X,Y]), X = 3, Y = 4.
```

```
X = 3
```

```
Y = 4
Yes (0.00s cpu)
[eclipse 23]: integers([X,Y]), X = 3, Y = 4.5.

No (0.00s cpu)
[eclipse 24]: reals(X), X = [1,2.1,4].

X = [1, 2.1, 4]
Yes (0.00s cpu)
[eclipse 25]: reals(X), X = [1,2.1,a].

No (0.00s cpu)
```

Integrality can also be imposed implicitly on all the expressions in a constraint by using # instead of $:

```
[eclipse 26]: X $> 2, X = 2.5.

X = 2.5
Yes (0.00s cpu)
[eclipse 27]: X #> 2, X = 2.5.

No (0.00s cpu)
```

9.4.4 Reified constraints

Reified constraints are constraints that can be switched to **true** or **false** by setting an extra Boolean variable. All the core constraints mentioned above can be reified in this way, by adding an extra Boolean variable (so one taking a value 0 or 1) as an argument of the constraint. Here are a few examples, where we assume that the **suspend** library is loaded:

```
[eclipse 28]: $>(5, 4, 1).

Yes (0.00s cpu)
[eclipse 29]: $>(4, 5, 1).

No (0.00s cpu)
[eclipse 30]: $>(4, 5, Bool), Bool = 0.

Bool = 0
```

```
Yes (0.00s cpu)
[eclipse 31]: $>(3, Y, 1), Y = 2.


Y = 2
Yes (0.00s cpu)
[eclipse 32]: $::(X, 1..9, 0), X = 10.


X = 10
Yes (0.00s cpu)
[eclipse 33]: or(1,0,B).


B = 1
Yes (0.00s cpu)
```

In the last example the binary disjunction or/2 is reified to the ternary one, or/3.

9.5 User defined suspensions

The suspend library supports all the core constraints, but occasionally we also need to suspend user-defined goals. This can be done in ECL^{i}PS^e using the built-in **suspend/3** that allows us to suspend arbitrary atomic goals.

To explain its use consider first an atomic goal referring to a built-in. Suppose, for example, we wish to suspend the atomic goal X =:= 10 until X is instantiated. To achieve this behaviour we pass the atomic goal as an argument to the **suspend/3** predicate:

```
[eclipse 34]: suspend(X =:= 10, 3, X -> inst).


X = X


Delayed goals:
        X =:= 10
Yes (0.00s cpu)
```

The suspended atomic goal is executed as soon as X becomes instantiated:

```
[eclipse 35]: suspend(X =:= 10, 3, X -> inst), X is 2+8.


X = 10
Yes (0.00s cpu)
```

The second argument to `suspend/3` is an integer (3 in the above examples), indicating the priority of the goal when it wakes up. When several goals wake up as the result of the same event (such as X becoming instantiated) the higher priority goals are executed earlier.

The third argument specifies the waking condition, written as `Term -> Cond`. (Alternatively a list of such conditions can be given.) The term `Term` can be any term that includes variables. The waking condition applies to all the variables appearing in the term. The condition `Cond` is normally `inst`.[1]

To illustrate the suspension of user-defined goals let us define a predicate `xor/2` that defines *exclusive or*. Of course it can be encoded simply as:

```
xor(1, 0).
xor(0, 1).
```

But this definition leads to an unnecessary backtracking search that we now wish to avoid. We do this by suspending the atomic goal `xor(X, Y)` and have it wake only after both variables are instantiated, by building a chain of suspensions. We achieve this by means of a predicate `susp_xor/2`, defined in Figure 9.2.

```
susp_xor(X, Y) :-
    ( nonvar(X) ->
      susp_y_xor(X, Y)
    ;
      suspend(susp_y_xor(X,Y), 3, X -> inst)
    ).

susp_y_xor(X, Y) :-
    ( nonvar(Y) ->
      xor(X, Y)
    ;
      suspend(xor(X,Y), 3, Y -> inst)
    ).

xor(1, 0).
xor(0, 1).
```

Fig. 9.2 Exclusive or with a suspension

---

[1] The full set of conditions can be found in the ECL^{i}PS^e documentation.

This predicate waits using the call

```
suspend(susp_y_xor(X,Y), 3, X -> inst)
```

until X is instantiated and then it calls the second predicate, **susp_y_xor/2**. (If X is already instantiated, then it calls **susp_y_xor/2** immediately.) This predicate in turn waits, using the call

```
suspend(xor(X,Y), 3, Y -> inst),
```

until Y is instantiated before finally calling **xor/2**. No matter in which order the variables X and Y become instantiated the **susp_xor/2** predicate behaves correctly:

```
[eclipse 36]: susp_xor(X, Y).

X = X
Y = Y

Delayed goals:
        susp_y_xor(X, Y)

Yes (0.00s cpu)
[eclipse 37]: susp_xor(X, Y), X = 0.

X = 0
Y = Y

Delayed goals:
        xor(0, Y)
Yes (0.00s cpu)
[eclipse 38]: susp_xor(X, Y), Y = 1.

X = X
Y = 1

Delayed goals:
        susp_y_xor(X, 1)
Yes (0.00s cpu)
[eclipse 39]: susp_xor(X, Y), Y = 1, X = 0.

X = 0
```

```
Y = 1
Yes (0.00s cpu)
```

This should be contrasted with the behaviour of xor/2: the corresponding queries (so queries 37–39 with susp_xor replaced by xor) all succeed, but each time a backtracking takes place.

Finally, of course there is no need to delay an atomic goal by means of suspend/3 until *all* its arguments are instantiated. In fact, a more general use of suspend/3 allows us to suspend an atomic goal until some of its arguments are instantiated.

To explain the syntax and its use let us suspend the xor(X, Y) goal until *either* X *or* Y have been instantiated:

```
[eclipse 40]:  suspend(xor(X, Y), 2, [X, Y] -> inst).

X = X
Y = Y

Delayed goals:
        xor(X, Y)
Yes (0.00s cpu)
[eclipse 41]: suspend(xor(X, Y), 2, [X, Y] -> inst), X = 1.

X = 1
Y = 0
Yes (0.00s cpu)
[eclipse 42]: suspend(xor(X, Y), 2, [X, Y] -> inst), Y = 1.

X = 0
Y = 1
Yes (0.00s cpu)
```

We shall discuss the suspend/3 built-in again in Subsection 10.3.1, where we shall review its behaviour in the presence of constraint propagation.

9.6 Generating CSPs

Now that we know how to create constraints using the suspend library let us see how we can generate specific CSPs. As an example, to generate the CSP

$$\langle x \neq y, y \neq z, x \neq z \; ; \; x \in \{0, 1\}, y \in \{0, 1\}, z \in \{0, 1\} \rangle$$

we use the following query:

```
[eclipse 43]: [X,Y,Z] :: 0..1, X #\= Y, Y #\= Z, X #\= Z.

X = X
Y = Y
Z = Z


Delayed goals:
        suspend : ([X, Y, Z] :: 0 .. 1)
        suspend : (X #\= Y)
        suspend : (Y #\= Z)
        suspend : (X #\= Z)
Yes (0.00s cpu)
```

So the 'delayed goals' correspond to the variable declarations and the unsolved constraints on these variables. In other words, the execution of the above query results in an answer that is a representation of the original CSP.

Note that the corresponding ECL^{i}PS^e query with #\= replaced by =\= yields a run-time error:

```
[eclipse 44]: [X,Y,Z] :: 0..1, X =\= Y, Y =\= Z, X =\= Z.
instantiation fault in X =\= Y
Abort
```

Indeed, during its execution the arithmetic comparison predicate =\= is applied to arguments that are not numbers.

So far, all the constraints were explicitly written. A powerful feature of ECL^{i}PS^e is that the constraints and whole CSPs can also be generated. Let us clarify it by the following example. Suppose we wish to generate the CSP

$$\langle x_1 < x_2, \ldots, x_{n-1} < x_n \; ; \; x_1 \in \{1..1000\}, \ldots, x_n \in \{1..1000\}\rangle,$$

where $n > 1$, independently of the value of n. This can be done by means of the program given in Figure 9.3 that should be compared with the ORDERED program from Figure 7.6 on page 127.

We can now run the query

```
List :: 1..1000, ordered(List).
```

with an arbitrary list of variables List. Each such query generates an appropriate CSP. For example, to generate the CSP

```
% ordered(Xs) :- Xs is an <-ordered list of numbers.


ordered(List) :-
    ( List = [] ->
      true
    ;
      ( fromto(List,[This,Next | Rest],[Next | Rest],[_])
      do
        This $< Next
      )
    ).
```

Fig. 9.3 Another ORDERED program

$$\langle x < y, y < z, z < u, u < v\,;\ x \in \{1..1000\}, y \in \{1..1000\},$$
$$z \in \{1..1000\}, u \in \{1..1000\}, v \in \{1..1000\}\rangle$$

we use the following query:

```
[eclipse 45]: [X,Y,Z,U,V] :: 1..1000, ordered([X,Y,Z,U,V]).

X = X
Y = Y
Z = Z
U = U
V = V


Delayed goals:
        suspend : ([X, Y, Z, U, V] :: 1 .. 1000)
        suspend : (X < Y)
        suspend : (Y < Z)
        suspend : (Z < U)
        suspend : (U < V)
Yes (0.00s cpu)
```

Earlier we used a query (query No. 43 on page 171) that given a list of three variables posted a disequality constraint between each pair of elements of the list. Now we show how to define a generic version that we call diff_list/1 that does the same with a list of any number of variables. This predicate corresponds to the all_different constraint introduced in Subsection 6.4.2. It is defined in Figure 9.4 using the `fromto/4` and `foreach/2` iterators.

```
% diff_list(List) :-
%     List is a list of different variables.

diff_list(List) :-
    ( fromto(List,[X|Tail],Tail,[])
    do
      ( foreach(Y, Tail),
        param(X)
      do
        X $\= Y
      )
    ).
```

Fig. 9.4 The DIFF_LIST program

For example, the query

```
length(List, 3), List:: 1..100, diff_list(List).
```

produces a list `List` of three anonymous variables, each with the domain `1..100`, and subsequently generates the disequality constraints between these three variables. Recall from Section 7.3 that `length/2` is a Prolog built-in that given a list as the first argument computes its length, or given a natural number `n` as the second argument generates a list of anonymous (and thus distinct) variables of length `n`.

Here is the outcome of the interaction with ECL^{i}PS^e:

```
[eclipse 46]: length(List, 3), List:: 1..100, diff_list(List).

List = [_268, _330, _242]

Delayed goals:
        suspend : ([_268, _330, _242] :: 1 .. 100)
        suspend : (_268 =\= _330)
        suspend : (_268 =\= _242)
        suspend : (_330 =\= _242)
Yes (0.00s cpu)
```

As a final example consider the problem of generating a constraint of the form

$$\sum_{i=1}^{n} a_i \cdot x_i \leq v,$$

where $n \geq 1$, all a_is are given parameters and all x_is and v are variables ranging over an integer interval. Recall that we used this constraint when discussing the knapsack problem in Subsection 6.5.1. This constraint can be generated in ECL^{i}PS^e as follows:

```
sigma(As, Xs, V) :-
    sum(As, Xs, Out),
    eval(Out) #=< V.


sum([], [], 0).
sum([A|As], [X|Xs], A*X + Y) :-
    sum(As, Xs, Y).
```

Note the use of the `eval/1` built-in in the constraint `eval(Out) #=< V`. It is a 'wrapper' used to indicate that a variable that occurs inside an arithmetic constraint, here `Out`, will be bound to an expression at the run-time. So it is only used in programs which generate constraints at run-time, like the above clause defining `sigma/3`.

Now, during the execution of the query

```
[X,Y,Z,U] :: 1..1000, sigma([1,2,3,4], [X,Y,Z,U], V).
```

the local variable `Out` becomes instantiated to the sum `1*X + 2*Y + 3*Z + 4*U` that is subsequently passed to the constraint `eval(Out) $<= V` and we get the following outcome:

```
[eclipse 47]: [X,Y,Z,U] :: 1..1000,
               sigma([1,2,3,4], [X,Y,Z,U], V).


X = X
Y = Y
Z = Z
U = U
V = V


Delayed goals:
    suspend : ([X, Y, Z, U] :: 1 .. 1000)
    suspend : (eval(1 * X + (2 * Y + (3 * Z + (4 * U + 0)))))
```

```
                    #=< V)
Yes (0.00s cpu)
```

9.7 Using the suspend library

Any program behaviour that can be achieved using the **suspend** library can be equally achieved without it. However, reordering of the atomic goals so that they are evaluated as soon as their arguments have become instantiated requires careful programming. The key benefit of the **suspend** library is that such a reordering can be achieved in a straightforward way. So using this library flexible programs can be written in a simple and readable way. To illustrate this point we now discuss three programs that compute solutions to the CSPs studied in Section 6.4.

9.7.1 Map colouring problems

Recall that the problem was specified by

- a set of regions,
- a (smaller) set of colours,
- a neighbour relation between pairs of regions.

The problem was to associate a colour with each region so that no two neighbours have the same colour.

To model this problem in ECL^{i}PS^e we simply generate the appropriate CSP discussed in Subsection 6.4.1 by means of an ECL^{i}PS^e program. So each region is represented by a decision variable. The value of the variable, when it is finally instantiated, is the colour chosen for that region.

Because the core constraints are numeric, the program has to use numbers for the colours. So we represent the data as follows:

```
no_of_regions(4).

neighbour(1, 2).
neighbour(1, 3).
neighbour(1, 4).
neighbour(2, 3).
neighbour(2, 4).

colour(1). % red
colour(2). % yellow
colour(3). % blue
```

If the neighbours are recorded in a predicate, this problem is difficult to solve in ECL^{i}PS^e without using the **suspend** library. The difficulty is that as soon as a region is coloured the disequality should be checked between that region's variable and the already instantiated variables of its neighbours. This form of control is awkward to express and difficult to modify in case the programmer decides to instantiate the variables in a different order.

In contrast, using the **suspend** library the map colouring program can be written in a simple and generic way. It is presented in Figure 9.5. The variable declarations are omitted as the variable domains are used only within the search, through the calls of `colour(R)`. In the program the counter variables I and J have the same start and stop values so we use the intuitively clear shorthand `multifor([I,J],1,Count)` available in ECL^{i}PS^e.

```
% colour_map(Regions) :- Regions is a colouring of
%      the map represented by the neighbour/2 predicate.

colour_map(Regions) :-
    constraints(Regions),
    search(Regions).

constraints(Regions) :-
    no_of_regions(Count),
    dim(Regions,[Count]),
    ( multifor([I,J],1,Count),
      param(Regions)
    do
      ( neighbour(I, J) ->
        Regions[I] $\= Regions[J]
      ;
        true
      )
    ).

search(Regions) :-
    ( foreacharg(R,Regions) do colour(R) ).
```

Fig. 9.5 The MAP_COLOURING program

The suspend implementation of $\= ensures that the disequalities be-
tween the neighbouring countries are automatically tested as soon as both
neighbours are instantiated. The separation of the constraint generation
phase from the search allows us to modify the search routine, for example
to take into account a specific structure of the map, without any need to
change the constraint handling.

For the above data six solutions listed in Subsection 6.4.1 are generated,
starting with:

```
[eclipse 48]: colour_map(Regions).
```

```
Regions = [](1, 2, 3, 3)
Yes (0.00s cpu, solution 1, maybe more) ? ;
```

9.7.2 *SEND + MORE = MONEY* puzzle

Recall from Subsection 6.4.2 that the problem is to replace each letter by a
different digit so that the above sum is correct. The appropriate ECL^{i}PS^e
program consists simply of the formulation of the constraints followed by
the systematic selection of possible values for all variables. We choose here,
as an illustration, the third representation given in Subsection 6.4.2 with the
all_different constraint modelled by the earlier introduced diff_list/1
constraint. The program is given in Figure 9.6.

For compatibility with the next chapter we included in the program the
variable declarations even though they are not needed here. To generate
the possible values we use in the definition of search/1 the select_val/3
predicate from Figure 3.2 on page 46.

The following interaction with ECL^{i}PS^e shows that this a very inefficient
solution:

```
[eclipse 49]: send(List).
```

```
List = [9, 5, 6, 7, 1, 0, 8, 2]
Yes (176.60s cpu, solution 1, maybe more) ? ;
```

```
No (183.94s cpu)
```

The reason is that each constraint is activated only when all its variables
become ground. So the fact that these constraints were generated first is
only of a limited use. For example, the combination of values S = 1, E =
1, N = 1 is not generated, since a failure arises after trying S = 1, E = 1.

```
% send(List):-  List is a solution to
%     the SEND + MORE = MONEY puzzle.

send(List):-
    List = [S,E,N,D,M,O,R,Y],
    List :: 0..9,
    diff_list(List),
                1000*S + 100*E + 10*N + D
              + 1000*M + 100*O + 10*R + E
    $= 10000*M + 1000*O + 100*N + 10*E + Y,
    S $\= 0,
    M $\= 0,
    search(List).

search(List) :-
    ( foreach(Var,List) do select_val(0, 9, Var) ).
```

augmented by the DIFF_LIST program of Figure 9.4 and the SELECT
program of Figure 3.2.

Fig. 9.6 The SEND_MORE_MONEY program

However, all possible value combinations for the variables that are pairwise
different are still generated since the crucial equality constraint is used only
for testing. In the next chapter we shall see that in the presence of constraint
propagation this approach becomes considerably more realistic and efficient.

9.7.3 The n-queens problem

To solve this problem using the suspend library we use the second for-
malisation of it given in Subsection 6.4.3. So we assume that the solution
is generated in the form of a one-dimensional array QueenStruct of size
[1..Number] and just need to generate the following disequality constraints
for I ∈ [1..Number] and J ∈ [1..I-1]:

- QueenStruct[I] $\= QueenStruct[J],
- QueenStruct[I]-QueenStruct[J] $\= I-J,
- QueenStruct[I]-QueenStruct[J] $\= J-I.

The corresponding program is given in Figure 9.7. Again, for compatibility with the next chapter we included in the program the variable declarations, in the line

```
QueenStruct[I] :: 1..Number,
```

even though they are not needed.

```
% queens(QueenStruct, Number) :- The array QueenStruct
%     is a solution to the Number-queens problem.

queens(QueenStruct, Number) :-
    dim(QueenStruct,[Number]),
    constraints(QueenStruct, Number),
    search(QueenStruct).

constraints(QueenStruct, Number) :-
    ( for(I,1,Number),
      param(QueenStruct,Number)
    do
      QueenStruct[I] :: 1..Number,
      ( for(J,1,I-1),
        param(I,QueenStruct)
      do
        QueenStruct[I] $\= QueenStruct[J],
        QueenStruct[I]-QueenStruct[J] $\= I-J,
        QueenStruct[I]-QueenStruct[J] $\= J-I
      )
    ).

search(QueenStruct) :-
    dim(QueenStruct,[N]),
    ( foreacharg(Col,QueenStruct),
      param(N)
    do
      select_val(1, N, Col)
    ).
```

augmented by the SELECT program of Figure 3.2.

Fig. 9.7 Another QUEENS program

The structure of this program is different from that of the QUEENS program given in Figure 7.7 on page 130. Namely, first constraints are generated and then systematically the values for the subscripted variables are generated. Unfortunately, because each constraint is activated only when the variable QueenStruct becomes ground (i.e., when every queen has been placed) this program is very inefficient:

```
[eclipse 50]: queens(QueenStruct, 8).

QueenStruct = [](1, 5, 8, 6, 3, 7, 2, 4)
Yes (341.84s cpu, solution 1, maybe more) ?
```

In the next chapter we shall reevaluate this approach in the presence of constraint propagation. The reader should also consult Exercise 9.3.

9.8 Summary

In this chapter we discussed the **suspend** library of ECL^{i}PS^e. It provides a support for passive constraints through a dynamic reordering of the atomic goals. In the case of arithmetic constraints this prevents the occurrence of run-time errors.

We introduced the following core constraints that are available in the **suspend** library:

- Boolean constraints:
  and/2, or/2, neg/1, =>/2,
- arithmetic comparison constraints on reals:
  $<, $=<, $=, $\=, $>=, $>,
- arithmetic comparison constraints on integers:
  #<, #=<, #=, #\=, #>=, #>,
- variable declarations:
  range (::, $::, #::, for example M..N), **integers/1** and **reals/1**.

We also discussed the **suspend/3** built-in that allows us to delay arbitrary atomic goals. Further, we introduced the **eval/1** built-in used to indicate that a variable within an arithmetic constraint will be bound to an expression at the run-time.

We also explained how CSPs can be generated and illustrated the introduced facilities by presenting three programs that provide solutions to the CSPs studied in Section 6.4.

9.9 Exercises

Exercise 9.1 The META_INTERPRETER program for the suspend library given in Figure 9.1 on page 159 outputs the suspended atomic goals in the reverse order:

```
[eclipse 1]: solve((suspend:(2 < Y + 1), suspend:(X > 3)),
                   true, SuspOut).

Y = Y
X = X
SuspOut = suspend : (X > 3), suspend : (2 < Y + 1), true
Yes (0.00s cpu)
```

while we have

```
[eclipse 2]: suspend:(2 < Y + 1), suspend:(X > 3).

Y = Y
X = X

Delayed goals:
        suspend : (2 < Y + 1)
        suspend : (X > 3)
Yes (0.00s cpu)
```

Propose a modification that deals with this problem and that reproduces the output of the suspend library, through a call of a solve/1 predicate.

Exercise 9.2 Write a version of the diff_list/2 predicate from Figure 9.4 on page 173 that uses recursion instead of iteration.

Exercise 9.3 As already mentioned, the QUEENS program from Figure 9.7 on page 179 is very inefficient because each constraint is activated only when the variable QueenStruct becomes ground. Propose a modification of this program in which each binary constraint is activated as soon as both of its variables are ground.

Exercise 9.4 By a *clause* we mean a disjunction of Boolean variables. We represent it is a list. The clause is then *true* if at least one variable in it is identical to 1.

Using the **suspend/3** built-in write a procedure **test_cl/1** that implements the test whether a clause is true, by suspending on just one Boolean variable.

Hint. Use the following **filter/3** predicate in your implementation:

```
filter([], [], unsat).
filter([H | T], [H | Rest], Sat) :-
    var(H), !, filter(T, Rest, Sat).
filter([0 | T], Rest, Sat) :- !,
    filter(T, Rest, Sat).
filter([1 |_], [], sat).
```

The call **filter(List, Rest, Sat)** filters the instantiated variables (1 or 0) out of the clause **List**, leaving the remaining variables in **Rest**, and recording in **Sat** if the clause is already satisfied.

Exercise 9.5 Modify the **ORDERED** program from Figure 9.3 on page 172 using the **suspend/3** built-in so that it fails as early as possible. For example the query **ordered([W,X,Y,Z])**, **W = 2**, **Z = 2** should fail.

Part IV

Programming with active constraints

10

Constraint propagation in ECL^iPS^e

10.1 Introduction

A SIGNIFICANT LIMITATION of the support for constraint processing provided by the **suspend** library is that only passive constraints are admitted. As a result some obvious conclusions cannot be inferred without search. As an example, recall that the query No. 5:

```
suspend:(X or Y), X = 0.
```

from page 160 did not allow us to infer that Y = 1. Such a conclusion could only be established by explicitly instantiating Y and testing whether the instantiation is correct.

Starting with this chapter we discuss libraries of ECL^iPS^e that provide a more powerful support for constraint processing by admitting active constraints. So an evaluation of a constraint can affect its variables. In particular inferences such as Y = 1 above can be made automatically. This additional support is called ***constraint propagation*** and, as already mentioned in Section 6.6, involves removal from the domains of variables some values that do not participate in any solution. In the above example constraint propagation results in removing the value 0 from the domain of Y which leaves 1 as the only possible alternative. As a result Y gets instantiated to 1.

The constraint propagation is activated in an 'eager' way: as soon as a new constraint is encountered, a new round of the constraint propagation process is triggered. This may reduce the domains of the previously considered variables and lead in turn to a renewed activation of the already considered constraints. The formal details of this process are omitted but are illustrated by several examples.

In this chapter we introduce two libraries that support active constraints. They are called **sd** and **ic**. The first one deals with constraints defined over symbolic values, while the second deals with the core constraints, so constraints defined over Booleans, integers and reals, and reified constraints. We focus here on the built-in facilities concerned with the constraint propagation. The facilities supporting search will be discussed in the next chapter.

10.2 The sd library

We introduce here the ECL^{i}PS^e library **sd** (standing for symbolic domains) which supports symbolic domains such as {a,b,c,d,e}. In **sd** the variables are declared as follows:

```
X &:: [a,b,d],
[Y,Z] &:: [a,b,c,d]
```

In all examples below we assume that the **sd** library is loaded. Two binary constraints are available on symbolic finite domains. These are:

- equality, written as &=
- disequality, written as &\=.

To generate the CSP

$$\langle x = y, y \neq z \; ; \; x \in \{a,c,d\}, y \in \{a,b,c,d\}, z \in \{c\}\rangle$$

we thus use the following query:

```
[eclipse 1]: X &:: [a,c,d], Y &:: [a,b,c,d], Z &:: [c],
             X &= Y, Y &\= Z.


X = X{[a, d]}
Y = Y{[a, d]}
Z = c


Delayed goals:
        X{[a, d]} &= Y{[a, d]}
Yes (0.00s cpu)
```

We see here an important difference in ECL^{i}PS^e behaviour with respect to the **suspend** library. Indeed, different variable domains from the declared ones are produced. In fact, the produced answer corresponds to the following CSP:

$$\langle x = y \ ; \ x \in \{a, d\}, y \in \{a, d\}, z \in \{c\}\rangle.$$

So in the presence of the **sd** library an inference was made that led to a removal of the value c from the domain of X and the values b,c from the domain of Y. This inference can be easily justified by noting that because of the equality constraint X &= Y the domains of X and Y have to be equal. Further, because of the disequality constraint Y &\= Z the value c can be removed from the domain of Y and hence the domain of X. At this moment the disequality constraint Y &\= Z becomes solved (i.e., all possible variable combinations satisfy it) so it is deleted. In the **sd** library such inferences are done automatically.

In some situations, thanks to constraint propagation, all constraints become solved and a solution is obtained. As an example reconsider the CSP

$$\langle x = y, y \neq z, z \neq u \ ; \ x \in \{a, b, c\}, y \in \{a, b, d\}, z \in \{a, b\}, u \in \{b\}\rangle$$

from Section 6.3. To generate it in ECL^{i}PS^e we use the following query:

```
[eclipse 2]: X &:: [a,b,c], Y &:: [a,b,d], Z &:: [a,b],
             U &:: [b], X &= Y, Y &\= Z, Z &\= U.


X = b
Y = b
Z = a
U = b
Yes (0.00s cpu)
```

So this query actually produces a unique solution to the CSP in question.

Finally, it is important to note that the constraint propagation for the equality and disequality constraints considers each constraint separately (and iterates the inferences until no new ones can be made). For example, even though it is possible to infer that the CSP

$$\langle x \neq y, y \neq z, x \neq z \ ; \ x \in \{a, b\}, y \in \{a, b\}, z \in \{a, b\}\rangle$$

has no solution, the **sd** library cannot make this inference:

```
[eclipse 3]: [X,Y,Z] &:: [a,b],
             X &\= Y, Y &\= Z, X &\= Z.
```

```
X = X{[a, b]}
Y = Y{[a, b]}
Z = Z{[a, b]}

Delayed goals:
        X{[a, b]} &\= Y{[a, b]}
        Y{[a, b]} &\= Z{[a, b]}
        X{[a, b]} &\= Z{[a, b]}
Yes (0.00s cpu)
```

As in the case of the **suspend** library we can also generate sequences of constraints by means of ECL^{i}PS^e programs. For example, to generate the CSP

$$\langle x_1 = x_2, \ldots, x_{n-1} = x_n \; ; \; x_1 \in \{\mathtt{l,r}\}, x_2 \in \{\mathtt{l,r},\mathtt{'+'}\}, \ldots, x_n \in \{\mathtt{l,r},\mathtt{'+'}\}\rangle$$

where $n > 1$, independently of the value of n, we can use the following program:

```
equal([]).
equal([H | Ts]) :- equal(H, Ts).

equal(_, []).
equal(H, [Y | Ts]) :- H &= Y, equal(Y, Ts).
```

Then for each variable H and a list of variables **List** the query

```
H :: [l,r], List :: [l,r,'+'], equal([H | List])
```

generates an appropriate CSP on the variables in [H | List]. For example, we have

```
[eclipse 4]: H &:: [l,r], [X,Y,Z] &:: [l,r,'+'],
             equal([H | [X,Y,Z]]).

H = H{[l, r]}
X = X{[l, r]}
Y = Y{[l, r]}
Z = Z{[l, r]}

Delayed goals:
        H{[l, r]} &= X{[l, r]}
        X{[l, r]} &= Y{[l, r]}
        Y{[l, r]} &= Z{[l, r]}
```

`Yes (0.00s cpu)`

So here, like in the previous examples of this section, an inference was made that automatically led to reduced variable domains.

10.3 The ic library

We now move on to discuss the library ic (standing for interval constraints). It greatly enhances the capabilities provided by the **suspend** library. The ic library, just as the **suspend** library, supports all the core constraints, originally introduced in Section 9.4. Recall that these constraints comprise the variable declarations (viewed as unary constraints), Boolean constraints, arithmetic constraints and reified constraints.

ic also supports a more powerful syntax for variable declarations. In addition to the **suspend** library variable declarations we can also declare variables ranging over more complex domains than ranges, for instance:

```
X :: [3,4,5,6,8,9],
[Y,Z] :: [1..3,5,7..9],
```

and use an alternative syntax for ranges:

```
Z :: [3..9].
```

In the case of other core constraints, the same syntax as in the **suspend** library is used. However, in contrast to the **suspend** library, the constraint propagation is now triggered. We now illustrate the resulting effect for the Boolean constraints and arithmetic constraints.

10.3.1 Constraint propagation for Boolean constraints

To see the difference between the **suspend** and ic libraries let us return to the query

```
X or Y, X = 0
```

already discussed in Section 9.4. We noted there that the **suspend** library does not allow us to deduce that Y = 1. In contrast, once the ic library is loaded this inference is made:

```
[eclipse 5]: ic:(X or Y), X = 0.


X = 0
Y = 1
Yes (0.00s cpu)
```

Analogous inferences are automatically made for other Boolean constraints. In what follows we assume that all Boolean constraints are taken from the `ic` library, so the explicit module qualification can be dropped.

To illustrate the cumulated effect of the underlying constraint propagation consider digital circuits built out of the AND, OR and XOR gates. Each gate generates an output value given two input values. In particular, recall that XOR stands for the *exclusive or* defined by the following table:

XOR	0	1
0	0	1
1	1	0

We can view these gates as ternary (so reified) Boolean constraints. Therefore the circuits built out of these gates can be naturally represented by a sequence of such ternary constraints. In particular, consider the circuit depicted in Figure 10.1.

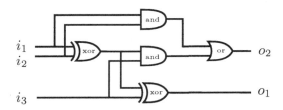

Fig. 10.1 Full adder circuit

This circuit is called **full adder** as it computes the binary sum $i_1 + i_2 + i_3$ in the binary word $o_2 o_1$. For example $1 + 1 + 0$ yields 10. To reason about this circuit we can use the following program:[1]

```
fullAdder(I1, I2, I3, O1, O2) :-
    xor3(I1, I2, X1),
    and(I1, I2, Y1),
    xor3(X1, I3, O1),
    and(I3, X1, Y2),
    or(Y1, Y2, O2).

xor3(X, Y, Z) :- neg(X, X1), neg(Y, Y1), and(X, Y1, Z1),
                 and(X1, Y, Z2), or(Z1, Z2, Z).
```

---

[1] In ECL^{i}PS^e xor/3 is a built-in with a different meaning, so we need to use another name to define XOR.

The last rule defines `xor3/3` by means of the `and/3`, `or/3` and `neg/2` constraints using the equivalence

$$X \text{ xor3 } Y \text{ iff } (X \text{ and not } Y) \text{ or } (Y \text{ and not } X).$$

We would like now to show that $i_3 = 0$ and $o_2 = 1$ implies that $i_1 = 1, i_2 = 1$ and $o_1 = 0$. To this end we simply execute the appropriate query:

```
[eclipse 6]: fullAdder(I1, I2, 0, O1, 1).

I1 = 1
I2 = 1
O1 = 0
Yes (0.00s cpu)
```

So we reached the desired conclusion using constraint propagation only. Note that no backtracking takes place here. To run this query in Prolog instead of using the constraints `xor3/3`, `and/3` and `or/3` we would have to define them as predicates, listing the facts that represent their truth tables. This would yield the same outcome at the cost of a considerable number of backtracks that would start as soon as the first atomic goal, `xor3(I1, I2, X1)`, is encountered.

Let us discuss now an alternative definition of `xor/3` using the `suspend/3` built-in defined in Section 9.5. The following code generates the appropriate constraints as soon as one argument of `xor/3` is ground:

```
xor3(X, Y, Z) :-
    [X,Y,Z]::0..1,
    ( ground(X) -> xor3g(X,Y,Z) ;
      ground(Y) -> xor3g(Y,X,Z) ;
      ground(Z) -> xor3g(Z,X,Y) ;
      true -> suspend(xor3(X,Y,Z),2, [X,Y,Z] -> inst)
    ).

xor3g(0, Y, Z) :- Y = Z.
xor3g(1, Y, Z) :- neg(Y, Z).
```

Note that the `xor3g/3` predicate is called each time with the arguments appropriately swapped. For example, if `X` and `Y` are not ground and `Z` is, the call `xor3g(Z,X,Y)` takes place. Then, if `Z=0`, the constraint `X = Y` is generated and if `Z=1`, the constraint `neg(X, Y)` is generated.

10.3.2 Constraint propagation for linear constraints

In the `ic` library a built-in constraint propagation mechanism is also available for arithmetic constraints. Recall that the `suspend` library provided the possibility to use # instead of $ when writing these constraints. Both versions are allowed in `ic`, as well. If the '#' syntax is used, all subexpressions on both sides of the constraint are also constrained to be integral. Thus we have

```
[eclipse 10]: [X,Y]::1..4, X/2 - Y/2 #= 1.
```

```
X = 4
Y = 2
Yes (0.00s cpu)
```

That is, this query has only one solution, X = 4 and Y = 2. The solution X = 3 and Y = 1 is excluded since then X/2 and Y/2 are not integers.

Below we use the '$' syntax rather than the '#' syntax so as to allow us to freely switch between integer, finite domains and real, continuous domains. If a variable without a domain is encountered in an `ic` constraint, it is automatically initialised with an infinite domain `-1.0Inf .. 1.0Inf`.

Because of the built-in constraint propagation the generated CSP can differ from the one actually written down in ECL^{i}PS^e. Since the constraint propagation maintains equivalence, the resulting CSP is always equivalent to the original one (i.e., it has the same set of solutions). As an example involving linear constraints reconsider the predicate **ordered/2** from Figure 9.3 on page 172. To generate the CSP

$$\langle x < y, y < z, z < u, u < v \,;\; x \in \{1..1000\}, y \in \{1..1000\},$$
$$z \in \{1..1000\}, u \in \{1..1000\}, v \in \{1..1000\}\rangle$$

we used there the query

```
[X,Y,Z,U,V] :: 1..1000, ordered([X,Y,Z,U,V]).
```

Now, however, a different, though equivalent, CSP is generated:

```
[eclipse 11]: [X,Y,Z,U,V] :: 1..1000, ordered([X,Y,Z,U,V]).
```

```
X = X{1 .. 996}
Y = Y{2 .. 997}
Z = Z{3 .. 998}
U = U{4 .. 999}
V = V{5 .. 1000}
```

```
Delayed goals:
        ic : (Y{2 .. 997} - X{1 .. 996} > 0)
        ic : (Z{3 .. 998} - Y{2 .. 997} > 0)
        ic : (U{4 .. 999} - Z{3 .. 998} > 0)
        ic : (V{5 .. 1000} - U{4 .. 999} > 0)
Yes (0.00s cpu)
```

The first five lines report the new domains of the considered variables.

Sometimes this built-in constraint propagation can result in solving the generated constraints, that is, in producing a solved CSP. In this case the final domains of its variables are generated. Here is an example:

```
[eclipse 12]: X :: [5..10], Y :: [3..7], X $< Y, X $\= 6.
```

```
X = 5
Y = Y{[6, 7]}
Yes (0.00s cpu)
```

Here X = 5 is a shorthand for X = X{[5]}, i.e., it stands for the 'degenerated' variable declaration X :: [5..5]. So the answer corresponds to the CSP $\langle \, ; \, x \in \{5\}, y \in \{6,7\}\rangle$ with no constraints. If in the solved CSP all the variable domains are singletons, a customary Prolog answer is produced. For instance, we have

```
[eclipse 13]: X :: [5..10], Y :: [3..6], X $< Y.
```

```
X = 5
Y = 6
Yes (0.00s cpu)
```

Note that the corresponding ECL^{i}PS^e query

```
X :: [5..10], Y :: [3..6], X < Y
```

yields a run-time error:

```
[eclipse 14]: X :: [5..10], Y :: [3..6], X < Y.
instantiation fault in X{5 .. 10} < Y{3 .. 6}
Abort
```

So the use of the constraint $</2 instead of the arithmetic comparison predicate </2 is essential here. Further, in some circumstances the constraint propagation can detect that the generated CSP is inconsistent, like in this example:

```
[eclipse 15]: [X,Y,Z] :: [1..1000], X $> Y, Y $> Z, Z $> X.
```

```
No (0.01s cpu)
```

Also here the replacement of $> by > leads to a run-time error.

So using the constraints and constraint propagation only we can solve more queries than using Prolog and also more queries than using the **suspend** library.

Finally, let us return to the problem of generating a constraint of the form

$$\Sigma_{i=1}^n a_i \cdot x_i \le v,$$

where $n \ge 1$, all a_is are given parameters and all x_is and v are variables ranging over an integer interval. We explained in Section 9.6 how to generate it using the **suspend** library. Using the **ic** library and the **foreach/2** iterator this can be also done by means of the following non-recursive program:

```
sigma(As, Xs, V) :-
    ( foreach(A,As),
      foreach(X,Xs),
      foreach(Expr,Exprs)
    do
      Expr = A*X
    ),
    sum(Exprs) $=< V.
```

We use here the built-in **sum/1**. In the context of the **ic** library the call **sum(List)** returns the sum of the members of the list **List**.

Now, during the execution of the query

```
[X,Y,Z,U] :: 1..1000, sigma([1,2,3,4], [X,Y,Z,U], V)
```

the local variable **Exprs** becomes instantiated to the list [1*X, 2*Y, 3*Z, 4*U] that is subsequently passed to the constraint **sum(Exprs) $=< V**. Additionally, some constraint propagation is automatically carried out and we get the following outcome:

```
[eclipse 16]: [X,Y,Z,U] :: 1..1000,
              sigma([1,2,3,4], [X,Y,Z,U], V).
```

```
X = X{1..1000}
Y = Y{1..1000}
Z = Z{1..1000}
U = U{1..1000}
```

```
V = V{10.0..1.0Inf}
```

```
Delayed goals:
        ic : (4*U{1..1000} + 3*Z{1..1000} + 2*Y{1..1000} +
              X{1..1000} - V{10.0..1.0Inf} =< 0)
```

So the original, implicit, domain of V, -1.0Inf..1.0Inf, got reduced to 10.0..1.0Inf. Recall that when the **suspend** library was used no domain reduction was achieved.

10.3.3 *SEND + MORE = MONEY* puzzle revisited

A dramatic effect of the constraint propagation for linear constraints in combination with the disequality constraints can be demonstrated using the *SEND + MORE = MONEY* puzzle introduced in Subsection 6.4.2 and encoded in ECL^{i}PS^e in Figure 9.6 on page 178. Thanks to the constraint propagation process all the variable domains become reduced before the search process is launched. Indeed, given the variable declarations and constraints as in Figure 10.2 (the diff_list/1 predicate is defined in Figure 9.4 on page 173) we get the following interaction with ECL^{i}PS^e:

```
[eclipse 17]: send(List).
```

```
List = [9, E{4..7}, N{5..8}, D{2..8}, 1, 0, R{2..8}, Y{2..8}]
```

```
There are 11 delayed goals.
```

```
send(List):-
    List = [S,E,N,D,M,O,R,Y],
    List :: 0..9,
    diff_list(List),
                1000*S + 100*E + 10*N + D
              + 1000*M + 100*O + 10*R + E
    $= 10000*M + 1000*O + 100*N + 10*E + Y,
    S $\= 0,
    M $\= 0.
```

Fig. 10.2 Domains and constraints for the SEND_MORE_MONEY puzzle

In fact, now, because of the constraint propagation the solution is found almost instantaneously. Indeed for the SEND_MORE_MONEY program from Figure 9.6 on page 178 (the one in which the definition of **send/1** ends with the call to **search/1**) we get:

```
[eclipse 18]: send(L).

L = [9, 5, 6, 7, 1, 0, 8, 2]
Yes (0.00s cpu, solution 1, maybe more) ? ;

No (0.00s cpu)
```

Recall that with the **suspend** library loaded instead of **ic** we got the final answer after more than three minutes of CPU time.

It is important to realise that this significant domain reduction is achieved thanks to the integrality constraints on the variables used. If we drop them by changing the declaration

```
List :: 0..9
```

to

```
List :: 0.0..9.0,
```

very little can be inferred since there are many non-integer solutions to the problem. Indeed, the only domain that gets reduced then is that of M which becomes 0.0..1.102.

Finally, let us mention that the **diff_list/1** predicate is available in the **ic** library as the **alldifferent/1** built-in.

10.3.4 The n-queens problem revisited

Let us return now to the QUEENS program presented in Figure 9.7 on page 179. We noted there that it took more than 341 seconds of CPU time to generate the first solution to the 8-queens problem. Now, thanks to the constraint propagation the first solution is generated almost instantaneously:

```
[eclipse 19]: queens(QueenStruct, 8).

QueenStruct = [](1, 5, 8, 6, 3, 7, 2, 4)
Yes (0.01s cpu, solution 1, maybe more) ?
```

Here, in contrast to the program that solves the $SEND + MORE = MONEY$ puzzle, the constraint propagation has no effect before the search process is launched. In fact, in the QUEENS program the constraint propagation is activated only when a variable gets instantiated. This happens for the first time during the search process. Each time a subscripted variable QueenStruct[I] gets instantiated to a value some, possibly different, values are removed from the domains of other subscripted variables by virtue of the constraint propagation that is activated by the disequality constraints in which QueenStruct[I] occurs.

10.3.5 Constraint propagation for non-linear constraints

The constraint propagation is also activated by non-linear arithmetic constraints, as the following three examples show.

```
[eclipse 20]:   [X,Y] :: [1.0..1000.0], X*X + Y*Y $= 1000.


X = X{1.0 .. 31.606961258558218}
Y = Y{1.0 .. 31.606961258558218}


Delayed goals:
        ic : (Y{1.0 .. 31.606961258558218} =:=
              rsqr(_740{1.0 .. 999.0}))
        ic : (X{1.0 .. 31.606961258558218} =:=
              rsqr(_837{1.0 .. 999.0}))
        ic : (_740{1.0 .. 999.0} + _837{1.0 .. 999.0} =:=
              1000)
Yes (0.00s cpu)
```

The delayed goals show how each constraint was internally rewritten by means of the auxiliary variables.

Integrality and non-linearity can be combined freely. Adding integrality to the previous example tightens the bounds – not just to the next integer – but, in this case, even further because additional constraint propagation can take place:

```
[eclipse 21]:   [X,Y] :: [1..1000], X*X + Y*Y $= 1000.
X = X{10 .. 30}
Y = Y{10 .. 30}


Delayed goals:
    ic : (Y{10 .. 30} =:= rsqr(_657{100.0 .. 900.0}))
    ic : (X{10 .. 30} =:= rsqr(_754{100.0 .. 900.0}))
```

```
        ic : (_657{100.0 .. 900.0} + _754{100.0 .. 900.0} =:= 1000)
Yes (0.00s cpu)
```

In some examples constraint propagation alone is sufficient to solve non-linear constraints:

```
[eclipse 22]: X :: [1..20], Y :: [9..11], Z :: [155..161],
              X*Y $= Z.
```

```
X = 16
Y = 10
Z = 160
Yes (0.00s cpu)
```

In general, however, constraint propagation can only narrow the domain bounds without determining a solution. For example, consider the following integer constraint:

```
[eclipse 23]: X :: 1..1000, X*(X+1)*(X+2) $=< 1000.
```

```
X = X{1 .. 22}
```

```
There are 6 delayed goals.
```

Additional constraint propagation can be achieved by trying values near the boundary of a variable's domain, and narrowing the bounds if no solution is found. The `ic` built-in to perform this kind of constraint propagation is `squash/3`.

```
[eclipse 24]: X :: 1..1000, X*(X+1)*(X+2) $=< 1000,
              squash([X],0.1,lin).
```

```
X = X{1 .. 9}
```

```
There are 6 delayed goals.
Yes (0.00s cpu)
```

The second parameter of **squash/3** specifies how near the bounds to test for infeasibility, and the third argument specifies whether to divide up the domain linearly (**lin**), or logarithmically (**log**), which can work better for large domains. We shall discuss this predicate in more detail in Section 13.5.

10.3.6 Direct variable domain modification

Finally, let us discuss the effect of a direct modification of a variable domain. We say that an unsolved arithmetic constraint is **attached** to a variable, say V, if V occurs in this constraint. Normally if the domain of V is reduced, all the constraints attached to V are woken and may cause further domain reductions through constraint propagation.

In ECL^{i}PS^e one can reduce the domain of a variable using the exclude/2 built-in. For a variable X the query exclude(X,El) removes the element El from the domain of X. If the resulting domain is empty, a failure arises. However, if the domain is reduced by the call exclude(X,El), the constraints attached to X are not automatically woken. This enables the programmer to control the program execution more precisely. To wake the constraints attached to X the programmer needs to call explicitly the built-in wake/0.

To see this consider the following two queries (till the end of this subsection we simplify displayed information about the delayed goals):

```
[eclipse 25]: X :: 4..10, Y :: 3..7, X $< Y.

X = X{4 .. 6}
Y = Y{5 .. 7}

There is 1 delayed goal.
Yes (0.00s cpu)
[eclipse 26]: X :: 4..10, Y :: 3..7, X $< Y, X $\= 4.

X = X{[5, 6]}
Y = Y{[6, 7]}

There is 1 delayed goal.
Yes (0.00s cpu)
```

So the constraint X $\= 4, through constraint propagation, led to a reduction of the domain of Y from 5..7 to 6..7.

Now suppose that instead of using the constraint X $\= 4 we explicitly remove 4 from the domain of X using the call exclude(X,4):[2]

```
[eclipse 27]: X :: 4..10, Y :: 3..7,
              X $< Y, ic_kernel:exclude(X,4).
```

---

[2] The exclude/2 command is 'hidden' in the ECL^{i}PS^e module ic_kernel because its behaviour is non-standard. This explains the use of the 'ic_kernel:' prefix.

```
X = X{[5, 6]}
Y = Y{5 .. 7}
```

```
There is 1 delayed goal.
Yes (0.00s cpu)
```

So, since no `wake/0` has been invoked, the final round of the constraint propagation is not performed and the domain of Y remains here 5..7. The constraint propagation takes place only after calling `wake/0`:

```
[eclipse 28]: X :: 4..10, Y :: 3..7,
              X $< Y, ic_kernel:exclude(X,4), wake.
```

```
X = X{[5, 6]}
Y = Y{[6, 7]}
```

```
There is 1 delayed goal.
Yes (0.00s cpu)
```

In summary, the constraint propagation is triggered as soon as the CSP represented by the set of unsolved constraints, i.e., delayed goals, is modified. This modification can result from an addition of a constraint or from a removal of an element from the domain of a variable. The set of delayed constraints is usually called the **constraint store**. It is helpful to view the corresponding variable declarations as part of the constraint store, that is to view the constraint store as a CSP.

The constraint store dynamically changes during the computation. If, due to constraint propagation, a delayed constraint becomes solved, it is removed from the constraint store. If, due to the constraint propagation, the constraint store becomes failed, a failure arises (which can trigger backtracking). In the presence of constraints a computation is successful if it yields an answer (i.e., does not fail) and the constraint store is empty. These remarks about the constraint store apply to arbitrary type of constraints used in ECL^{i}PS^e.[3]

10.4 Disjunctive constraints and reification

So far, the ECL^{i}PS^e programs that generated constraints were deterministic, in the sense that part of the program used for generating constraints left no choice points. This is good constraint programming practice.

---

[3] In practice, for efficiency reasons, ECL^{i}PS^e does not always detect immediately whether a constraint is solved.

In this section we shall discuss how to set up *disjunctive constraints*. The easiest way is to use multiple clauses to define the constraint. Consider for example the dist(X, Y, Z) constraint that states that |X-Y| $= Z. It can be naturally defined by the following two clauses:

```
% dist(X, Y, Z) :- |X-Y| $= Z.

dist(X, Y, Z) :- X-Y $= Z.
dist(X, Y, Z) :- Y-X $= Z.
```

But this is not good constraint programming practice as it introduces a choice point during the constraint setup. We now have

```
[eclipse 29]: X :: [1..4], Y :: [3..6], dist(X, Y, 1).

X = 4
Y = 3
Yes (0.00s cpu, solution 1, maybe more) ? ;

X = X{2 .. 4}
Y = Y{3 .. 5}

Delayed goals:
        ic : (X{2 .. 4} - Y{3 .. 5} =:= -1)
Yes (0.00s cpu, solution 2)
```

This shows that first a solution to the alternative X-Y $= 1, is generated and subsequently, upon hitting ";" (that occurs in the

```
Yes (0.00s cpu, solution 1, maybe more) ? ;
```

line), a solution to the second alternative, X-Y $= -1, is generated.

The reason it is not good practice is because choice points belong to the search routine, after all the constraints have been set up. A key advantage of constraint programming is that each choice is made *after* the constraint propagation takes place. Making choices before all the constraints have been set up reduces the amount of constraint propagation that can occur and therefore reduces the chances of making the right choice. More importantly, it does not allow dynamic reordering of choices at execution time, which we shall see later is crucial to the design of an efficient search routine.

For the above example it is possible to set up this same disjunctive constraint deterministically using the built-in mathematical operator abs/1:

```
% dist(X, Y, Z) :- |X-Y| $= Z.

dist(X, Y, Z) :- abs(X-Y) $= Z.
```

This implementation of dist/3 leads to domain reductions through constraint propagation before any choices are made:

```
[eclipse 30]: X :: [1..4], Y :: [3..6], abs(X-Y) $= 1.

X = X{2 .. 4}
Y = Y{3 .. 5}

Delayed goals:
        ic : (_706{-1 .. 1} - X{2 .. 4} + Y{3 .. 5} =:= 0)
        ic : (1 =:= abs(_706{-1 .. 1}))
        ic : (_706{-1 .. 1} =:= +- 1)
Yes (0.00s cpu)
```

To get all solutions, it is necessary at search time to split a domain, for example by choosing either X $> 3 or X $=< 3.

A more general way to handle disjunctive constraints is by using reification, originally introduced in Subsection 9.4.4. Recall that for each of the arithmetic constraints $=, $>, $=< etc. there is a ternary, reified, version with an extra argument. This argument indicates whether the constraint holds or not. Setting this extra argument to 1 enforces the constraint, while setting it to 0 enforces its negation. Now, our example constraint dist(X, Y, Z) can be imposed without introducing any choice points by exploiting these additional variables. Indeed, if B1 is the extra argument indicating the truth or falsity of one constraint, and B2 is the extra argument for the second constraint, then adding the constraint B1+B2 $= 1 enforces their disjunction:

```
dist(X, Y, Z) :-
    $=(X-Y, Z, B1),
    $=(Y-X, Z, B2),
    B1+B2 $= 1.
```

To save introducing these extra arguments we can use the Boolean constraint or/2. Thus we can simply write:

```
dist(X, Y, Z) :- X-Y $= Z or Y-X $= Z.
```

To properly understand this definition recall that or/2 can be written in the infix form and that on the account of the ambivalent syntax the arguments of or/2 can be queries. The interaction with ECL^{i}PS^e reveals that this version is actually implemented by translating it into the previous one using reified constraints:

```
[eclipse 31]: X :: [1..4], Y :: [3..6], X-Y $= 1 or Y-X $= 1.

X = X{1 .. 4}
Y = Y{3 .. 6}

Delayed goals:
        =:=(-(Y{3 .. 6}) + X{1 .. 4}, 1, _914{[0, 1]})
        =:=(Y{3 .. 6} - X{1 .. 4}, 1, _1003{[0, 1]})
        -(_1003{[0, 1]}) - _914{[0, 1]} #=< -1
Yes (0.00s cpu)
```

We stress that or/2 is different from the Prolog disjunction ;/2. In fact, the latter creates a choice point and if we used it here instead of or/2, we would have reintroduced the initial dist/3 constraint.

Just as or/2 above, other Boolean constraints, i.e. neg/1, and/2, and =>/2, can be used to form logical combinations of arbitrary constraints without introducing any choice points.

The additional Boolean variables used in a reified constraint can be used after all the constraints have been set up, during search, to make the choices that were postponed during constraint setup.

Finally, let us mention that reified constraints cannot be further reified. For example, the following query yields a run-time error:

```
[eclipse 32]: and(X, Y, 0) or neg(X, Y).
calling an undefined procedure and(X, Y, 0, _394)
in module eclipse
Abort
```

because of a failed attempt to reify the arguments of or/2.

10.5 Summary

In this chapter we discussed various facilities present in the libraries sd and ic.

In the case of the sd library we explained how variables ranging over finite symbolic domains can be introduced and how constraints on these variables can be generated. In the case of the ic library we explained Boolean constraints and arithmetic constraints on integers and reals. Finally, we discussed reification as a means to handle disjunctive constraints.

From the point of view of programming two features were of crucial importance: the built-in facilities allowing us to generate CSPs, and the built-in constraint propagation for the considered classes of constraints.

In the process we also introduced the following built-ins of ECL^{i}PS^e relevant for constraint programming:

- alldifferent/1,
- sum/1,
- abs/1,
- squash/3,
- exclude/2,
- wake/0.

10.6 Exercises

Exercise 10.1 Suppose that the library ic is loaded. What is the ECL^{i}PS^e output to the following queries? (Note that these are the queries from Exercise 3.1 with is replaced by #=.)

1. X #= 7, X #= 6.

2. X #= 7, X #= X+1.

3. X #= X+1, X #= 7.

4. X #= 3, Y #= X+1.

5. Y #= X+1, X #= 3.

Exercise 10.2 Write a program that formalizes representation No. 4 of the *SEND + MORE = MONEY* puzzle from Subsection 6.4.2 using the ic library.

Exercise 10.3 Write a program that formalizes the first representation of the *n*-queens problem from Subsection 6.4.3 using the ic library.

11

Top-down search with active constraints

11.1 Introduction

THE PROBLEM OF solving finite CSPs is central to this book. Initially, in Chapter 8, we explained how to solve them in Prolog. In Chapter 10 we noted that it is considerably more efficient to rely on the constraint propagation automatically provided in the ic library. However, in the presence of constraint propagation the domains of the variables shrink and it is important to organise the top-down search in such a manner that during the search only the reduced domains and not the original domains are considered. Additionally, as already mentioned in Chapter 6, the top-down search can be complete or incomplete and can be set up in several ways by specifying the variable ordering and the ordering of the domain values. The ic library provides a support for these aspects of top-down search. The purpose of this chapter is to explain these facilities and illustrate them by discussing various forms of top-down search.

Throughout the chapter we assume that the ic library is loaded. We illustrate the impact of various heuristics by discussing corresponding solutions to the n-queens problem and considering in each case the number

205

of backtracks. To this end we use the 'clever' way of counting discussed in Section 8.6.

11.2 Backtrack-free search

We begin our exposition by programming in ECL^{i}PS^e the **backtrack-free search**. It attempts to construct a solution to a finite CSP as follows.

We assume some fixed variable ordering. We start with the empty assignment (of values to decision variables). Then successively we try to extend the current *partial assignment* defined on some variables to the next variable in the assumed ordering. This is done by assigning to each variable the minimum (or maximum) value in its *current* domain. If by proceeding this way the final variable gets instantiated, a solution is found. Otherwise a failure is reported.

This search procedure relies crucially on the constraint propagation in that each time the current and *not* the original variable domain is used. This makes it a meaningful search procedure, as opposed to the corresponding backtrack-free search in Prolog. However, this search procedure is clearly incomplete in that it may not find a solution if one exists. Indeed, it can take a 'wrong' turn already at the beginning, by instantiating the first variable to a value that does not participate in a solution.

This procedure can be implemented using the get_min/2 built-in. Given a variable X, the query get_min(X, Min) returns in Min the minimum value in the *current* domain of X. So the query get_min(X, X) instantiates X to the minimum value in its current domain. The dual built-in get_max/2 returns the maximum value in the current variable domain.

To illustrate the use of the backtrack-free search let us return to the definition of the variable domains and constraints for the *n*-queens problem given in the program from Figure 9.7 on page 179. By combining it with an appropriate use of the get_min/2 built-in we obtain a program that realises for the *n*-queens problem the backtrack-free search in the presence of the constraint propagation for arithmetic constraints. It is given in Figure 11.1.

Interestingly, this program generates a solution for only two values of N < 500, namely 5 and 7. For N equal to 7 we get the following solution:

```
[eclipse 1]: queens(QueenStruct, 7).

QueenStruct = [](1, 3, 5, 7, 2, 4, 6)
Yes (0.00s cpu, solution 1, maybe more) ?
```

In fact, for N equal to 7, after placing the first three queens the constraint

```
queens(QueenStruct, Number) :-
    dim(QueenStruct,[Number]),
    constraints(QueenStruct, Number),
    backtrack_free(QueenStruct).

constraints(QueenStruct, Number) :-
    ( for(I,1,Number),
      param(QueenStruct,Number)
    do
      QueenStruct[I] :: 1..Number,
      (for(J,1,I-1),
       param(I,QueenStruct)
      do
        QueenStruct[I] $\= QueenStruct[J],
        QueenStruct[I]-QueenStruct[J] $\= I-J,
        QueenStruct[I]-QueenStruct[J] $\= J-I
      )
    ).

backtrack_free(QueenStruct):-
    ( foreacharg(Col,QueenStruct) do get_min(Col,Col) ).
```

Fig. 11.1 A backtrack-free solution to the n-queens problem

propagation already determines the unique positions for the remaining four queens. This can be seen by omitting the final call to the `backtrack_free/1` and by executing the following query:

```
[eclipse 2]: queens([](1,3,5,X4,X5,X6,X7), 7).

X4 = 7
X5 = 2
X6 = 4
X7 = 6
Yes (0.00s cpu)
```

In case the decision variables are organised in a list, the backtrack-free search procedure is defined as follows:

```
backtrack_free(List) :-
    ( foreach(Var,List) do get_min(Var,Var) ).
```

The following query illustrates the effect of this search procedure:

```
[eclipse 3]: List = [X,Y,Z], List :: 1..3,
            alldifferent(List), backtrack_free(List).
```

```
List = [1, 2, 3]
X = 1
Y = 2
Z = 3
Yes (0.00s cpu)
```

11.3 Shallow backtracking search

By a *shallow backtracking search* we mean a search that differs from
the backtrack-free search in that only a limited form of backtracking is
allowed, inside the value selection process. More precisely, in the shallow
backtracking search, when we try to assign a value to the current variable,
the constraint propagation process is automatically triggered. If it yields a
failure, the next value is tried. This process continues until the first value
is found for which the constraint propagation does not yield a failure. Once
such a value is found its choice is final and we proceed to the next variable.
As before, if by proceeding this way the final variable gets instantiated, a
solution is found. Otherwise a failure is reported.

Again, this search procedure is incomplete so a failure does not necessarily
mean that no solution exists. To encode this search we need built-ins that
allow us to access the *current* variable domain.

One of such built-ins is `get_domain_as_list/2` that takes as the first
argument a finite domain variable X and generates in the second argument
the ordered list of the values of the *current* domain of X. For example:

```
[eclipse 4]: X :: [1..4], get_domain_as_list(X, Domain),
            X #\= 2, get_domain_as_list(X, NewDomain).
```

```
X = X{[1, 3, 4]}
Domain = [1, 2, 3, 4]
NewDomain = [1, 3, 4]
Yes (0.00s cpu)
```

Once the list `Domain` is produced, we can enumerate all its members by means of the `member/2` predicate, as in the following query:

```
[eclipse 5]: X :: [1..4], X #\= 2,
             get_domain_as_list(X, Domain), member(X, Domain).


X = 1
Domain = [1, 3, 4]
Yes (0.00s cpu, solution 1, maybe more) ? ;


X = 3
Domain = [1, 3, 4]
Yes (0.00s cpu, solution 2, maybe more) ? ;


X = 4
Domain = [1, 3, 4]
Yes (0.00s cpu, solution 3)
```

This combination of `get_domain_as_list/2` and `member/2` is so often used that ECL^{i}PS^e provides a built-in `indomain/1`, defined logically as

```
indomain(X) :-
    get_domain_as_list(X, Domain),
    member(X, Domain).
```

but implemented more efficiently, without constructing the `Domain` list.

We can now define the shallow backtracking search for a list of variables by means of the following procedure:

```
shallow_backtrack(List) :-
    ( foreach(Var,List) do once(indomain(Var)) ).
```

Recall from Section 4.2 that `once(Q)` generates only the first solution to the query `Q`.

The following two queries illustrate the difference between the backtrack-free search and shallow backtracking:

```
[eclipse 6]: List = [X,Y,Z], X :: 1..3, [Y,Z] :: 1..2,
             alldifferent(List), backtrack_free(List).


No (0.00s cpu)
[eclipse 7]: List = [X,Y,Z], X :: 1..3, [Y,Z] :: 1..2,
             alldifferent(List), shallow_backtrack(List).
```

```
List = [3, 1, 2]
X = 3
Y = 1
Z = 2
Yes (0.00s cpu)
```

As an example of the use of shallow backtracking, let us return to the
SEND + MORE = MONEY puzzle and reconsider the send/1 procedure
from Figure 10.2 on page 195, the one in which only the variable domains
and constraints were defined. Then the unique solution to this puzzle can be
generated by adding to it the shallow backtracking search, that is by means
of the program in Figure 11.2.

```
send(List):-
    List = [S,E,N,D,M,O,R,Y],
    List :: 0..9,
    diff_list(List),
                1000*S + 100*E + 10*N + D
            + 1000*M + 100*O + 10*R + E
    $= 10000*M + 1000*O + 100*N + 10*E + Y,
    S $\= 0,
    M $\= 0,
    shallow_backtrack(List).

shallow_backtrack(List) :-
    ( foreach(Var,List) do once(indomain(Var)) ).
```
augmented by the diff_list/2 procedure of Figure 9.4.

Fig. 11.2 The SEND_MORE_MONEY program with shallow backtracking

Indeed, we have then:

```
[eclipse 8]: send(L).

L = [9, 5, 6, 7, 1, 0, 8, 2]
Yes (0.00s cpu)
```

11.4 Backtracking search

We considered already the backtracking search for CSPs on finite domains in the example programs discussed in Section 9.7. In these programs the backtracking search was realised by a systematic enumeration of the *original* variable domains. This ensured completeness of this search procedure.

However, in the presence of the `ic` library this approach does not take into account the fact that the domains of the variables shrink during the constraint propagation phase. As a result, during the so defined search procedure values are generated that lie outside the current variable domains, which is completely unneeded. A more appropriate approach consists of enumerating the *current* variable domains. This brings us to a revision of the generic search procedure introduced in Figure 8.6 on page 138.

Recall that this procedure required the *initial* domain to be explicitly associated with each variable and the `choose_val/2` predicate used the variable domain as an input argument. With the `ic` library loaded we can access instead the *current* variable domain using the `get_domain_as_list/2` built-in. However, for the purpose of the backtracking process it is more efficient to use instead the `indomain/1` built-in which both retrieves a value from the current domain and instantiates the variable to that value.

As a result, we can simplify the generic search procedure from Figure 8.6 to the one shown in Figure 11.3. In the presence of finite domains this procedure emerged as a standard in constraint programming.

```
% search(List) :- Assign values from their domains
%                 to all the variables in List.

search_with_dom(List) :-
        ( fromto(List, Vars, Rest, [])
        do
          choose_var(Vars, Var, Rest),
          indomain(Var).
        ).

choose_var(List, Var, Rest) :- List = [Var | Rest].
```

Fig. 11.3 Generic search using associated variable domains

Because this generic search procedure is so common, it is available as a built-in predicate in the `ic` library that for historical standardisation reasons is named `labeling/1`. (`indomain/1` and `labeling/1` built-ins are also available in the **sd** library.) As in the `choose_var/2` procedure the variable ordering of the original input list is adopted, the definition of `labeling/1` can be simplified to

```
labeling(List):- ( foreach(Var,List) do indomain(Var) ).
```

The following query illustrates this form of search:

```
[eclipse 9]: List = [W,X,Y,Z], W::1..4, [X,Y,Z] :: 1..3,
             alldifferent(List), labeling(List).

List = [4, 1, 2, 3]
W = 4
X = 1
Y = 2
Z = 3
Yes (0.00s cpu, solution 1, maybe more) ? ;
```

In total 6 solutions are produced. In contrast, `backtrack-free/1` and `shallow_backtrack/1` procedures both fail here.

Conceptually, for a list of variables `List`, the query `labeling(List)` realises a backtracking search for the generated CSP on the variables in `List` that takes into account the underlying constraint propagation process. To illustrate the gain achieved by the presence of constraint propagation consider the following query:

```
[eclipse 10]: List = [X,Y,Z], List :: 1..100,
              X $> Y, Y*Y $>= Z, Y + Z $>= 2*X + 50.

List = [X{5 .. 49}, Y{4 .. 48}, Z{12 .. 100}]
X = X{5 .. 49}
Y = Y{4 .. 48}
Z = Z{12 .. 100}

There are 4 delayed goals.

Yes (0.00s cpu)
```

So the constraint propagation led to a substantial domain reduction but was not sufficient to find a solution and we need to perform a search. This can be done by just invoking `labeling/1`:

```
[eclipse 11]: List = [X,Y,Z], List :: 1..100,
             X $> Y, Y*Y $>= Z, Y + Z $>= 2*X + 50,
             labeling(List).
```

```
List = [9, 8, 60]
X = 9
Y = 8
Z = 60
Yes (0.00s cpu, solution 1, maybe more) ?
```

Several more solutions are returned upon backtracking.

During the execution of this query the call `labeling(List)` unfolds into

`indomain(X), indomain(Y), indomain(Z),`

so the backtracking involves the enumeration of the elements of the *current* domain of X, which is [5..49]. Additionally, each time the calls `indomain(Y)` and `indomain(Z)` are reached, the current domains of Y and Z are reduced to respective subsets of [4..48] and [12..100] because of the triggered constraint propagation process. If we used here instead the backtracking search as in Section 9.7, the search would involve the original, larger, domains of X, Y and Z which are all [1..100].

As another illustration of the difference between the backtracking search here considered and the one used in Chapter 9 let us return again to the definition of the domains and constraints for the *n*-queens problem used in the program from Figure 9.7 on page 179. By combining it with an appropriate use of `indomain/1` we obtain a program that takes full advantage of the constraint propagation during the search process. The program is given in Figure 11.4.

With the `ic` library loaded this program is considerably faster than the one given in Figure 9.7 on page 179 in which the search involved the enumeration of the original domains. For example, it finds the first solution to the 20-queens problem 21 times faster.

In general it is important to realise which variables should be passed as arguments to the `labeling` procedure. To see this recall from Subsection 10.3.2 the `sigma/3` predicate that was defined by

```
sigma(As, Xs, V) :-
   ( foreach(A,As),
     foreach(X,Xs),
     foreach(Expr,Exprs)
   do
```

```
queens(QueenStruct, Number) :-
    dim(QueenStruct,[Number]),
    constraints(QueenStruct, Number),
    backtrack_search(QueenStruct).

constraints(QueenStruct, Number) :-
    ( for(I,1,Number),
      param(QueenStruct,Number)
    do
      QueenStruct[I] :: 1..Number,
      (for(J,1,I-1),
       param(I,QueenStruct)
      do
        QueenStruct[I] $\= QueenStruct[J],
        QueenStruct[I]-QueenStruct[J] $\= I-J,
        QueenStruct[I]-QueenStruct[J] $\= J-I
      )
    ).

backtrack_search(QueenStruct):-
    ( foreacharg(Col,QueenStruct) do indomain(Col) ).
```

Fig. 11.4 A backtracking solution to the n-queens problem

```
    Expr = A*X
  ),
  sum(Exprs) $=< V.
```

and that generated the constraint

$$\Sigma_{i=1}^{n} a_i \cdot x_i \leq v.$$

Here $n \geq 1$, all a_is are given parameters and all x_is and v are variables ranging over an integer interval.

The appropriate labelling involves here only the variables in the list Xs and V. Indeed, first of all we wish to call **sigma/3** with the first argument instantiated, so the variables in As do not need to be enumerated. Second, the local variables A,X,Expr and Exprs are only used to construct the relevant constraint and should not be enumerated. Finally, if we always call **sigma/3** with the last argument V instantiated, its enumeration is not needed either.

11.5 Variable ordering heuristics

In the implementations of search provided so far, i.e. in `backtrack_free/1`, `shallow_backtrack/1` and the `labeling/1` procedures, the ordering of the variables as in the input variable list is adopted and in each domain the values are enumerated proceeding from the smallest one to the largest one. To solve a computationally intensive problem it is often useful to use different heuristics that allow us to alter these orderings. They naturally fall into two categories: the variable ordering heuristics and the value ordering heuristics.

To illustrate the possible choices for the first category we construct a generic n-queens program with a parameter `Heur` that we will use to distinguish between alternative heuristics. We use the definition of the domains and constraints for the n-queens problem as in the program from Figure 11.4 but add a call to the `struct_to_list/2` predicate that converts a structure (here an array) to a list by simply stepping through the arguments and copying them into a list. The generic `search/2` procedure has now the extra parameter `Heur`. The program is given in Figure 11.5. To complete it we now systematically add to it the clauses defining the `search/2` procedure.

naive heuristic

This heuristic simply reproduces the behaviour of the built-in `labeling/1`. So it labels the variables in the order they appear in the list and tries values starting with the smallest element in the current domain and trying the rest in increasing order.

Let us call this heuristic **naive** and define the first clause of `search/2` accordingly:

```
search(naive, List) :- labeling(List).
```

The **naive** heuristic reproduces the behaviour of the program from Figure 11.4 on page 214 and finds a solution to the 8-queens problem after only 10 backtracks, and can solve the 16-queens problems with 542 backtracks, but the number of backtracks grows very quickly with an increasing number of queens. With a limit of 50 seconds, even the 32-queens problem times out.

middle_out heuristic

For the n-queens problem it makes sense to start labelling queens near the centre of the board earlier. Indeed, a queen placed near the centre of the board tends to constrain the others more than a queen near the edge and

```
% queens(Heur, Queens, Number) :-
%              Solve the Number-queens problem using
%              heuristic Heur, generating answer Queens.

queens(Heur, Queens, Number) :-
    dim(QueenStruct,[Number]),
    constraints(QueenStruct, Number),
    struct_to_list(QueenStruct, Queens),
    search(Heur, Queens).

constraints(QueenStruct, Number) :-
    ( for(I,1,Number),
      param(QueenStruct,Number)
    do
      QueenStruct[I] :: 1..Number,
      (for(J,1,I-1),
       param(I,QueenStruct)
      do
        QueenStruct[I] $\= QueenStruct[J],
        QueenStruct[I]-QueenStruct[J] $\= I-J,
        QueenStruct[I]-QueenStruct[J] $\= J-I
      )
    ).

struct_to_list(Struct, List) :-
    ( foreacharg(Arg,Struct),
      foreach(Var,List)
    do
      Var = Arg
    ).
```

Fig. 11.5 Generic *n*-queens search program

hence yields a stronger constraint propagation. This can be achieved by re-ordering the list of queens so as to start with the middle queen and hop back and forth to the next queen before and the next queen after. The reordering is encoded using three predefined predicates, defined in an ECL^{i}PS^e library called lists:

```
:- lib(lists).

middle_out(List, MOutList) :-
    halve(List, FirstHalf, LastHalf),
    reverse(FirstHalf, RevFirstHalf),
    splice(LastHalf, RevFirstHalf, MOutList).
```

The call `halve(List, Front, Back)` splits its first argument in the middle while the call `splice(Odds, Evens, List)` merges the first two lists by interleaving their elements.

The `middle_out` heuristic simply reorders the list of queens and labels them as before:

```
search(middle_out, List) :-
    middle_out(List, MOutList),
    labeling(MOutList).
```

Interestingly, the query `queens(middle_out, Queens, 8)` succeeds without any backtracking, and a first solution to the 16-queens problem now needs only 17 backtracks. However, for 32 queens the search still times out after 50 seconds.

first_fail heuristic

`first_fail` is a widely applicable heuristic that selects as the next variable to label the one with the fewest values remaining in its domain. This is a dynamic heuristic, as the sizes of the domains of the unlabelled variables are reduced during search. Indeed, for the n-queens problem all the variables initially have domains of the same size, so any improvement in efficiency brought by the `first_fail` heuristic depends upon changes in the domain sizes which have occurred earlier during the search.

This heuristic is supported by the **delete/5** built-in of the library **ic**. The call

```
delete(Var, Vars, Rest, Arg, Heur)
```

removes a variable `Var` from a list of variables `Vars`, leaving the remaining list `Rest`. The parameter `Arg` enables this predicate to handle not only lists of variables, but more generally lists of compound terms in which the variable occurs as an argument. The final parameter `Heur` is the criterion used to select the variable to remove. For our current heuristic this parameter is input as `first_fail`.

This heuristic is encoded as the following clause for **search/2**:

```
search(first_fail, List) :-
   ( fromto(List, Vars, Rest, [])
   do
      delete(Var, Vars, Rest, 0, first_fail),
      indomain(Var)
   ).
```

On the small problem instances of the n-queens problem – such as 8-queens – the impact of **first_fail** is unspectacular. Indeed, the search requires 10 backtracks to find the first solution to 8-queens, which is no better than the naive heuristic. However, on larger instances its impact is dramatic. Indeed, this heuristic enables a first solution to the 32-queens problem to be found with only four backtracks. Even the 75-queens problem succumbs after 818 backtracks.

middle_out combined with first_fail (moff) heuristic

Naturally, the static variable ordering heuristic **middle_out** can be combined with the dynamic **first_fail** heuristic, to create a new heuristic, which we shall call here **moff**. The following clause for **search/2** encodes this combined heuristic:

```
search(moff,List) :-
    middle_out(List, MOutList),
   ( fromto(MOutList, Vars, Rest, [])
   do
      delete(Var, Vars, Rest, 0, first_fail),
      indomain(Var)
   ).
```

The **moff** heuristic solves the 8-queen and 16-queen problem without any backtracking, and also solves the 75-queens problem, but it still needs 719 backtracks before finding the first solution.

11.6 Value ordering heuristics

The **middle_out** heuristic was motivated by our observation that the middle queens had more impact on the remaining queens. This also holds for value choice: choosing a location near the centre of the board will also lead to more conflicts. Since the middle positions must be filled sooner or later, it makes sense to try and fill them earlier and propagate the consequences of these choices.

ECL^{i}PS^e provides an `indomain/2` built-in whose second argument gives the programmer control over the order in which values are tried. In particular `indomain(Var,middle)` tries first values near the middle of the current domain of `Var`, and only explores the minimum and maximum values after all the others. In turn, `indomain(Var,min)` reproduces the behaviour of `indomain(Var)` while `indomain(Var,max)` starts the enumeration from the largest value downwards.

Our final heuristic for the n-queens problem combines the `moff` variable ordering heuristic (i.e., the middle-out static variable ordering combined with the first-fail dynamic variable ordering) and the middle-out value ordering heuristic. We call it the `moffmo` heuristic and encode it as follows:

```
search(moffmo, List) :-
    middle_out(List, MOutList),
    ( fromto(MOutList, Vars, Rest, [])
    do
      delete(Var, Vars, Rest, 0, first_fail),
      indomain(Var,middle)
    ).
```

The number of backtracks for each introduced heuristic on various sizes of the n-queens problem is summarised in Table 11.6.

	naive	middle_out	first_fail	moff	moffmo
8-queens	10	0	10	0	3
16-queens	542	17	3	0	3
32-queens	—	–	4	1	7
75-queens	—	–	818	719	0
120-queens	—	–	—	—	0

Table 11.1 Number of backtracks for solving n-queens with different heuristics

Of course for different combinatorial problems different value ordering heuristics may be advantageous. For example, for graph colouring problems the value ordering heuristic which works best is to try to avoid re-using colours. Since a standard value ordering method – such as the one used in `indomain/1` – will always try the colours in the same order, it leads to colour reuse by default. A better value ordering heuristic for graph-colouring is therefore `indomain(Var,random)`.

For scheduling and packing problems it is usually best to label each variable by its smallest possible value, so using `indomain(Var,min)`. (In fact `indomain(Var)` uses this same value ordering.)

11.7 Constructing specific search behaviour

The n-queens problem is symmetrical in that you can either place a queen in every column, or equivalently place a queen in every row. Indeed, if the problem is solved by placing a queen at the n_ith square in each column i, it is also solved by placing a queen in the n_ith square in every row. The solutions can be shown to be the same by just turning the board 90 degrees.

Consequently, when the `middle_out` variable ordering heuristic finds a solution without backtracking, then so should the `indomain(Var,middle)` value ordering heuristic. We can now take a step further and create a modification of the `indomain(Var,middle)` value ordering heuristic that backtracks in exactly the same way as the `middle_out` variable ordering heuristic. By 'rotating' the output the resulting program produces the same solutions in the same order.

To achieve this search behaviour we use the `middle_out/2` predicate defined on page 216 but this time to appropriately reorder the domain values, through a call

```
middle_out(OrigDom, MOutDom).
```

Next, instead of iterating over the list of decision variables (using `foreach(Var,MOutList)` for the `middle_out` variable ordering heuristics) we now iterate over the domain values (using `foreach(Val,MOutDom)`). Further, instead of selecting a value for the current decision variable through a call to `indomain/1`, we now select a variable to which a given value is assigned, through an appropriate call to `member/2`, as in:

```
[eclipse 12]: member(2, [X,Y,Z]).

X = 2
Y = Y
Z = Z
Yes (0.00s cpu, solution 1, maybe more) ? ;

X = X
Y = 2
Z = Z
```

```
Yes (0.00s cpu, solution 2, maybe more) ? ;

X = X
Y = Y
Z = 2
Yes (0.00s cpu, solution 3)
```

Finally, to make the output the same, we 'rotate' the board at the end, so that if in the solution the ith queen is in square j, then in the output the jth queen is in square i.

Accordingly, the n-queens program in Figure 11.6 produces exactly the same results in the same order as the `middle_out` variable ordering heuristic, that is the queries

```
queens(middle_out, Queens, Number).
```

and

```
queens(rotate, Queens, Number).
```

produce the same solutions in the same order. Surprisingly, when we count the number of backtracks required to find the first solution, we get the results in Table 11.2.

	middle_out	rotate
8-queens	0	0
16-queens	17	0
24-queens	194	12
27-queens	1161	18
29-queens	25120	136

Table 11.2 Number of backtracks for solving n-queens with `middle_out` and `rotate` heuristics

This difference occurs because the constraint propagation behaviour is not the same for columns and for rows. In our model we have a single (queen) variable for each column whose value is the square that the queen occupies in that column. If all the values for a column (i.e. for a variable) are excluded except one, then this variable is immediately instantiated to the remaining value. This is the behaviour exhibited by the `rotate` variable ordering heuristics.

However, if all the values in a row are excluded except one, then in our

```
queens(rotate, Queens, Number) :-
    dim(QueenStruct,[Number]),
    constraints(QueenStruct, Number),
    struct_to_list(QueenStruct, QList),
    search(rotate, QList),
    rotate(QueenStruct, Queens).

search(rotate, QList) :-
    middle_out_dom(QList, MOutDom),
    ( foreach(Val,MOutDom),
      param(QList)
    do
      member(Val, QList)
    ).

middle_out_dom([Q | _], MOutDom) :-
    get_domain_as_list(Q,OrigDom),
    middle_out(OrigDom, MOutDom).

rotate(QueenStruct, Queens) :-
    dim(QueenStruct,[N]),
    dim(RQueens,[N]),
    ( foreachelem(Q,QueenStruct,[I]),
      param(RQueens)
    do
      subscript(RQueens,[Q],I)
    ),
    struct_to_list(RQueens, Queens).
```

augmented by the **constraints/2** and **struct_to_list/2** procedures of
Figure 11.5 and **middle_out/2** procedure from page 216.

Fig. 11.6 Rotated **middle_out** heuristic for n-queens

model it means that only one (queen) variable remains which still has a
square in that row in its domain. In this case, which corresponds to the
middle_out variable ordering heuristics, constraint propagation does not
instantiate the variable. This phenomenon is illustrated in Figure 11.7. In
row 5 only the field **e5** is available. Since in every row exactly one queen

needs to be placed, it follows that in column **5** the queen has to be placed in the field **e5**. However, the variables represent columns, so the constraint propagation only reduces the domain of the variable representing column **e** to the set {2,3,5}.

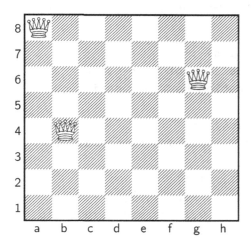

Fig. 11.7 Limitation of constraint propagation

The way to achieve the same amount of constraint propagation – and ultimately the same number of backtracks – for the two symmetrical heuristics is to add another board and link the two, so that if queen i is placed on square j on one board, then queen j is automatically placed on square i on the other. This redundant modelling of the problem improves all the n-queens problem benchmark results, and is a typical way to improve problem solving efficiency.

11.8 The search/6 generic search predicate

The different variable and value choice heuristics, together with a number of incomplete search options are provided through a single generic ECL^{i}PS^e predicate called **search/6**. The six arguments of

search(List, Arg, VarChoice, ValChoice, Method, Options)

are best illustrated by some examples of its use.

The first argument, **List**, is a list of decision variables when the second argument, **Arg**, is 0 or a list of compound terms when the second argument, **Arg**, is > 0. Assume for a moment that **Arg = 0**. By instantiating appropriately the third argument, **VarChoice**, to the (predicate) name of a predefined or user-defined variable ordering heuristic and the fourth argument, `ValChoice`, to the (predicate) name of a predefined or user-defined value ordering heuristic, we can encode different combinations of heuristics. As an example in Figure 11.8 we define using the `search/6` predicate the already discussed heuristics for the n-queens problem.

```
% search(Heur, List) :-
%      Find a labelling of List using
%      the combination Heur of heuristics.

search(naive, List) :-
    search(List,0,input_order,indomain,complete,[]).

search(middle_out, List) :-
    middle_out(List, MOutList),
    search(MOutList,0,input_order,indomain,complete,[]).

search(first_fail, List) :-
    search(List,0,first_fail,indomain,complete,[]).

search(moff, List) :-
    middle_out(List, MOutList),
    search(MOutList,0,first_fail,indomain,complete,[]).

search(moffmo, List) :-
    middle_out(List, MOutList),
    search(MOutList,0,first_fail,
           indomain_middle,complete,[]).
```
augmented by the `middle_out/2` procedure from page 216.

Fig. 11.8 Generic search for solving n-queens

So `input_order` and `first_fail` are predefined variable ordering heuristics corresponding to `naive` and `first_fail`, while `indomain` and `indomain_middle` are predefined value ordering heuristics corresponding to `indomain(Var,min)` (i.e., `indomain(Var)`) and `indomain(Var,middle)`.

In all the clauses the fifth argument, `Method`, is instantiated to `complete` which refers to a complete search. Other, incomplete, forms of search are also allowed. For example, by instantiating `Method` to `lds(2)` we specify a limited discrepancy search with up to two discrepancies (see Section 8.4).

The sixth argument, `Options`, allows the programmer to specify options, such as counting backtracks, or drawing the search tree as a graph. An example use might be as in the following query:

```
search(Queens,0,first_fail,
       indomain_middle,lds(2),[backtrack(B)]),
writeln(backtracks - B).
```

Finally, consider the second argument, `Arg`, of `search/6` when `Arg > 0`. As already mentioned in that case the first argument, `List`, should be a list of compound terms. The idea is that from an object-oriented viewpoint it makes sense to admit any list of compound terms (representing objects) as input, as long as during search we can extract the decision variable from the current compound term. This is done by instantiating the second argument, `Arg`, to the argument of each term that contains the decision variable.

Suppose for example that we keep with each queen variable an integer recording which column this queen belongs to. Each queen will then be represented by the term `q(Col,Q)`, where `Col` is an integer recording the column and `Q` a domain variable which will represent the queen's position. The first argument, `List`, of `search/6` will then be a list of such terms. In this case the decision variable is the second argument of each term, so the second argument of `search/6` is set to 2.

We mentioned already that the `VarChoice` and `ValChoice` parameters of `search/6` can be instantiated to user-defined heuristics. Let us illustrate now the usefulness of this facility. Suppose that for performance debugging purposes of a variable ordering heuristic for a given search method (such as limited discrepancy search) we want to output the column and the position whenever a queen is labelled, so that we know the order in which the queens are being selected for labelling. To do this we introduce a user-defined `show_choice` value ordering heuristic that displays the choice currently being made, and set the fourth argument, `ValChoice`, of `search/6` to `show_choice`. The resulting program is shown in Figure 11.9.

The following example interaction with this program illustrates the behaviour of the `first_fail` variable ordering heuristic for `lds(2)`, the limited discrepancy search with up to two discrepancies.

```
[eclipse 13]: queens(debug, Queens, first_fail, lds(2), 6).
col(1) - square(1)
col(2) - square(3)
```

```
queens(debug, Queens, VarChoice, Method, Number) :-
    dim(QueenStruct,[Number]),
    constraints(QueenStruct, Number),
    struct_to_list(QueenStruct, Queens),
    struct_to_queen_list(QueenStruct, QList),
    search(QList, 2, VarChoice, show_choice, Method, []).

struct_to_queen_list(Struct, QList) :-
    ( foreacharg(Var,Struct),
      count(Col,1,_),
      foreach(Term,QList)
    do
      Term = q(Col, Var)
    ).

show_choice(q(I, Var)) :-
    indomain(Var),
    writeln(col(I):square(Var)).
```

augmented by the **constraints/2** and **struct_to_list/2** procedures of Figure 11.5.

Fig. 11.9 Code for performance debugging of *n*-queens

```
col(1) - square(1)
col(2) - square(3)
col(2) - square(4)
col(1) - square(2)
col(2) - square(4)
col(3) - square(6)
col(4) - square(1)
col(5) - square(3)
col(6) - square(5)

Queens = [2, 4, 6, 1, 3, 5]
Yes (0.00s cpu, solution 1, maybe more) ?
```

We can now illustrate the flexibility of the **search/6** predicate, by using it to run our own credit based value ordering heuristic procedure. The procedure **share_credit/2** defined in Figure 8.11 on page 143 assigned more credit to our earlier choices and less to later ones. To interface to such procedures the fourth argument, ValChoice, of search/6 allows us to thread an extra argument, for example the initial credit Var, through the procedure. An example interface is shown in Figure 11.10 where the ValChoice argument of search/6 is instantiated to our_credit_search(Var, _). The resulting search/2 procedure also uses the first_fail variable choice heuristic, to show the orthogonality of variable and value ordering heuristics, however complex these heuristics may be.

To complete the chapter we present experimental results in Table 11.3 that show that each time we change the amount of credit, we also get different backtracking behaviour. This suggests that insufficient credit is eliminating some correct choices, and consequently suggests that our credit based search is not a good heuristic for solving the n-queens problem.

Credit(N)	N=10	N=20	N=40	N=100
8-queens	failed	6	10	16
16-queens	7	13	25	45
32-queens	9	9	14	21
75-queens	failed	failed	7	6
120-queens	failed	failed	21	3

Table 11.3 Number of backtracks for solving n-queens with different credit limits

11.9 Summary

In this chapter we studied the support provided in the ic library for top-down search for finite CSPs in the presence of constraint propagation. We discussed in turn the backtrack-free search, shallow backtracking and backtracking search. We also defined various variable and value ordering heuristics and showed how by using them specific forms of search behaviour can be defined.

Further, we discussed a generic search procedure search/6 that allows us to customise the top-down search process by using predefined or user-defined variable ordering and value ordering heuristics, and various, possibly incomplete, forms of search.

In our presentation we introduced the following ic library built-ins:

• get_min/2,

```
% search(our_credit_search(Var,_), List) :-
%     Find a labelling of List using our own credit based
%     search procedure with an initial credit of Var.

search(our_credit_search(Var,_), List) :-
    search(List, 0, first_fail,
            our_credit_search(Var,_), complete, []).

% our_credit_search(Var, TCredit, NCredit) :-
%     Select a value for Var reducing the remaining
%     credit from TCredit to NCredit.

our_credit_search(Var, TCredit, NCredit) :-
    get_domain_as_list(Var,Domain),
    share_credit(Domain, TCredit, DomCredList),
    member(Val-Credit, DomCredList),
    Var = Val,
    NCredit = Credit.

% share_credit(DomList, InCredit, DomCredList) :-
%     Share the credit in InCredit amongst the
%     values in DomList producing DomCredList.

share_credit(DomList, InCredit, DomCredList) :-
    ( fromto(InCredit, TCredit, NCredit, 0),
      fromto(DomList, [Val | Tail], Tail, _),
      foreach(Val-Credit, DomCredList)
    do
      Credit is fix(ceiling(TCredit/2)),
      NCredit is TCredit - Credit
    ).
```

Fig. 11.10 Credit based search for solving n-queens

- get_max/2,
- get_domain_as_list/2,
- indomain/1,
- labeling/1,

- delete/5,
- indomain/2,
- search/6.

Throughout the chapter we assumed that the domain splitting consists of an enumeration of all the domain elements. But other natural possibilities exist. For example, instead of such a complete domain decomposition we could instead split the domain only into two parts, one consisting of a single element and the other of the remaining elements. Alternatively, we could split the domain into two, roughly equal parts.

These alternatives can be programmed in ECL^{i}PS^e in a straightforward way. We shall return to the last one in Chapter 13 on solving continuous CSPs, as for finite domains this approach can be easily obtained by a minor modification of the corresponding domain splitting method there defined.

11.10 Exercises

Exercise 11.1 Write a version of the queens/2 predicate from Figure 11.4 on page 214 that uses lists instead of arrays and recursion instead of iteration.

Exercise 11.2 Write an ECL^{i}PS^e program that solves the problem from Exercise 6.1 on page 108.

Exercise 11.3 Write an ECL^{i}PS^e program that solves the problem from Exercise 6.2 on page 109.

Exercise 11.4 Write an ECL^{i}PS^e program that generates magic squares of order ≤ 5. (For their definition see Exercise 6.3 on page 109.)

Optimisation with active constraints

L ET US TURN our attention now to the problem of solving finite constrained optimisation problems (COPs) as defined in Section 6.5. ECL^{i}PS^e allows us to solve them by combining constraint propagation with various forms of the branch and bound search. This form of search does not need to be programmed explicitly as it is supported by the `branch_and_bound` library. In this chapter we discuss two main built-ins available in this library.

12.1 The `minimize/2` built-in

The most common built-in in this library is `minimize/2`. Its appropriate use is best explained by recalling from Chapter 9 the general form of an ECL^{i}PS^e program that solves a constrained optimisation problem with finite domains. In the current context it looks as follows:

```
:- lib(ic).
:- lib(branch_and_bound).

solveOpt(List):-
```

```
declareDomains(List),
generateConstraints_and_Cost(List, Cost),
minimize(search(List), Cost).
```

The call **generateCons_and_Cost(List, Cost)** generates the constraints and defines the cost function that is subsequently used to find the optimal solution. The call

```
minimize(search(List), Cost)
```

realises in ECL^{i}PS^e the basic branch and bound algorithm discussed in Section 6.6, augmented with the constraint propagation for constraints on finite domains. It computes, using the call **search(List)**, a solution to the generated CSP for which the value of the cost function defined in **Cost** is minimal. At the time of the call **Cost** has to be a variable, i.e., it should not be instantiated.

To illustrate the internal working of **minimize/2** consider the following query:

```
[eclipse 1]: minimize(member(X,[5,6,5,3,4,2]), X).
Found a solution with cost 5
Found a solution with cost 3
Found a solution with cost 2
Found no solution with cost -1.0Inf .. 1

X = 2
Yes (0.00s cpu)
```

So ECL^{i}PS^e reports information about each newly found improved value of the cost function. The **member/2** built-in generates upon backtracking the successive elements of the input list, so only the solutions with the cost **5**, **3** and **2** are reported. Upon termination of the search the values of the variables for the first optimal solution found are printed.

If we need to use a non-variable cost function, we introduce it by means of a constraint, as in the following example:

```
[eclipse 2]: Cost #= X+1,
             minimize(member(X,[5,6,5,3,4,2]), Cost).
Found a solution with cost 6
Found a solution with cost 4
Found a solution with cost 3
Found no solution with cost -1.0Inf .. 2
```

```
Cost = 3
X = 2
Yes (0.00s cpu)
```

In general, to solve a constrained optimisation problem we need to launch a complete top-down search, for example using the `labeling/1` built-in, in the presence of the cost function. As an example consider the following artificial problem.

Problem Find a solution to the equation $x^3 + y^2 = z^3$ such that $x, y, z \in [100..500]$, with the minimal value of $z - x - y$.

Here is a solution in ECL^{i}PS^e:

```
find(X, Y, Z) :-
    [X,Y,Z] :: [100..500],
    X*X*X + Y*Y #= Z*Z*Z,
    Cost #= Z-X-Y,
    minimize(labeling([X,Y,Z]), Cost).
```

The interaction with ECL^{i}PS^e yields the following outcome:

```
[eclipse 3]: find(X, Y, Z).
Found a solution with cost -180
Found a solution with cost -384
Found no solution with cost -1.0Inf .. -385

X = 110
Y = 388
Z = 114
Yes (12.34s cpu)
```

Of course, in general the efficiency of the program and the order in which the values of the cost function are generated depend on the adopted search strategy.

12.2 The knapsack problem

We now explain how to solve in ECL^{i}PS^e the knapsack problem introduced in Subsection 6.5.1. Let us recall first its formulation as a COP.

We have n objects with volumes $a_1, ..., a_n$ and values $b_1, ..., b_n$ and the knapsack volume v. Further, we have n Boolean variables $x_1, ..., x_n$. The inclusion of the object i in a collection is modelled by setting the value of x_i to 1.

So we have just one constraint:

$$\sum_{i=1}^{n} a_i \cdot x_i \leq v \tag{12.1}$$

that models the requirement that the collection fits in the knapsack. The cost function which we wish to minimise is:

$$-\sum_{i=1}^{n} b_i \cdot x_i.$$

It models the requirement that we seek a solution to (12.1) for which the sum is maximal.

The appropriate program is given in Figure 12.1. It uses twice the predicate sigma/3. Its variant was originally discussed in Subsection 10.3.2, where we explained how the constraint (12.1) can be generated in the ic library. The discussion at the end of Section 11.4 explains why the labeling procedure is applied only to the list Xs.

```
knapsack(Volumes, Values, Capacity, Xs) :-
    Xs :: [0..1],
    sigma(Volumes, Xs, Volume),
    Volume $=< Capacity,
    sigma(Values, Xs, Value),
    Cost $= -Value,
    minimize(labeling(Xs), Cost).

sigma(List1, List2, Value) :-
    ( foreach(V1,List1),
      foreach(V2,List2),
      foreach(Prod,ProdList)
    do
      Prod = V1*V2
    ),
    Value $= sum(ProdList).
```

Fig. 12.1 The KNAPSACK program

As an example assume we have a knapsack with capacity 60 and that we have five objects with the volumes and values as given in Table 12.1.

volume	value
52	100
23	60
35	70
15	15
7	15

Table 12.1 Volumes and values of knapsack objects

We get then:

```
[eclipse 4]: knapsack([52,23,35,15,7], [100,60,70,15,15],
                       60, [X1,X2,X3,X4,X5]).

Found a solution with cost 0
Found a solution with cost -15
Found a solution with cost -30
Found a solution with cost -70
Found a solution with cost -85
Found a solution with cost -100
Found a solution with cost -130
Found no solution with cost -260.0 .. -131.0

X1 = 0
X2 = 1
X3 = 1
X4 = 0
X5 = 0
Yes (0.01s cpu)
```

12.3 The coins problem

To see another example of the use of the `minimize/2` built-in let us return now to the coins problem introduced in Subsection 6.5.2. Recall that the task was to find the minimum number of euro cent coins that allows us to pay exactly any amount smaller than one euro.

We formalized this problem using six variables $x_1, x_2, x_5, x_{10}, x_{20}, x_{50}$ ranging over the domain $[0..99]$ that denote the appropriate amounts of the coins, and for each $i \in [1..99]$ six variables $x_1^i, x_2^i, x_5^i, x_{10}^i, x_{20}^i, x_{50}^i$ that are used to state that the amount of i cents can be exactly paid. The appropriate constraints are:

$$x_1^i + 2x_2^i + 5x_5^i + 10x_{10}^i + 20x_{20}^i + 50x_{50}^i = i,$$

$$0 \leq x_j^i,$$

$$x_j^i \leq x_j$$

for all $i \in [1..99]$ and $j \in \{1, 2, 5, 10, 20, 50\}$ and the cost function is

$$x_1 + x_2 + x_5 + x_{10} + x_{20} + x_{50}.$$

The program is a direct translation of this representation into ECL^{i}PS^e. So we use a list `Coins` of six variables corresponding to the variables x_1, x_2, $x_5, x_{10}, x_{20}, x_{50}$, each ranging over the domain `0..99`.

Then for each price between 1 and 99 we impose the above three constraints using the predicate `price_cons/4`. The variables $x_1^i, x_2^i, x_5^i, x_{10}^i, x_{20}^i$, x_{50}^i are kept in the list `CoinsforPrice` and the complete list of these lists, with $i \in [1..99]$, is kept in the list `Pockets`. Though we are not interested in the values of the variables assembled in the list `Pockets`, we keep them so as to be able to ensure there really is a feasible labelling for them after setting the appropriate amounts of the coins to variables in the list `Coins`. Finally, we use `sum(Coins)` as the cost function. The program is given in Figure 12.2.

This optimisation problem is easy to solve. The optimal solution of 8 is found very quickly:

```
[eclipse 5]: solve(Coins, Min).
Found a solution with cost 8
Found no solution with cost 1.0 .. 7.0

Coins = [1, 2, 1, 1, 2, 1]
Min = 8
Yes (0.08s cpu)
```

12.4 The currency design problem

In the last problem the values of the six coins were fixed: 1, 2, 5, 10, 20 and 50. But suppose now that we have the freedom of choosing the values

```
solve(Coins, Min) :-
    init_vars(Values, Coins),
    coin_cons(Values, Coins, Pockets),
    Min #= sum(Coins),
    minimize((labeling(Coins), check(Pockets)), Min).

init_vars(Values, Coins) :-
    Values = [1,2,5,10,20,50],
    length(Coins, 6),
    Coins :: 0..99.

coin_cons(Values, Coins, Pockets) :-
    ( for(Price,1,99),
      foreach(CoinsforPrice,Pockets),
      param(Coins,Values)
    do
      price_cons(Price, Coins, Values, CoinsforPrice)
    ).

price_cons(Price, Coins, Values, CoinsforPrice) :-
    ( foreach(V,Values),
      foreach(C,CoinsforPrice),
      foreach(Coin,Coins),
      foreach(Prod,ProdList)
    do
      Prod = V*C,
      0 #=< C,
      C #=< Coin
    ),
    Price #= sum(ProdList).

check(Pockets) :-
    ( foreach(CoinsforPrice,Pockets)
    do
      once(labeling(CoinsforPrice))
    ).
```

Fig. 12.2 The COINS program

of these six coins. Can we then design a set of six coins for which we can solve the above problem with fewer than eight coins? This is the currency design problem introduced in Subsection 6.5.2. Computationally this is a much more challenging problem. The reason is that the constraints become now non-linear. Indeed, recall that each previous constraint

$$x_1^i + 2x_2^i + 5x_5^i + 10x_{10}^i + 20x_{20}^i + 50x_{50}^i = i$$

becomes now

$$v_1 \cdot x_1^i + v_2 \cdot x_2^i + v_3 \cdot x_3^i + v_4 \cdot x_4^i + v_5 \cdot x_5^i + v_6 \cdot x_6^i = i,$$

where $v_1, \ldots, v_6$ are the values of the coins and for each $i \in [1..99]$, $x_1^i, \ldots, x_6^i$ are the numbers of these coins that allow one to pay the amount i.

On the other hand, from the programming point of view the solution is a minor modification of the previous program. Indeed, to solve this problem instead of the list of coin values

```
Values = [1,2,5,10,20,50]
```

we simply use now the list

```
Values = [V1, V2, V3, V4, V5, V6]
```

of six constraint variables such that 0 #< V1 #< ... #< V6 #< 100, that represent the values of the coins for which an optimal solution is sought.

Unfortunately, even though the resulting program finds a solution with eight coins relatively quickly, the computation concerned with the proof of optimality takes an excessive amount of time.

A remedy consists of using implied constraints that make a big difference to performance. The idea is that if we have coins with value $V1$ and $V2$, where $V1 < V2$, then it is never needed to have enough coins with value $V1$ to equal or exceed the value $V2$. Indeed, if we had so many $V1$-valued coins, we could pay the amount that uses them using a $V2$-valued coin instead. The reason is that in any solution there are always enough coins to make up any amount up to $V1 - 1$.

Additionally, for the coin with the largest value we can impose the constraint that we only need to pay amounts smaller than 100. The resulting program is presented in Figure 12.3. The additional constraints are generated using the predicate `clever_cons/2`. The `increasing/1` predicate is a simplified version of the `ordered/1` predicate introduced in Figure 9.3 on page 172, in which we do not deal with the case of the empty lists.

The following interaction with ECL^{i}PS^e shows that no solution with seven coins exists.

```
design_currency(Values, Coins) :-
    init_vars(Values, Coins),
    coin_cons(Values, Coins, Pockets),
    clever_cons(Values, Coins),
    Min #= sum(Coins),
    minimize((labeling(Values), labeling(Coins),
                                check(Pockets)), Min).

init_vars(Values, Coins) :-
    length(Values, 6),
    Values :: 1..99,
    increasing(Values),
    length(Coins, 6),
    Coins :: 0..99.

increasing(List) :-
    ( fromto(List,[This,Next | Rest],[Next | Rest],[_])
    do
      This #< Next
    ).

clever_cons(Values, Coins) :-
    ( fromto(Values,[V1 | NV],NV,[]),
      fromto(Coins,[N1 | NN],NN,[])
    do
      ( NV = [V2 | _] ->
        N1*V1 #< V2
      ;
        N1*V1 #< 100
      )
    ).
```

augmented by the procedures **coin_cons/3** and **check/1** of Figure 12.2.

Fig. 12.3 The CURRENCY program

```
[eclipse 6]: design_currency(Values, Coins).
Found a solution with cost 19
[...]
```

```
Found a solution with cost 8
Found no solution with cost 1.0 .. 7.0

Values = [1, 2, 3, 4, 11, 33]
Coins = [1, 1, 0, 2, 2, 2]
Yes (297.98s cpu)
```

In other words, it is impossible to design a set of values for 6 coins such that a set of 7 coins would allow us to pay exactly any amount smaller than one euro.

Call now a collection of n (possibly identical) coins of some values an n **coins system** if it allows us to pay exactly any amount smaller than one euro. Using the COINS program we showed that an eight coins system exists.

Further, using the additional constraints that we formalized using the predicate clever_cons/2 we can prove that if an n coins system exists, then also an n coins system with all coins different exists. Indeed, if a V-valued coin appears more than once, say N times, then its Nth occurrence can be replaced by a different coin with face value $N \cdot V$. By the additional constraints it is a 'new' coin. Repeating this replacement process we end up with an n coins system with all coins different. For example, this transformation transforms the above solution with

```
Values = [1, 2, 3, 4, 11, 33]
Coins =  [1, 1, 0, 2,  2,  2]
```

into a solution with

```
Values = [1, 2, 4, 8, 11, 22, 33, 66]
Coins =  [1, 1, 1, 1,  1,  1,  1,  1].
```

So using the CURRENCY program we showed that no six coins system exists.

The final question is of course whether a seven coins system exists. To answer it, in view of the above transformation, it suffices to change in the CURRENCY program the parameter 6 to 7, add the constraint Min #= 7, and run the query design_currency(Values, [1,1,1,1,1,1,1]).

Note also that in this case the call of clever_cons/2 is unneeded. This yields after 5 seconds a solution

```
Values = [1, 2, 3, 6, 12, 25, 50].
```

So an optimal coin system consists of seven coins and 1, 2, 3, 6, 12, 25, 50 is one possible choice.

12.5 Generating Sudoku puzzles

Sudoku puzzles gained popularity in Japan in the eighties. They became recently extremely popular throughout the world and nowadays many newspapers publish them (often referring to some copyrighted websites). A Sudoku puzzle consists of a 9 by 9 grid divided into 9 squares of size 3 by 3, partially filled with the digits 1 through 9. The problem consists of filling the empty fields so that that every row, every column, and every 3 by 3 square contains the digits 1 through 9. It is required that the Sudoku puzzle has a unique solution. An example is given in Figure 12.4.

	2	1			7			
					8			
						9	3	
	8		9			6		1
				6			2	
					5			3
	9	4					5	6
7			3			8		
					2			

Fig. 12.4 A Sudoku puzzle

In this section we consider the problem of generating Sudoku puzzles. We begin with a simpler problem of solving Sudoku puzzles. We represent such puzzles by means of an 9 by 9 array partially filled with the digits 1 through 9, with the remaining fields filled by the anonymous variables. For example, here is the array representing the Sudoku puzzle from Figure 12.4:

```
[](
  [](_, 2, 1, _, _, 7, _, _, _),
  [](_, _, _, _, _, 8, _, _, _),
  [](_, _, _, _, _, _, 9, 3, _),
  [](_, 8, _, 9, _, _, 6, _, 1),
  [](_, _, _, _, 6, _, _, 2, _),
  [](_, _, _, _, _, 5, _, _, 3),
  [](_, 9, 4, _, _, _, _, 5, 6),
  [](7, _, _, 3, _, _, 8, _, _),
  [](_, _, _, _, _, 2, _, _, _))
```

The program solving Sudoku puzzles is very simple: it suffices to state the **alldifferent** constraints for each row, column and 3 by 3 square and launch the search. In the program we use the **alldifferent/1** built-in from the library **ic_global** that leads to a stronger constraint propagation than the **alldifferent/1** built-in from the **ic** library. For example, we have

```
[eclipse 7]: [X,Y,Z] :: [0..1], ic:alldifferent([X,Y,Z]).


X = X{[0, 1]}
Y = Y{[0, 1]}
Z = Z{[0, 1]}


There are 3 delayed goals.
Yes (0.00s cpu)
[eclipse 8]: [X,Y,Z] :: [0..1], ic_global:alldifferent([X,Y,Z]).


No (0.00s cpu)
```

The program is given in Figure 12.5. It uses two built-ins that were not discussed so far: **flatten/2** and **term_variables/2**. The former transforms a list of lists (in general, a list of lists of ... lists) into a list. So the query

```
S is Board[I..I+2,J..J+2], flatten(S, SubSquare).
```

assigns to the variable **SubSquare** the list of elements filling the subsquare **Board[I..I+2,J..J+2]** of **Board**. In turn, the **term_variables/2** built-in computes the list of variables that appear in a term. It is similar to the **vars/2** predicate defined in Figure 5.2 on page 83 (see also Exercise 5.2 on page 85). Finally, the **multifor([I,J],1,9,3)** shorthand stands for the iteration of I and of J from 1 to 9 in the increments of 3, i.e., through the values 1,4,7. The solution to the puzzle from Figure 12.4 is easily found:

```
[eclipse 9]: solve([](
       [](_, 2, 1, _, _, 7, _, _, _),
       [](_, _, _, _, _, 8, _, _, _),
       [](_, _, _, _, _, _, 9, 3, _),
       [](_, 8, _, 9, _, _, 6, _, 1),
       [](_, _, _, _, 6, _, _, 2, _),
       [](_, _, _, _, _, 5, _, _, 3),
       [](_, 9, 4, _, _, _, _, 5, 6),
       [](7, _, _, 3, _, _, 8, _, _),
       [](_, _, _, _, _, 2, _, _, _))).
```

```
solve(Board) :-
    sudoku(Board),
    print_board(Board).

sudoku(Board) :-
    constraints(Board),
    search(Board).

constraints(Board) :-
    dim(Board,[9,9]),
    Board[1..9,1..9] :: [1..9],
    ( for(I,1,9), param(Board)
    do
      Row is Board[I,1..9],
      alldifferent(Row),
      Col is Board[1..9,I],
      alldifferent(Col)
    ),
    ( multifor([I,J],1,9,3),
      param(Board)
    do
      S is Board[I..I+2,J..J+2],
      flatten(S, SubSquare),
      alldifferent(SubSquare)
    ).

search(Board) :-
    term_variables(Board, Vars),
    labeling(Vars).

print_board(Board) :-
    ( foreachelem(El,Board,[_,J])
    do
      ( J =:= 1 -> nl ; true ),
      write(' '),
      ( var(El) -> write('_') ; write(El) )
    ).
```

Fig. 12.5 The SUDOKU program

```
9  2  1  5  3  7  4  6  8
4  3  6  2  9  8  1  7  5
8  5  7  4  1  6  9  3  2
2  8  5  9  7  3  6  4  1
1  7  3  8  6  4  5  2  9
6  4  9  1  2  5  7  8  3
3  9  4  7  8  1  2  5  6
7  6  2  3  5  9  8  1  4
5  1  8  6  4  2  3  9  7
Yes (0.20s cpu)
```

To generate the Sudoku puzzles we consider two different approaches. The first program starts by randomly generating a solution to a Sudoku puzzle. Then repeatedly fields are randomly removed (i.e., replaced by an anonymous variable) until a problem with more than one solution is created. The problem just before the last one is then a Sudoku puzzle and is printed. Using the branch and bound search a Sudoku puzzle with the minimum number of filled fields is sought and each successively better solution is printed.

The resulting program is given in Figure 12.6. It relies on three supporting predicates, `remove_random/3`, `board_to_list/2` and `list_to_board/2` with the expected meaning. They are defined in Figure 12.8 on page 247.

The program performs the branch and bound search using the `minimize/2` built-in. The crucial procedure is `drop_until/3`. Its first argument, `List`, represents the contents of the initial solution while the second argument, `Final`, represents the contents of the final solution, both in a list form. The third argument, `Min`, represents the number of (non-dropped) values in the final solution.

To test that a puzzle has a unique solution we use within the `drop_until/3` procedure the predicate `one/1` defined in Figure 8.16 on page 149. Recall that the call `one(Q)` does not instantiate the variables of the query `Q`. If there is only one solution, the iteration continues by dropping further values. Otherwise, if there are multiple solutions, the iteration stops and returns the previous solution.

The search is launched by the query **generate**. It fairly quickly generates puzzles with 23–25 filled fields.

In the above approach each printed Sudoku puzzle is a 'subset' of the original randomly generated solution. The second program takes a 'dual' approach. It generates a Sudoku puzzle by repeatedly randomly filling fields

```
generate :-
    sudoku_random(Board),
    minimize(search(Board,Min), Min).

sudoku_random(Board) :-
    constraints(Board),
    term_variables(Board, Vars),
    ( foreach(X,Vars) do indomain(X,random) ).

search(Board, Min) :-
    board_to_list(Board, List),
    drop_until(List, Final, Min),
    list_to_board(Final, FinalBoard),
    print_board(FinalBoard), nl.

drop_until(List, Final, Min) :-
    ( fromto(List, This, Next, Final),
      fromto(ok, _, Cont, stop)
    do
      remove_random(This, _, Succ),
      list_to_board(Succ, Test),
      ( one(sudoku(Test)) ->
        Next = Succ, Cont = ok
      ;
        Next = This, Cont = stop
      )
    ),
    length(Final, Min).
```

augmented by the procedures constraints/1, sudoku/1 and
print_board/1 of Figure 12.5; board_to_list/2, list_to_board/2
and remove_random/3 given below in Figure 12.8;
and one/1 of Figure 8.16.

Fig. 12.6 The GEN_SUDOKU program

until a Sudoku puzzle (i.e., a puzzle with a unique solution) is created. The
generated puzzle is printed. Subsequently, using the branch and bound
search a Sudoku puzzle with the minimum number of filled fields is sought.
The program is given in Figure 12.7.

```
generate :-
    constraints(Board),
    minimize(search2(Board,Min), Min).

search2(Board, Min) :-
    board_to_list(Board, List),
    add_until(Board, List, Final, Min),
    list_to_board(Final, FinalBoard),
    print_board(FinalBoard), nl.

add_until(Board, List, Final, Min) :-
    ( fromto([], Used, [[I,J]-Val | Used], Final),
      fromto(List, TFree, NFree, _),
      fromto(ok, _, Cont, stop),
      count(Ct,1,Min),
      param(Board, Min)
    do
      Min #>= Ct,
      remove_random(TFree, [I,J]-Val, NFree),
      var(Val),
      indomain(Val,random),
      ct(search(Board), N),
      ( N = 1         -> Cont = stop ;
        N = multiple -> Cont = ok )
    ).

ct(Q, N) :-
    ( not twice(Q) -> getval(x,N) ; N = multiple ).
```

augmented by the procedures **constraints/1**, **search/1** and
print_board/1 of Figure 12.5; **board_to_list/2**, **list_to_board/2**
and **remove_random/3** given below in Figure 12.8;
and **twice/1** of Figure 8.16.

Fig. 12.7 Another GEN_SUDOKU program

The crucial procedure, **add_until/4**, is now more involved. Its first argument, **Board**, represents the constrained Sudoku board. The second argument, **List**, is a list of the remaining unfilled squares in the board. The third argument, **Final**, as before represents the contents of the final solution in a list form, and the fourth argument, Min, is the number of entries in this final solution.

In contrast to the previous program the search for the minimum uses a constraint, Min #>= Ct, to prune the search tree, which is needed to curtail fruitless searches for solutions that have too many entries.

The call remove_random(TFree, [I,J]-Val, NFree) removes an(other) entry from the board. The test if Val is a variable avoids explicitly selecting entries whose values are already entailed by constraint propagation from the previously chosen entries. In turn, the call ct(search(Board), N) is used to complete the board after instantiating the next value. Since the constraints were posted at the start, this program uses the search/1 procedure instead of the more costly sudoku/1.

Also ct/2 is used instead of one/1, because this enables the program to distinguish the case where the current board has multiple solutions from the case where there are none. (Recall that x is the non-logical variable used in the procedure one/2 defined in Figure 8.16.) Finally, the statement

```
( N = 1        -> Cont = stop ;
  N = multiple -> Cont = ok )
```

is used to avoid extending a partial assignment that is not a partial solution. (Note that if N = 0 a failure arises.) If there are no solutions, the program immediately backtracks and finds a different value for Val.

The program can be easily modified to one in which one first randomly generates a solution to a Sudoku puzzle and then randomly copies its fields into the Board array until a Sudoku puzzle is created.

We conclude by listing in Figure 12.8 the supporting predicates needed for the two previous programs.

12.6 The bb_min/3 built-in

In general, the computation of a solution to an optimisation problem consists of:

- the process of finding successively better solutions, before an optimum solution is found,
- the proof of optimality, obtained by searching for an even better solution, and ultimately failing.

For problems such as the currency design problem from the last section, where the optimum is almost exactly known in advance, the first process can be avoided by constraining the cost function to be at or near the optimum.

```
remove_random(List, Val, Next) :-
    length(List, Len),
    Index:: 1..Len,
    indomain(Index,random),
    remove_nth(Index, List, Val, Next).

remove_nth(1, [H | T], H, T) :- !.
remove_nth(N, [H | T], Val, [H | Tail]) :-
    N1 is N-1,
    remove_nth(N1, T, Val, Tail).

board_to_list(Board, List) :-
    ( foreachelem(Val,Board,[I,J]),
      foreach([I,J]-Val,List)
    do
      true
    ).

list_to_board(List, Board) :-
    dim(Board,[9,9]),
    ( foreach([I,J]-Val,List),
      param(Board)
    do
      subscript(Board,[I,J],Val)
    ).
```

Fig. 12.8 Supporting predicates for GEN_SUDOKU

Benchmark optimisation problems are typically of this kind. For most optimisation problems, however, it is necessary to trawl through a sequence of better and better solutions en route to the optimum. Here is a trace of a scheduling program:

```
Cost: 863 in time: 0.110000000000582
... [20 intermediate solutions found in quick succession]
Cost: 784 in time: 2.04300000000148
... [10 more solutions - the time for each is growing]
Cost: 754 in time: 7.65100000000166
Cost: 752 in time: 8.75300000000061
```

```
Cost: 750 in time: 21.8120000000017
Cost: 743 in time: 30.8549999999996
Cost: 742 in time: 32.3169999999991
... [5 solutions found quickly]
Cost: 723 in time: 34.2400000000016
Cost: 716 in time: 34.3600000000006
Cost: 710 in time: 34.5900000000001
Cost: 709 in time: 42.1610000000001
... [5 more solutions found quickly]
Cost: 685 in time: 44.5740000000005
Cost: 684 in time: 44.8050000000003
Cost: 683 in time: 51.7350000000006
Cost: 677 in time: 58.1140000000014
Found no solution with cost 349.0 .. 676.0
```

The uneven progress is typical: it takes some 13 seconds to improve the cost from 752 to 750, but the improvement from 723 to 710 takes under half a second. It took 7 seconds to improve the second best solution to an optimal one and the time to prove optimality (not shown above) was also around 7 seconds.

To better manage the computation process concerned with an optimisation problem ECL^{i}PS^e offers the bb_min/3 built-in. The minimize/2 built-in is a special case of bb_min/3. However, bb_min/3 has one extra argument which allows the programmer to specify a number of options, some of which we discussed in Subsection 6.6.3, and which can be used to reduce the computation time needed for finding an optimal solution or a solution the cost of which is close to the optimum.

We begin by exploring the following two options:

- delta,
- factor,

that are concerned with the improvement of the cost of each new solution. Such options for bb_min are specified using a special syntax which we explain by returning to the trivial matter of finding the minimal element in the list [5,6,5,3,4,2].

Let us specify that in the branch and bound search the cost of each new solution has to be better by the value of 3 w.r.t. the previous one. This is done by means of the following query:

```
[eclipse 10]: bb_min(member(X,[5,6,5,3,4,2]),
                X,
```

```
                      bb_options{delta:3}).
Found a solution with cost 5
Found a solution with cost 2
Found no solution with cost -1.0Inf .. -1


X = 2
Yes (0.00s cpu)
```

Note that in the search the solution with cost 3 was skipped. Of course, the branch and bound search with such an option can cease to be complete:

```
[eclipse 11]: bb_min(member(X,[5,6,5,3,4,2]),
                      X,
                      bb_options{delta:4}).
Found a solution with cost 5
Found no solution with cost -1.0Inf .. 1


X = 5
Yes (0.00s cpu)
```

Still we can conclude that the cost of the generated solution is at most `delta` from the optimum.

A more important option is **factor** that governs how much better the next solution should be than the last. The improvement **factor** is a number between 0 and 1, which relates the improvement to the current cost upper bound and lower bound.

Setting the **factor** to 1 puts the new upper bound at the last found best cost – this is the default used by the standard **minimize/2** predicate. Setting the factor to 0.01 sets the new upper bound almost to the cost lower bound (factor 0.0 is not accepted by **bb_min/3**): typically it is easy to prove there is no solution with a cost near this lower bound, and the optimisation terminates quickly. More interesting is a setting around 0.9, which looks for a 10% improvement at each step. In the case of our scheduling example this factor gives the following trace:

```
Cost: 863 in time: 0.120000000002619
Cost: 811 in time: 0.200000000004366
Cost: 764 in time: 0.30000000000291
Cost: 716 in time: 0.430000000000291
Cost: 677 in time: 2.95400000000518
Found no solution with cost 349.0 .. 644.2
```

This represents a tremendous saving in the time taken to improve, from the same initial solution as before 863, to the optimal solution of 677. Notice that the cost lower bound is 349. So after finding an initial solution of 863, the new cost bound is set to $349 + 0.9 \cdot (863 - 349) = 811.6$. The next bounds are successively 764.8, 722.5, 679.3, 644.2, the last one being below the optimum and therefore yielding no solution.

In this example the optimum solution is found, but in fact this search only proves there is no solution better than 644: had there been further solutions between 677 and 644 they would not have been found by this procedure.

What we get is a guarantee that the best solution 677 is within 10% – or more precisely within $0.1 \cdot (677 - 349)$ – of the optimum.

The benefit is that not only is the time taken for the improvement process much shorter (it is reduced from 58 seconds to around 3 seconds), but also the time taken for the proof of optimality. It is reduced from 7 seconds to around 0.2 seconds. The reason is that it is much easier to prove there is no solution better than 644.2 than to prove there is no solution better than 677.

As another example let us modify the CURRENCY program from Figure 12.3 on page 238 so that we call for an improvement by a factor of 2/3. To this end we replace the call

```
minimize((labeling(Values), labeling(Coins), check(Pockets)),
         Min)
```

by

```
bb_min((labeling(Values), labeling(Coins), check(Pockets)),
       Min,
       bb_options{factor:0.666}).
```

An optimal solution is found then considerably faster:

```
[eclipse 12]: design_currency(Values, Coins).
Found a solution with cost 19
Found a solution with cost 12
Found a solution with cost 8
Found no solution with cost 1.0 .. 5.662

Values = [1, 2, 3, 4, 11, 33]
Coins = [1, 1, 0, 2, 2, 2]
Yes (29.26s cpu)
```

On the other hand, with the option `factor:0.2` instead of `factor:0.666` the above query exhibits the following behaviour:

```
[eclipse 13]: design_currency(Values, Coins).
Found a solution with cost 19
Found no solution with cost 1.0 .. 4.6

Values = [1, 2, 3, 4, 5, 6]
Coins = [1, 1, 0, 1, 0, 16]
Yes (8.78s cpu)
```

This confirms that, just as the **delta** option, the **factor** option can lead to incompleteness.

Other important options for **bb_min/2** control the strategy used in the branch and bound search and are in this sense more fundamental than **delta** and **factor**. These strategy options are:

- strategy:continue,
- strategy:restart,
- strategy:dichotomic.

The **continue** strategy is the default used by **minimize/2**: when a new optimum is found search continues from the same point as before. The **restart** strategy restarts the search whenever a new optimum is found. The consequence can be that parts of the search tree that have already been explored previously are explored again. However, because of the dynamic variable choice heuristics, restarting can be more efficient than continuing, if the tightened cost focusses the heuristic on the 'right' variables.

As an example consider the following quotation from Hardy [1992]:

I had ridden in taxi cab number 1729 and remarked that the number seemed to me rather a dull one, and that I hoped it was not an unfavorable omen. "No," he [Srinivasa Ramanujan] replied, "it is a very interesting number; it is the smallest number expressible as the sum of two cubes in two different ways."

To prove this property of 1729 it suffices to use the predicate **hardy/2** defined in Figure 12.9 in which the **restart** strategy is employed.

The answer is produced instantaneously:

```
[eclipse 14]: hardy([X1,X2,Y1,Y2], Z).
Found a solution with cost 1729
Found no solution with cost 2.0 .. 1728.0

X1 = 1
```

```
hardy([X1,X2,Y1,Y2], Z) :-
    X1 #> 0, X2 #> 0,
    Y1 #> 0, Y2 #> 0,
    X1 #\= Y1, X1 #\= Y2,
    X1^3 + X2^3 #= Z,
    Y1^3 + Y2^3 #= Z,
    bb_min(labeling([X1,X2,Y1,Y2]),
           Z,
           bb_options{strategy:restart}).
```

Fig. 12.9 The `hardy/2` predicate

```
X2 = 12
Y1 = 9
Y2 = 10
Z = 1729

Yes (0.01s cpu)
```

In contrast, if we try to solve this problem using the `continue` strategy instead, i.e., using the `minimize/2` built-in, the optimality of the solution is not computed in a meaningful amount of time.

Finally, the `dichotomic` strategy, like the `factor` option, seeks a faster improvement of the cost but without sacrificing optimality. With this strategy the search can seek improvements of the cost by, say, 10% or more, but if no solution is found, then the failed upper bound is set as a new lower bound, and the search resumes within the gap. On our scheduling example, dichotomic search with factor 0.9 gives the following trace:

```
Cost: 863 in time: 0.120999999999185
Cost: 811 in time: 0.201000000000931
Cost: 764 in time: 0.290999999997439
Cost: 716 in time: 0.421000000002095
Cost: 677 in time: 2.92500000000291
Found no solution with cost 349.0 .. 644.2
Found no solution with cost 644.2 .. 673.72
Found no solution with cost 673.72 .. 676
```

Other options are available and so are other versions of bb_min with more arguments that give the programmer even more control over the computations that deal with the optimisation.

12.7 When the number of variables is unknown

It is useful to realise that some constrained optimisation problems with finite domains cannot be solved by means of the branch and bound search. This is the case for COPs with an unknown number of variables. Such COPs can be easily generated in ECL^{i}PS^e. They still can be solved by means of the customary backtracking combined with the constraint propagation, without any use of the minimize/2 or bb_min/3 built-ins. As an example consider the following problem concerning natural numbers:

Problem Given m check whether it can be written as a sum of at least two different cubes. If yes, produce the smallest solution in the number of cubes.

Even if m is fixed, say 100, it is not clear what the number of variables of the corresponding CSP is. In other words, it not clear how to set up a CSP for which we are to find an optimal solution. In this case the most natural solution consists of systematically picking a candidate number n ∈ [2..m] and of trying to find an appropriate combination of n different cubes. This boils down to solving a CSP with n variables. If no such combination exists, the candidate number is incremented and the procedure is repeated.

We can limit the variable domains by noting that

$$x_1^3 + \cdots + x_n^3 = M \text{ and } 0 < x_1 < x_2 < \cdots < x_n$$

implies

$$x_n \le \lfloor \sqrt[3]{M} \rfloor \text{ and } n \le \lfloor \sqrt[3]{M} \rfloor,$$

where the latter holds since $n \le x_n$. To keep things simple in the program presented in Figure 12.10 we actually use $\lfloor \sqrt{M} \rfloor$ (as the expression fix(round(sqrt(M)))) as the bound, since the computation of $\lfloor \sqrt[3]{M} \rfloor$ would have to be programmed explicitly.

Then the following interaction with ECL^{i}PS^e shows that a solution exists for N equal to 1000 000, in contrast to N equal to 1000:

```
[eclipse 15]: cubes(1000000, Qs).

Qs = [16, 68, 88]
```

```
cubes(M, Qs) :-
    K is fix(round(sqrt(M))),
    N :: [2..K],
    indomain(N),
    length(Qs, N),
    Qs :: [1..K],
    increasing(Qs),
    ( foreach(Q,Qs),
      foreach(Expr,Exprs)
    do
      Expr = Q*Q*Q
    ),
    sum(Exprs) #= M,
    labeling(Qs), !.
```

augmented by the procedure **increasing/1** of Figure 12.3.

Fig. 12.10 The CUBES program

```
Yes (0.28s cpu)
[eclipse 16]: cubes(1000, Qs).

No (0.07s cpu)
```

12.8 Summary

In this chapter we explained how finite COPs can be solved using ECL^iPS^e. To this end we studied the facilities provided by the **branch_and_bound** library, notably the **minimize/2** built-in. It realises the basic form of the branch and bound search. We illustrated the use of **minimize/2** by considering the knapsack problem, the coins problem and the currency design problem originally introduced in Section 6.5. Also we showed how Sudoku puzzles can be generated in a simple way by combining constraint propagation with the branch and bound search.

Further, we introduced the **bb_min/3** built-in, of which **minimize/2** is a special case, that allows us to program various versions of the branch and bound search by selecting appropriate options. We also clarified that some finite domain COPs cannot be solved by means of the branch and bound search when the number of variables can be unknown. In that case the search for an optimal solution can be programmed using the customary backtracking combined with the constraint propagation.

12.9 Exercises

Exercise 12.1 Solving an optimisation problem sometimes requires a bit of experimentation. Consider the following program:

```
create_list_exprlist(N, List, ExprList) :-
    length(List, N),
    Max is 2*N,
    List :: 0 .. Max,
    alldifferent(List),
    ( for(C,1,N),
      for(D,N,1,-1),
      foreach(Var,List),
      foreach(Expr,ExprList)
    do
      Expr #= C*D*Var
    ).
```

Find minimal solutions to the following two problems:

(i) `prob1(List, Min) :-`
        `create_list_exprlist(9, List, ExprList),`
        `Min #= sum(ExprList).`

(ii) `prob2(List, Min) :-`
        `create_list_exprlist(16, List, ExprList),`
        `maxlist(ExprList,Min).`

`maxlist/2` is a built-in in the `ic` library for which `maxlist(List,X)` holds if X the maximum value of the list `List`.

Hint. Each of these problems calls for different `search/6` and `bb_min/3` strategies.

Exercise 12.2 Given an $n \times n$ chess board, find the *domination number*, which is the minimum number of queens needed to attack or occupy every square. For the 8×8 chess board, the queen's domination number is 5.

Exercise 12.3 Given an integer-sized square and a list of integer-sized square tiles pack the square with the tiles so that the number of uncovered unit squares is minimal.

13

Constraints on reals

13.1 Introduction

I N THE PREVIOUS three chapters we have assumed that the variables have finite domains. Accordingly all the problems have a finite search space which can be explored by instantiating the variables in all possible ways. In the next two chapters we will consider problems involving variables with infinite domains. Because the problem search space is no longer always finite, we may need to resort to different ways of solving these problems. In this chapter we consider constraints on reals, sometimes called constraints over ***continuous variables***.

Constraints on reals are sometimes handled by artificially discretising the domain, for example by only allowing 60 time points per hour, or distances in multiples of a metre. The resulting problem has finite domain variables and can be solved by labelling and propagation.

However, such a discretisation is artificial. More importantly, if an accurate solution is needed the discretisation needs to be fine, and then the variable domain sizes become huge, making the search space for labelling too large. The most important drawback of discretisation is that it may eliminate solutions completely! For example, suppose we discretise a continuous domain by admitting points which are exactly representable with N decimal places. Then any problem whose solutions are not exactly representable in this way becomes insoluble. A simple example would be to find a right angle triangle with two equal sides, and return the length of the hypotenuse: this has no solutions representable exactly to N decimal places.

Consequently, instead of the discretisation we rather modify the ingredients of the approach used so far, i.e. top-down search and constraint propagation.

13.2 Three classes of problems

In general, it is useful to distinguish three classes of problems involving continuous variables:

- those whose continuous variables are all dependent on other, finite domain, variables. These can be solved by searching for the values of the finite domain variables and then deriving the values of the continuous variables,
- those which have a finite search space, but involve mathematical constraints which yield real number values for the variables,
- those which have an infinite search space, and possibly infinitely many solutions, which can only be represented intensionally by means of formulas, for instance $0.0 \leq X \leq 10.0$.

Let us illustrate these problems by means of examples.

13.2.1 A problem with dependent continuous variables

We wish to build a cylindrical compost heap using a length of chicken wire. The volume of compost should be at least 2 cubic metres. The wire comes in lengths of 2, 3, 4 and 5 metres, and widths of 50, 100 and 200 centimetres. Which length and width of wire do we need?

The variables in this problem are the length of wire, L, the width W and the volume surrounded by the wire, V, see Figure 13.1.

The constraints are $L \in \{2, 3, 4, 5\}$, $W \in \{50, 100, 200\}$, $V \geq 2$ and $V = (W/100) * (L^2/(4 * \pi))$.

This problem can be solved in the usual way using search and propagation, as follows:

```
:- lib(ic).
:- lib(branch_and_bound).
```

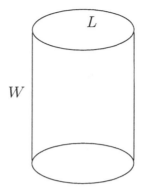

Fig. 13.1 A cylinder

```
compost_1(W, L, V) :-
    W :: [50, 100, 200],
    L :: 2..5,
    V $>= 2.0,
    V $= (W/100)*(L^2/(4*pi)),
    minimize(labeling([W,L]),V).
```

Notice that in ECL^{i}PS^e pi/0 is a built-in constant which returns the value of π.

We get then:

```
[eclipse 1]: compost_1(W, L, V).
Found a solution with cost
                  2.5464790894703251__2.546479089470326
Found no solution with cost
                  2.5464790894703251 .. 1.546479089470326

W = 200
L = 4
V = 2.5464790894703251__2.546479089470326

There are 6 delayed goals.
Yes (0.00s cpu)
```

So the generated solution reports a number of delayed goals. The reasons for this will be explained in Section 13.5. Also, the value of V is returned in the form of an interval.

13.2.2 A problem with a finite search space involving continuous variables

To illustrate this class of problems we use a simple geometrical problem. It involves two circles of radius 2, the first one centered on (0,0) and the second one centered on (1,1). We seek a pont that lies on both circles, and additionally lies to the right of the line $X = Y$:

```
circles(X, Y) :-
    4 $= X^2 + Y^2,
    4 $= (X - 1)^2 + (Y - 1)^2,
    X $>= Y.
```

The conjunction of these three constraints has exactly one solution, see Figure 13.2.

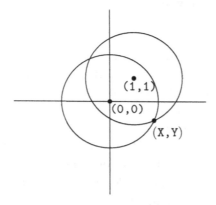

Fig. 13.2 Two intersecting circles

To solve this problem we must specify a form of search that focusses on the finite set of (two) potential solutions where the circles intersect. One form of search which achieves this is described in Section 13.4 below.

13.2.3 A problem with infinitely many solutions

The most general class of problems with continuous variables are problems that have an infinite space of potential – or actual – solutions.

By changing an input parameter, or a finite domain variable, into a continuous variable, many problems can be made infinite in this sense. For example, suppose in the compost heap problem the length and width of chicken wire are both continuous variables. We then seek pairs of values that yield a volume of 2:

```
compost_2(W, L) :-
    W :: 50.0..200.0,
    L :: 2.0..5.0,
    V $= 2.0,
    V $= (W/100)*(L^2/(4*pi)).
```

In this case ECL^{i}PS^e returns an interval of possible values for W and L:

```
[eclipse 2]: compost_2(W, L).

W = W{100.53096491487334 .. 200.0}
L = L{3.5449077018110313 .. 5.0}

There are 11 delayed goals.
Yes (0.00s cpu)
```

So, as in the discrete case, ECL^{i}PS^e returns a number of delayed goals. This answer means that there is no width below 100.53096491487334 and no length below 3.5449077018110313 from which we can build a 2 cubic metre compost heap. However, it is not possible to list all the pairs of values for W and L within the above intervals that yield a volume of 2 cubic metres. Instead, the delayed goals record additional constraints on the variables W and L that must be satisfied in any solution.

In this example *every* value for W in the final interval has a compatible value for L which together make up a solution to the problem. In general, it is not the case that all values in the final intervals form part of a solution. A trivial example is:

```
[eclipse 3]: [X, Y] :: -10.0 .. 10.0, X $= 1/Y.

X = X{-10.0 .. 10.0}
Y = Y{-10.0 .. 10.0}

There are 3 delayed goals.
Yes (0.00s cpu)
```

Clearly the delayed goals on X and Y are unsatisfiable for any value of Y in the interval -0.1 .. 0.1. We shall see in Section 13.4, to elicit compatible solutions for X and Y, this example requires some additional search and constraint propagation.

13.3 Constraint propagation

In principle to solve the constraints on continuous variables we can use the same constraint propagation techniques as the ones used before for finite domain variables. However, because the variable domains are infinite, additional complications can arise. First of all constraint propagation for the constraints on reals can be computationally costly because a single constraint propagation step may yield a very small reduction in the domain size of the variables. We can illustrate this very simply using an inconsistent pair of constraints. Consider the following definition:

```
incons(X, Y, Diff) :-
    [X,Y] :: 0.0..10.0,
    X $>= Y + Diff,
    Y $>= X + Diff.
```

If Diff > 0, then the query incons(X, Y, Diff) should fail even without any information about the domains of X and Y since X \$>= Y + Diff and Y \$>=X + Diff implies X \$>= X + 2*Diff. However, in the ic library each constraint is considered separately and the inconsistency is achieved only by the repeated shaving of the domain bounds of X and Y by the amount Diff. We can try smaller and smaller values of Diff and see how the time needed to detect the inconsistency grows. (The term 1e-n represents in ECL^{i}PS^e 10^{-n}.)

```
[eclipse 4]: incons(X, Y, 1e-4).
No (0.09s cpu)

[eclipse 5]: incons(X, Y, 1e-5).
No (0.82s cpu)

[eclipse 6]: incons(X, Y, 1e-6).
No (8.40s cpu)

[eclipse 7]: incons(X, Y, 1e-7).
No (159.81s cpu)

[eclipse 8]: incons(X, Y, 1e-8).

X = X{0.0 .. 10.0}
Y = Y{0.0 .. 10.0}
```

```
Delayed goals:
        ic : (Y{0.0 .. 10.0} - X{0.0 .. 10.0} =< -1e-8)
        ic : (-(Y{0.0 .. 10.0}) + X{0.0 .. 10.0} =< -1e-8)
Yes (0.00s cpu)
```

The increasing amount of time required to recognise the inconsistency for each query is due to the increasing number of constraint propagation steps required. The last query, shockingly, does not fail because instead of evaluating the constraints ECL^{i}PS^e delays them. This is, arguably, the most convenient behaviour because it would have taken an excessive amount of time to detect the inconsistency by means of the built-in constraint propagation.

The mechanism governing this process is a setting termed the **propagation threshold** which specifies a maximum amount by which the bounds of a variable may change without ECL^{i}PS^e actually updating the bounds and waking any delayed goals. The default propagation threshold is `1e-8`. The last query does not perform any constraint propagation because the change at the first step is too small and consequently no bound updates are performed.

For some applications the default threshold of `1e-8` is already too small (or too costly), and so the programmer has a facility to change this setting using the **set_threshold/1** built-in, for example:

```
[eclipse 9]: set_threshold(1e-3), incons(X, Y, 1e-4).

X = X{0.0 .. 10.0}
Y = Y{0.0 .. 10.0}

Delayed goals:
        ic : (Y{0.0 .. 10.0} - X{0.0 .. 10.0} =< -0.0001)
        ic : (-(Y{0.0 .. 10.0}) + X{0.0 .. 10.0} =< -0.0001)
Yes (0.00s cpu)
```

Controlling constraint propagation using the threshold is a question of experimentation, to be used in case the default threshold yields poor performance. One important point, however, is that changing the threshold cannot generate wrong answers. Any goals that are delayed are reported in the solution, and should remind the programmer that the solution is only true subject to these delayed constraints being satisfied.

13.4 Splitting one domain

Constraint propagation alone is not enough to solve constraint satisfaction problems on reals. Take for example the predicate `circles/2` discussed in Section 13.2. Constraint propagation produces an interval for each variable which includes both solutions and all the points in between:

```
[eclipse 10]:  circles(X, Y).


X = X{-1.0000000000000004 .. 2.0000000000000004}
Y = Y{-1.0000000000000004 .. 2.0000000000000004}


There are 13 delayed goals.
Yes (0.00s cpu)
```

To isolate the unique solution properly it is necessary to split the domain of X into two halves and try each domain separately:

```
[eclipse 11]:  circles(X, Y), (X $>= 1.5 ; X $=< 1.5).


X = X{1.8228756488546369 .. 1.8228756603552694}
Y = Y{-0.82287567032498 .. -0.82287564484820042}


There are 12 delayed goals.
Yes (0.00s cpu, solution 1, maybe more) ? ;


No (0.00s cpu)
```

So the first subdomain, with X >= 1.5, tightens the lower bound on X and enables the constraint propagation to reduce the domain of X to the interval

```
1.8228756488546369 .. 1.8228756603552694
```

and the domain of Y to the interval

```
-0.82287567032498 .. -0.82287564484820042.
```

The second subdomain, with X =< 1.5, tightens the upper bound on X and enables the constraint propagation to detect that there is no solution in this domain for X. Supplementing this computation by a reasoning showing that a unique solution exists we can conclude that this solution lies in the rectangle determined by the above two intervals. So even though we did not compute the precise solution we could determine its location with a very high degree of precision.

Domain splitting can also be effective for problems with infinitely many solutions, as illustrated by the example $X = 1/Y$ introduced in Section 13.2. In this case we need to split the domain into three subdomains, $X \leq -\epsilon$, $-\epsilon \leq X \leq \epsilon$ and $\epsilon \leq X$ for some small ϵ. With this splitting we can achieve a precise cover of the solution set:[1]

```
[eclipse 12]: [X, Y] :: -10.0..10.0, X $= 1/Y,
              (X :: -inf .. -0.001
              ;
               X :: -0.001 .. 0.001
              ;
               X :: 0.001 .. inf
              ).


X = X{-10.0 .. -0.099999999999999992}
Y = Y{-10.0 .. -0.099999999999999992}


There are 4 delayed goals.
Yes (0.00s cpu, solution 1, maybe more) ? ;


X = X{0.099999999999999992 .. 10.0}
Y = Y{0.099999999999999992 .. 10.0}


There are 4 delayed goals.
Yes (0.00s cpu, solution 2)
```

13.5 Search

For continuous variables a general search method is to associate with each variable a domain in the form of an interval of possible values, and at each search node to narrow one interval. Complete search can be maintained by exploring a different subinterval at each subbranch, but ensuring that the union of the subintervals covers the input interval at the node.

Because the domains are continuous, this search tree is infinitely deep: you can go on dividing an interval forever without reducing it to a point. Consequently a *precision* has to be specified which is the maximum allowed width of any interval on completion of the search. During the search, when the interval associated with a variable is smaller than this precision, this

---

[1] inf is the built-in representation of the infinity.

variable is never selected again. Search stops when all the variables have intervals smaller than the precision.

If the search fails after exploring all the alternative subintervals at each node, then (assuming the subintervals cover the input interval at the node) this represents a proof that the problem has no solution. In other words, the search failure for continuous variables is sound.

On the other hand if the search stops without failure, this is no guarantee that there really is a solution within the final intervals of the variables (unless they are all reduced by constraint propagation to a single point). A similar phenomenon has already been illustrated in Section 13.3 using the `incons/3` predicate, where constraint propagation stops even though there is no solution satisfying the constraints.

Accordingly each answer to a problem on reals is in fact only a ***conditional solution***. It has two components:

- A real interval for each variable. Each interval is smaller than the given precision.
- A set of constraints in the form of delayed goals. These constraints are neither solved nor unsatisfiable when considered on the final real intervals.

An example is the answer to the query No. 9 in the previous section.

13.6 The built-in search predicate `locate`

Naturally ECL^{i}PS^e provides a built-in predicate `locate/2` that makes it easy to search over continuous variables. This built-in recursively splits the domains of specified variables until their sizes fall within the specified precision.

The simplest version of `locate/2` has two arguments, specifying a list of variables to search on, and a final precision. Let us illustrate its use by considering the problem of finding zeroes of the polynomial $2*x^5-5*x^4+5$, depicted in Figure 13.3.

The difficulty lies in the fact that in general, by the celebrated Galois' theorem, the zeroes of polynomials of degree higher than four cannot be expressed as radicals, that is by means of the four arithmetic operations and the root extraction. In fact, $2*x^5-5*x^4+5$ is one of such polynomials, found in the nineteenth century by the Norwegian mathematician Niels Henrik Abel. To cope with this problem we shall ask for the (conditional) solutions in the form of intervals. To ensure an acceptable computation time we search for solutions within the interval `-1000000.0 .. 1000000.0`. In ECL^{i}PS^e

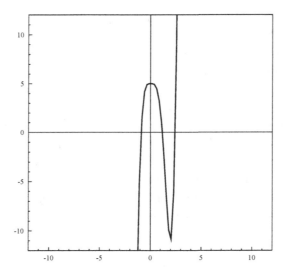

Fig. 13.3 The diagram of the polynomial $2 * x^5 - 5 * x^4 + 5$

we can represent this interval using the syntax 1e-6 .. 1e6, and so the problem is set up as follows:

```
abel(X) :-
    X :: -1e6 .. 1e6,
    2*X^5 - 5*X^4 + 5 $= 0.
```

Firstly we set the search precision to 1.0. This is sufficient to distinguish one of the solutions from the others:

```
[eclipse 13]: abel(X), locate([X], 1.0).

X = X{-0.92435801492603964 .. -0.92435801492602809}

There are 5 delayed goals.
Yes (0.00s cpu, solution 1, maybe more) ;

X = X{1.1711620684831605 .. 2.4280727927074546}

There are 5 delayed goals.
Yes (0.00s cpu, solution 2)
```

The delayed goals specify the additional conditions on X under which the query is satisfied. To separate out all three solutions we use a smaller precision, such as 0.001:

```
[eclipse 14]: abel(X), locate([X], 0.001).
```

```
X = X{-0.92435801492603964 .. -0.92435801492602809}
```

```
There are 5 delayed goals.
Yes (0.00s cpu, solution 1, maybe more) ;
```

```
X = X{1.1711620684831605 .. 1.1711620684832094}
There are 5 delayed goals.
Yes (0.00s cpu, solution 2, maybe more) ;
```

```
X = X{2.4280727927071966 .. 2.4280727927074546}
There are 5 delayed goals.
Yes (0.01s cpu, solution 3)
```

13.7 Shaving

While constraint propagation and domain splitting work fine on many problems, there are problems where even for very narrow intervals constraint propagation is unable to recognise infeasibility. The consequence is that too many alternative conditional solutions are returned.

The following predicate encodes the so-called Reimer's system:

```
reimer(X, Y, Z) :-
    [X,Y,Z] :: -1.0 .. 1.0,
    X^2 - Y^2 + Z^2 $= 0.5,
    X^3 - Y^3 + Z^3 $= 0.5,
    X^4 - Y^4 + Z^4 $= 0.5.
```

We will search for the solutions using the ECL^{i}PS^e query

```
reimer(X, Y, Z), locate([X,Y,Z], Prec).
```

for different levels of precision Prec. The number of conditional solutions returned for different levels of precision – i.e. different final interval widths – are presented in Table 13.1.

For the wide intervals it is clear that several solutions are being captured within a single interval, and decreasing the interval width increases the number of distinct conditional solutions. At a width of around 1e-10 the intervals are narrow enough to detect that certain conditional solutions are infeasible,

search precision	solution count	CPU seconds
1.0	6	0.09
0.01	8	2.08
1e-5	13	5.41
1e-8	11	7.23
1e-10	10	7.80
1e-12	11	8.25
1e-14	24	8.61

Table 13.1 Reimer's problem without shaving

so the number of distinct conditional solutions decreases. However, as the intervals become narrower many narrow intervals are returned in the vicinity of each actual solution. These figures would lead one to believe that the problem has 10 distinct real solutions, but this is surprisingly not the case.

To clarify these matters we return to the predicate `squash/3` which we encountered previously in Subsection 10.3.2. This predicate implements a special form of constraint propagation, called **shaving**, where a variable is constrained to take a value – or to lie within a narrow interval – near its bound (upper or lower), and the results of this constraint are propagated to the other variables to determine whether the problem is still feasible. If not, the domain of the original variable is reduced to exclude the infeasible region and constraint propagation continues.

For constraints on continuous variables shaving is a very important technique. Recall that the arguments of the `squash/3` predicate are:

- a list of variables to which this constraint propagation technique is applied,
- an interval width – the size of the region within which the variable is constrained to lie during propagation,
- a parameter which can take two values, `lin` or `log`. This parameter guides the way domains are split. If it is set to `lin`, the split is linear (i.e. the arithmetic mean of the bounds is used). If it is set to `log`, the split is logarithmic (i.e., the geometric mean of the bounds is used).[2]

To demonstrate its effect we will tackle Reimer's problem again, but this time applying shaving to the intervals returned by the search routine. We will again try different precisions for `locate/2` and for `squash/3` we will use

---

[2] Recall that the arithmetic mean of a and b is $(a + b)/2$ while the geometric mean of a and b is $\sqrt{a \cdot b}$.

an interval width of 1e-15. For the third parameter we will always choose
the value `lin`. The query is thus:

```
reimer(X, Y, Z), locate([X,Y,Z], Prec),
squash([X,Y,Z], 1e-15, lin).
```

search precision	solution count	CPU seconds
1.0	4	6.34
0.01	4	7.56
1e-5	4	8.58
1e-10	4	8.66
1e-14	16	8.44

Table 13.2 Reimer's problem with shaving

Clearly there are at most four different solutions. The shaving procedure
removes infeasible intervals. Note, however, that very narrow intervals very
close to a real solution still cannot be removed by `squash/3`. In particular,
if we set the precision to 1e-14, then we get 16 conditional solutions.

Shaving can be used as a (polynomial) alternative to the (exponential)
interval splitting method of narrowing intervals. Because it does not introduce extra choice points it applies well to problems of the second class
introduced in Section 13.2, that is problems which have a finite search space
but involve mathematical constraints.

As another example of the use of shaving we shall consider a program that
has been often used to illustrate solving constraints on continuous variables.
The program specifies a financial application, concerning how to pay off a
mortgage, and is given in Figure 13.4.

It expresses the relationship between the four variables:

`Loan` (the loan),
`Payment` (the fixed monthly amount paid off),
`Interest` (fixed, but compounded, monthly interest rate),
`Time` (the time in months taken to pay off a loan).

Three of the variables are continuous, `Loan`, `Payment` and `Interest`, and
the other, `Time`, is integer valued.

This program can be used in many ways, for example to compute the
duration of a given loan. To answer this question we need to ask for the

```
mortgage(Loan, _Payment, _Interest, 0) :-
    Loan $= 0.

mortgage(Loan, Payment, Interest, Time) :-
    Loan $> 0,
    Time $>= 1,
    NewLoan $= Loan*(1+Interest) - Payment,
    NewTime $= Time - 1,
    mortgage(NewLoan, Payment, Interest, NewTime).
```

Fig. 13.4 The MORTGAGE program

amount of time needed to pay off *at least* the borrowed amount, as in the
following query:

```
[eclipse 15]: minimize((X $>= 50000, X$=< 50700,
                        mortgage(X, 700, 0.01, T)),
                       T).
Found a solution with cost 126
Found no solution with cost -1.0Inf .. 125

X = 50019.564804291353__50019.56480429232
T = 126
Yes (0.06s cpu)
```

Note that the query mortgage(50000, 700, 0.01, T) simply fails, since
the payments of 700 do not add up to 50000 precisely.

It is more difficult to compute the required regular payment from a fixed
loan, interest rate and payoff time. At least we know the payment is greater
than 0 and less than the total loan, so we can provide an initial interval for
it:

```
[eclipse 16]: Payment :: 0.0 .. 200000.0,
              mortgage(200000, Payment, 0.01, 360).

Payment = Payment{0.0 .. 200000.0}

There are 718 delayed goals.
Yes (0.02s cpu, solution 1, maybe more) ? ;
```

No (0.02s cpu)

This is completely uninformative. Similarly, we may want to compute the actual interest rate corresponding to a given loan, regular payment and time. Also here we can provide an initial interval for the interest rate, between 0.0 and 1.0:

```
[eclipse 17]: Interest :: 0.0 .. 1.0,
              mortgage(60000, 1500, Interest, 60).

Interest = Interest{0.0 .. 0.5}

There are 257 delayed goals.
Yes (0.01s cpu, solution 1, maybe more) ? ;

No (0.01s cpu)
```

Again the answer is completely uninformative. However, using shaving we can extract solutions to both queries with a high degree of precision:

```
[eclipse 18]: Payment :: 0.0 .. 200000.0,
              mortgage(200000, Payment, 0.01, 360),
              squash([Payment], 1e-5, log).

Payment = Payment{2057.1348846043343 .. 2057.2332029240038}

There are 360 delayed goals.
Yes (3.72s cpu, solution 1, maybe more) ? ;

No (3.72s cpu)

[eclipse 19]: Interest :: 0.0 .. 1.0,
              mortgage(60000, 1500, Interest, 60),
              squash([Interest], 1e-5, log).

Interest = Interest{0.0143890380859375 .. 0.01439666748046875}

There are 237 delayed goals.
Yes (14.48s cpu, solution 1, maybe more) ? ;

No (14.48s cpu)
```

13.8 Optimisation on continuous variables

The branch and bound procedure embodied in the `minimize/2` and `bb_min/3` built-ins introduced in Chapter 12 relies on the fact that the search procedure instantiates the variable constrained to the cost function. (Otherwise a run-time error results.) In the case of constraints on continuous variables this cannot be guaranteed. Indeed, in general the search stops when all the variables have intervals smaller than the chosen precision. As a result these two built-ins cannot be used directly for optimisation on continuous variables. In this section we will outline one way of adapting them to cope with a continuous optimisation function.

In the case of constraints on continuous variables the backtracking process systematically returns conditional solutions in the form of 'small' boxes (of size smaller than the precision). When searching for an optimum of a continuous cost function, with each box an interval for the cost function is returned. To ensure that the the variable constrained to the cost function is instantiated, we set it each time to the lower bound of this returned interval. After this modification we can reuse the previous routine.

What can we conclude about the results produced by a so-modified branch and bound procedure? If the sets of constraints associated with each returned box are all satisfiable, we know that upon termination of this modified branch and bound the minimum lies in the interval of the size of the set precision, with the lower bound `Min`.

However, if some (possibly all) of these sets of constraints are unsatisfiable, we can only use the final value `Min` of the cost function as a conditional lower bound: we do not know whether an actual solution exists, but if it does then the value of the cost function is at least `Min`.

To clarify this approach suppose, for example, we wish to minimize some expression involving the variables X and Y under the following constraints, expressed in ECL^iPS^e:

```
cons(X, Y) :-
    [X,Y] :: -100.0 .. 100.0,
    X*2 + 2*Y^2  $< 10,
    X + 3*Y $=< 5,
    2*X - Y $=< 10.
```

Suppose, furthermore, we search for a solution by using `locate/2` to recursively split the intervals associated with the variables X and Y, using

```
locate([X,Y], 0.01).
```

During branch and bound search, whenever a conditional solution is returned, it will associate an interval with each of X and Y. If we introduce a new variable OptExpr constrained to be equal to the expression being optimised, then constraint propagation will produce an interval for OptExpr. Since we are minimising, the lower bound of this interval is the best possible solution found so far – if it is feasible! We use this lower bound to constrain the value of the optimised expression from now on. If no better solution is found, then the conditional solution returned is the last returned best conditional solution.

The appropriate optimisation predicate opt_1 can be encoded using the minimize/2 built-in introduced in Section 12.1:

```
opt_1(Query, Expr, Min) :-
    OptExpr $= eval(Expr),
    minimize(( Query, get_min(OptExpr,Min) ), Min).
```

Recall from Section 9.6 that the eval/1 built-in indicates that its argument is a variable that will be bound to an expression at the run-time. We can now solve our constrained optimisation problem. To be specific suppose the optimisation function is 6-X:

```
[eclipse 20]: cons(X, Y),
              opt_1( locate([X,Y], 0.01), (6-X), Min ).

Found a solution with cost 5.9977375094284113
Found a solution with cost 4.9949650990605292
Found a solution with cost 3.9640446836405561
Found a solution with cost 2.9593568281590485
Found a solution with cost 1.9412953187340669
Found no solution with cost -1.0Inf .. 0.94129531873406691

X = X{3.9941057914745426 .. 4.0587046812659331}
Y = Y{-0.0012435228262296953 .. 0.0044940668232825009}
Min = 1.9412953187340669

There are 4 delayed goals.
Yes (6.08s cpu)
```

This output shows that optimality (even in the conditional sense) has not exactly been proven: there is no solution with a value less than 0.941 295 318 734 066 91, but there is a gap between this and the best conditional solution found, which is 1.941 295 318 734 0669. The reason is that the branch and bound default is tailored for integer problems: it seeks a

solution which is a whole unit (i.e., 1.0) better than the previous one. So we
can only conclude that no minimum below 0.941 295 318 734 066 91 exists.

For continuous problems it therefore makes sense to override the default
and specify a minimum improvement sought at each step. The smaller
the improvement the nearer the procedure can guarantee to come to the
actual optimum (if it exists). However, smaller improvements can result in
increased solving times.

We conclude this chapter by encoding a modified optimisation procedure
that gives the programmer control over the required improvement at each
step. The appropriate optimisation predicate uses the **bb_min/3** built-in:

```
opt_2(Query, Expr, Improvement, Min) :-
    OptExpr $= eval(Expr),
    bb_min(( Query, get_min(OptExpr,Min) ),
            Min,
            bb_options{delta:Improvement}).
```

By choosing an improvement of first 0.5 and then 0.1 we can illustrate the
advantage of smaller improvements:[3]

```
[eclipse 21]: cons(X, Y),
              opt_2(locate([X, Y], 0.01), (6-X), 0.5, Min).


Found a solution with cost 5.9977375094284113


... 9 intermediate solutions


Found no solution with cost -1.0Inf .. 0.7349623277551629


X = X{4.6891966915344225 .. 4.7650376722448371}
Y = Y{-0.0012435228262296953 .. 0.0044940668232825009}
Min = 1.2349623277551629


There are 4 delayed goals.
Yes (6.16s cpu)

[eclipse 22]: cons(X, Y),
              opt_2(locate([X, Y], 0.01), (6-X), 0.1, Min).
```

---

[3] In this problem both queries happen to take a similar time: this is because the branch and
bound is not causing any pruning of the search space. Sometimes a branch and bound search
with more intermediate solutions takes an exponentially longer time.

```
Found a solution with cost 5.9977375094284113

... 42 intermediate solutions

Found no solution with cost -1.0Inf .. 0.97958067273231519

X = X{4.8421052712298724 .. 4.9204193272676848}
Y = Y{-0.0012435228262296953 .. 0.0044940668232825009}
Min = 1.0795806727323152

There are 4 delayed goals.
Yes (6.02s cpu)
```

Because the computed minima are only conditional (subject to the delayed constraints) we can only conclude that no minimum below 0.979 580 672 732 315 19 exists.

13.9 Summary

In this chapter we discussed the problem of solving constraints on reals. To this end we considered in turn:

- three natural classes of problems involving continuous variables,
- constraint propagation on continuous variables,
- search,
- optimisation over continuous optimisation functions.

We also indicated the importance of a specialised constraint propagation technique, called shaving.

In the process we introduced the following built-ins:

- the constant **pi**, which represents in ECL^{i}PS^e π,
- the number and exponent syntax for real numbers, e.g. **1e-8**,
- **set_threshold/1**, used to set the propagation threshold,
- **locate/2**, to perform search over continuous variables,
- **squash/3**, to perform shaving.

13.10 Exercises

Exercise 13.1 When optimising using the predicate **opt_2/3** defined in Section 13.8, it is necessary to compromise. A tighter precision means more optimisation steps, but a looser precision means there may be no feasible solution in the conditional solution returned at each branch and bound step.

Extend the definition of opt_2(Query, Expr, Imp) to include a call to squash(Vars, 1e-8, log) each time a new conditional solution is returned by branch and bound. Apply it to the list of the variables appearing in Query.

Exercise 13.2 Apply the same modification to minimise the expression $X^2 + (1/Y)^2$ under the constraints $X, Y \in -10.0\ldots 10.0$, $X * Y = 1$.

Exercise 13.3 A piano with length L and width W has to be moved around a right-angle corner in a corridor, see Figure 13.5. Coming into the corner the corridor has width $Corr1$ and going out it has a possibly different width $Corr2$. Given $L = 2, W = 1$ and $Corr1 = 1.5$, what is the minimum value for $Corr2$?

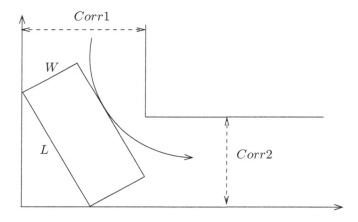

Fig. 13.5 A corridor

To make this a little easier here are the underlying mathematical constraints.

- The 'envelope' of the piano as it moves around the corner can be expressed in terms of a variable T. The envelope describes two coordinates X and Y as follows:
  $X = W * T^3 + L * (1 - T^2)^{1/2}$,
  $Y = L * T + W * (1 - T^2)^{3/2}$.
- At the critical point $X = Corr1$ and $Y = Corr2$.
- T can take values in the interval $MinT \,..\, MaxT$, where

$$MinT = \left(1/2 - \frac{(9*W^2 - 4*L^2)^{1/2}}{6*W}\right)^{1/2},$$

$$MaxT = \left(1/2 + \frac{(9*W^2 - 4*L^2)^{1/2}}{6*W}\right)^{1/2}.$$

The problem is then to write a predicate which finds the minimum possible value for $Corr2$, taking parameters W, L and $Corr1$.

Linear constraints over continuous and integer variables

14.1 Introduction

WE ALREADY DISCUSSED linear constraints on reals in Section 6.3 and used them in Subsection 6.5.4 to formalise the facility location problem. These constraints form an important class because of their wide range of applicability. As a result over many years in the field of operation research several efficient methods have been developed for handling them and ways of modelling problems using only constraints of this form have been devised. In contrast, the problem of solving linear constraints over integer variables is in general NP-complete and as a result can be used to express any constraint satisfaction problem.

There exist both scalable polynomial algorithms for solving linear constraints on reals and, in principle exponential, 'Simplex'-based algorithms which are both scalable and can be embedded in branch and bound algorithms for handling linear constraints over integer variables, see, e.g., Papadimitriou and Steiglitz [1982].

Linear constraints together with integrality constraints[1] are at the core of

---

[1] An integrality constraint on a variable enforces the variable to take an integer value.

Operational Research. There are several software packages available which perform constraint solving and search on problems expressed in terms of linear and integrality constraints. ECL^{i}PS^e provides an interface to the Xpress-MP package from Dash Optimisation, which was used to design and run the examples in this book. It also provides an interface to the CPLEX package from ILOG.

These interfaces are available through the ECL^{i}PS^e library **eplex** that consists of the **eplex** constraint mapping module augmented with a number of auxiliary built-ins that facilitate interaction with the external solver. In this chapter we discuss the **eplex** library and illustrate its use to solve problems that deal both with linear and non-linear constraints on integers and reals.

14.2 The eplex library

14.2.1 Motivation

To properly motivate the **eplex** library note first the following limitation of the **ic** library. Consider the predicate

```
incons(W, X, Y, Z) :-
    W+X+Y+Z $>= 10,
    W+X+Y $= 5,
    Z $=< 4.
```

Clearly the query incons(W, X, Y, Z) should fail. However, when we invoke it using the **ic** library we get the following outcome:

```
[eclipse 1]: [W,X,Y,Z]:: 0..10, incons(W, X, Y, Z).

W = W{0 .. 5}
X = X{0 .. 5}
Y = Y{0 .. 5}
Z = Z{0 .. 4}

Delayed goals:
        ic : (-(Z{0 .. 4}) - Y{0 .. 5} - X{0 .. 5} - W{0 .. 5}
            =< -10)
        ic : (Y{0 .. 5} + X{0 .. 5} + W{0 .. 5} =:= 5)
Yes (0.00s cpu)
```

So the inconsistency cannot be detected in `ic` without search. This is in contrast to the `eplex` solver. To execute the query `incons(W, X, Y, Z)` using `eplex` the appropriate ECL^{i}PS^e code is :

```
[eclipse 2]: eplex_solver_setup(min(0)),
             incons(W, X, Y, Z),
             eplex_solve(_).
```

```
No (0.00s cpu)
```

So the `eplex` solver correctly detects the inconsistency even without any initial domains for the variables.

A key difference is that, in contrast to `ic`, the `eplex` solver only handles constraints *after* it has been explicitly initialised by the program. (The rationale for this facility is that the same program can initialise more than one linear solver 'instance' through the `eplex` library, and send different constraints to different instances.) The first line initialises the `eplex` solver by stating whether one searches for a minimum of the cost function or a maximum.

In general, the argument of the `eplex_solver_setup/1` built-in is either `min(Cost)` or `max(Cost)`, where the `Cost` variable is constrained to the expression defining the cost function. In our example we are not interested in the finding an optimal solution, so just use `0` as the cost function. The last line launches the `eplex` solver using the `eplex_solve/1` built-in. In general its argument returns the optimal value of the expression defining the cost function and specified at setup time. Here we are not interested in the optimal value, so use an anonymous variable as the argument.

14.2.2 Accessing solver information

The `eplex` library admits variable declarations and a limited form of linear constraints, using the same syntax as the `ic` library. The following classes of constraints are not supported:

- the integer versions of linear constraints, such as `X #=< Y`,
- strict inequalities and disequality, so `X $< Y`, `X $\= Y`, `X $> Y`,
- Boolean constraints,
- reified constraints.

Let us give now an example of a successful evaluation using `eplex`:

```
[eclipse 3]: eplex_solver_setup(min(0)),
```

```
                    W+X+Y+Z $>= 10,
                    W+X+Y $= 5,
                    Z $=< 6,
                    eplex_solve(_).


W = W{-1e+20 .. 1e+20 @ 5.0}
X = X{-1e+20 .. 1e+20 @ 0.0}
Y = Y{-1e+20 .. 1e+20 @ 0.0}
Z = Z{-1e+20 .. 6.0 @ 5.0}
Yes (0.00s cpu)
```

The `eplex` solver does not tighten the domains of the variables, except for Z whose upper bound is explicitly set by the constraint `Z $=< 6`. However, it does compute a solution which satisfies all the constraints, and this solution is shown in the output, after the @ sign: `W = 5.0, X = 0.0, Y = 0.0, Z = 5.0`. In fact this is just one solution and there are many others, for example `W = 0.0, X = 5.0, Y = 0.0, Z = 5.0`.

In other words, the solution computed by `eplex` satisfies the constraints, but is not entailed by them. Many problems tackled by `eplex` have infinitely many solutions and it is impossible to generate all of them. Consequently `eplex` does not provide any means of computing alternative solutions, for example using backtracking. On the other hand, `eplex` does provide a mechanism for extracting the current solution, using the `eplex_var_get/3` built in:

```
[eclipse 4]: eplex_solver_setup(min(0)),
                    W+X+Y+Z $>= 10,
                    W+X+Y $= 5,
                    Z $=< 6,
                    eplex_solve(_),
                    eplex_var_get(W, typed_solution, Val).


...
Val = 5.0
Yes (0.00s cpu)
```

Alternatively, it is possible to extract information about the complete solver state using the `eplex_get/2` built-in:[2]

```
[eclipse 5]: eplex_solver_setup(min(0)),
```

---

[2] In this output, for brevity and clarity, we have set the variable printing options not to display any of the variable attributes.

```
                    W+X+Y+Z $>= 10,
                    W+X+Y $= 5,
                    Z $=< 6,
                    eplex_solve(_),
                    eplex_get(constraints, Cons),
                    eplex_get(vars, Vars),
                    eplex_get(typed_solution, Vals).
```

```
...
Cons = [Y + X + W =:= 5.0, Z + Y + X + W >= 10.0]
Vars = ''(W, X, Y, Z)
Vals = ''(5.0, 0.0, 0.0, 5.0)
Yes (0.00s cpu)
```

Often it is useful to instantiate the problem variables to the **eplex** solution, which can be done using the following predicate:

```
return_solution :-
    eplex_get(vars, Vars),
    eplex_get(typed_solution, Vals),
    Vars = Vals.
```

14.2.3 Integrality constraints

Handling integer variables dramatically increases the range of problems that can be solved using **eplex**, but they also require very different solving methods. Integrality constraints in the resulting class of optimisation problems, called *mixed integer programming* problems, cannot in general be solved without resorting to search. They are dealt with within the **eplex** solver using a search method transparent to the user.

A domain declaration with integer bounds does *not* automatically impose integrality within **eplex**, in order to leave the option open for the integrality to be imposed by another solver or search routine. To impose an integrality constraint on a list **List** of variables in **eplex** it is necessary to explicitly call **integers(List)**.

Consider a simple example:

```
lptest(W, X) :-
    eplex_solver_setup(min(X)),
    [W,X] :: 0..10,
    2*W+X $= 5,
```

```
eplex_solve(_),
return_solution.
```

Neither W nor X are constrained to be integers. The optimal solution returned by `eplex` is W = 2.5, X = 0.0. For this query ECL^{i}PS^e issues a warning:

```
[eclipse 6]: lptest(W, X).
```

```
WARNING: Imposing integer bounds on variable(s) [W, X]
for eplex instance eplex does not impose integer type.
```

```
W = 2.5
X = 0.0
Yes (0.02s cpu)
```

In the definition of `miptest/2` below, the integrality of W *is* enforced in `eplex`:

```
miptest(W, X) :-
    eplex_solver_setup(min(X)),
    [W,X] :: 0.0..10.0,
    integers([W]),
    2*W+X $= 5,
    eplex_solve(_),
    return_solution.
```

Now the solver performs a mixed integer programming algorithm and finds an optimal solution with W integral:

```
[eclipse 7]: miptest(W, X).
```

```
W = 2
X = 1.0
Yes (0.00s cpu)
```

The internal (branch and bound) search method involving integer variables is as follows.

(i) Solve the linear constraints in **eplex**, as if all the variables were continuous.

(ii) From the solution select an integer variable, W, whose **eplex** value *val* is non-integral. If there is no such variable the problem is solved.

(iii) Let val^{int} be the smallest integer larger than val and val_{int} the largest integer smaller than val. Then $val^{int} = val_{int} + 1$.

Make a search choice: add either the constraint $W \geq val^{int}$ or the constraint $W \leq val_{int}$. Return to (i). On backtracking try the alternative choice.

(iv) To find an optimal solution, use the branch and bound search described in Subsection 6.6.3.

14.3 Solving satisfiability problems using `eplex`

Thanks to the integrality constraints the `eplex` solver can also be used to solve sets of Boolean constraints. The underlying computation relies on the branch and bound search. Usually, a different representation is used, called a ***propositional satisfiability problem***. It involves Boolean variables and one deals with sets of ***clauses*** which in this case denote arbitrary disjunctions of literals. In turn, a ***literal*** is either a variable or a negated variable.

The encoding is simple: Boolean variables are modelled as 0-1 variables; a negated variable `not X` is modelled as `1-X` and a clause, say `X or Y or Z`, is encoded as an inequality `X+Y+Z $>= 1`. For example, the satisfiability problem

```
X or Y,
Y or Z,
Z or X,
not X or not Y,
not Y or not Z,
```

is modelled in `eplex` as follows:

```
sat(X, Y, Z) :-
    eplex_solver_setup(min(0)),
    integers([X,Y,Z]),
    [X,Y,Z] :: 0..1,
    X+Y $>= 1,   Y+Z $>= 1,   Z+X $>= 1,
    (1-X) + (1-Y) $>= 1, (1-Y) + (1-Z) $>= 1,
    eplex_solve(_),
    return_solution.
```

Running the query `sat(X, Y, Z)` yields a unique solution:

```
[eclipse 8]: sat(X, Y, Z).
```

```
X = 1
Y = 0
Z = 1
Yes (0.01s cpu)
```

14.4 Repeated solver waking

The most interesting uses of the linear constraint solver are ones where a set of linear constraints appears as part of a larger problem with other complicating constraints. One way of exploiting the linear constraints is to solve the linear subproblem at each node within a branch and bound search. New linear constraints may be added on the different branches below the node and an extended linear problem can be solved at each subnode.

14.4.1 A simple non-linear problem

To illustrate this on a toy example, we modify the previous problem and amend the minimisation expression, so as to minimise not X but $W + \sqrt{X}$ instead. Because the square root function is non-linear it cannot be represented within eplex. The simplest approach seems to be to minimise $W + X$, and instead of returning the value of $W + X$ as the optimum, to return $W + \sqrt{X}$. Unfortunately the solution that minimises $W + \sqrt{X}$ is not, in general, the solution that minimises $W + X$. Indeed, reconsider the constraints in our previous example:

```
cons(W, X) :-
    [W,X] :: 0..10,
    integers([W]),
    2*W+X $= 5.
```

The minimum value of $W + X$ is 3, when $X = 1$, but the minimum value of $W + \sqrt{X}$ is approximately 2.24, when $X = 5$. To find the true minimum we include a variable $SqrtX$ in our model, and use a *linear approximation* of the constraint $SqrtX = \sqrt{X}$. A linear approximation is, of course, a set of linear constraints that approximate the non-linear constraint.

For this problem we generate new linear constraints during search which are added to the initial linear approximation to make it better and better. Search stops when the optimal values of X and $SqrtX$ which satisfy the current linear approximation are 'near enough' in the sense that $abs(SqrtX - \sqrt{X}) \leq \epsilon$. In what follows we choose for ϵ the value 1e-5.

Our non-linear search `nlsearch/2` is thus defined by two clauses. The first one states that the search can halt when the absolute difference between $SqrtX$ and $\sqrt{X}$ is no more than ϵ:

```
nlsearch(X, SqrtX) :-
    eplex_var_get(X, solution, Val),
    eplex_var_get(SqrtX, solution, SqrtVal),
    abs(sqrt(Val)-SqrtVal) =< 1e-5, !,
    return_solution.
```

If the difference is not small enough, then search continues by making a choice, adding some additional linear constraints, and searching further. This is the second clause defining `nlsearch/2` which, because of the cut in the previous clause, is only taken if the gap is still not small enough:

```
nlsearch(X, SqrtX) :-
    make_choice(X),
    add_linear_cons(X, SqrtX),
    nlsearch(X, SqrtX).
```

The predicates used in this second clause are defined as follows.

- `make_choice/1`.

  The idea is to reduce the interval associated with X at each search step until the linear constraints on the square root sufficiently closely approximate the actual square root. This is achieved by simply splitting the interval associated with X at its current `eplex` value:

```
make_choice(X) :-
    eplex_var_get(X, solution, Val),
    ( X $>= Val ; X $=< Val ).
```

- `add_linear_cons/2`.

  This constraint adds a better and better approximation to the non-linear constraint $SqrtX = \sqrt{X}$. Because the square root of X increases with X, we can constrain the square root of X to fall within the range $[\sqrt{Min}..\sqrt{Max}]$, where $[Min..Max]$ is the current domain of X. Moreover, we also have $\sqrt{X} \cdot \sqrt{Min} \leq X$ and $\sqrt{X} \cdot \sqrt{Max} \geq X$.

  We can express these constraints using the `eplex_var_get_bounds/3` built-in that extracts the bounds of an `eplex` variable:

```
add_linear_cons(X, SqrtX) :-
    eplex_var_get_bounds(X, Min, Max),
    SqrtMin is sqrt(Min),
```

```
SqrtMax is sqrt(Max),
SqrtX $>= SqrtMin,
SqrtX $=< SqrtMax,
SqrtX*SqrtMin $=< X,
SqrtX*SqrtMax $>= X.
```

14.4.2 Setting up the eplex solver with triggers

The `nlsearch/2` predicate can be embedded in a branch and bound search in which the linear solver is invoked at each search node. To set up the linear solver so that it can be called again, automatically, whenever a new constraint is added, we use the `eplex_solver_setup/4` built-in. It does the job of both `eplex_solver_setup/1` and `eplex_solve/1`. It has four arguments:

```
eplex_solver_setup(OptFun, Cost, Options, Triggers),
```

where

- The optimisation function `OptFun` is as for `eplex_solver_setup/1` (for example `min(X)`).
- The `Cost` argument is the optimal value of this function, which is the same as the argument of `eplex_solve/1`. Because the solver runs immediately, as well as waking up and running again when an event triggers it, it is necessary to impose initial bounds on the optimisation variables, in this case `X` and `Cost`. They would normally be initialised to the same range.
- The third argument is a list of options. We will not choose any options for the considered example, so we will use the the empty list `[]`.
- The final argument specifies trigger conditions which will automatically wake the linear solver. We will specify two trigger conditions, **bounds** and **new_constraint**, which wake the solver whenever a variable bound is tightened, or a new linear constraint is imposed.

In the following we assume that we are dealing with a minimisation problem. The most important feature of `eplex_solver_setup/4`, which we will exploit immediately, is that each time the solver runs, and finds a new minimum, this is imposed as a new lower bound on the variable `Cost`. This lower bound is indeed a valid logical consequence of the optimisation procedure, and it remains a lower bound no matter how many more linear constraints are added to the problem (they can only make the problem 'harder' to solve, thus making the minimum value worse, i.e., higher).

14.4.3 Non-linear optimisation by branch and bound

Whilst the `eplex` solver imposes tighter lower bounds on the `Cost` variable, the branch and bound built-in `minimize(Query, Cost)` imposes a tighter upper bound on `Cost` each time a better solution has been found. If, at any point in the search tree, the lower bound on `Cost` imposed by the linear solver becomes greater than the upper bound imposed by the `minimize/2` predicate, the search fails at this point, and the whole subtree below the current node is pruned away.

The ECL^{i}PS^e predicate that employs this approach to solve our non-linear minimisation problem is defined as follows:

```
nonlin(W, X, Cost) :-
    Cost :: 0.0..inf,                              %1
    eplex_solver_setup(min(Cost),
                       Cost,
                       [],
                       [bounds, new_constraint]),  %2
    cons(W, X),                                    %3
    add_linear_cons(X, SqrtX),                     %4
    Cost $= W+SqrtX,                               %5
    minimize(nlsearch(X, SqrtX), Cost),           %6
    return_solution,                               %7
    eplex_cleanup.                                 %8
```

At the first line the optimisation variable is given an initial domain. At line 3 the problem constraints are imposed. Line 4 imposes the initial linear approximation to the square root. Line 5 constrains the optimisation variable W, and line 6 specifies the search.

At line 7 the predicate `return_solution` is invoked to instantiate to its `eplex` value any variables in the initial query `nonlin(W, X, Cost)` that were not already instantiated during search (in this case W).

Finally, at line 8, the final predicate `eplex_cleanup/0` is needed to stop the linear solver because otherwise it remains suspended even after the branch and bound search has ended, still waiting for a new event to activate it.

The initial non-linear optimisation problem can now be solved:

```
[eclipse 9]: nonlin(W, X, Cost).

W = 0
X = 5.0
```

```
Cost = 2.23606797749979
Yes (0.03s cpu)
```

14.5 The transportation problem

We now explain how to use the `eplex` to solve the facility location problem introduced in Subsection 6.5.4. Recall that the problem is concerned with a choice of a set of facilities, for instance warehouses, to best serve a given set of customers with a given set of demands. Each customer is characterised by its demand for the provided product. For each potential warehouse location and each client there are transportation costs of the product from the warehouse to the client, per unit of supplied quantity. The objective is to satisfy the demands of all customers minimising the total cost, including transportation costs.

We will tackle this problem in three stages, illustrating increasingly large and challenging classes of optimisation problems. The first stage is the *transportation* problem: how can a set of customers be served most efficiently from a set of warehouses. The second stage is the *facility location problem*: at which locations, from a finite set of alternatives, should we open warehouses so as to most efficiently serve a set of customers. Notice that the transportation problem is a subproblem of the facility location problem. The third stage is the *non-linear facility location problem*, a non-linear extension of the facility location problem where the capacity of each warehouse is a variable, and the cost of opening it has a non-linear relationship with its capacity. These three problems belong respectively to the following problem classes:

- *linear problems* that consists of linear constraints on continuous variables,
- *integer linear problems* that consists of linear constraints on both continuous and discrete variables,
- *non-linear problems* that consists of non-linear constraints on both continuous and discrete variables.

To represent the data of the transportation problem we use the following five predicates:

- `cust_count/1`; its argument is an integer, the number of customers,
- `warehouse_count/1`; its argument is an integer, the number of warehouses,
- `capacities/1`; its argument is a list of numbers, one for each warehouse,
- `demands/1`; its argument is a list of numbers, one for each customer,

- `transport_costs/1`; its argument is a two-dimensional array of numbers, one for each customer and warehouse.

Here is an example data file, illustrated in Figure 14.1:

```
cust_count(4).
warehouse_count(3).

capacities([600,500,600]).

demands([400,200,200,300]).

transport_costs([]([](5,4,1),
                   [](3,3,2),
                   [](4,2,6),
                   [](2,4,4))).
```

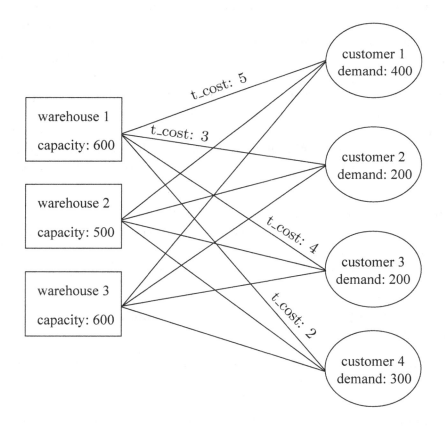

Fig. 14.1 A transportation problem

This problem has a decision variable for each customer and warehouse reflecting the amount of goods transported from the warehouse to the customer. To ensure the model is generic we use a matrix to hold all the decision variables. We solve it using the predicate **transport/2** defined by:

```
transport(Supplies, Cost) :-
    eplex_solver_setup(min(Cost)),
    init_vars(Supplies),
    supply_cons(Supplies),
    cost_expr(Supplies, Cost),
    eplex_solve(Cost),
    return_solution.
```

This has the usual structure of a constraint program, except the first and last lines which are specific to **eplex**. The arguments contain the decision variables, as discussed above. The objective is to minimise the variable **Cost**.

The data structures containing the decision variables are initialised as follows:

```
init_vars(Supplies) :-
    init_supplies(Supplies).

init_supplies(Supplies) :-
    cust_count(CustCt),
    warehouse_count(WCt),
    dim(Supplies,[CustCt,WCt]),
    ( foreachelem(S, Supplies)
    do
      0 $=< S
    ).
```

So to perform the initialisation we retrieve the number of customers from **cust_count/1** and the number of warehouses from **warehouse_count/1**. Notice that we have to explicitly constrain the supplied quantities, i.e., the **Supply** entries, to be non-negative.

The constraints are expressed more or less as they were written in the problem specification in Subsection 6.5.4. We formulate them using the **sum/1** built-in introduced in Subsection 10.3.2:

```
supply_cons(Supplies) :-
    capacity_cons(Supplies),
    demand_cons(Supplies).
```

```
capacity_cons(Supplies) :-
    capacities(Capacities),
    ( count(WHouse, 1, _),
      foreach(Cap, Capacities),
      param(Supplies)
    do
      cust_count(CustCt),
      Cap $>= sum(Supplies[1..CustCt, WHouse])
    ).

demand_cons(Supplies) :-
    demands(Demands),
    ( count(Cust, 1, _),
      foreach(Demand, Demands),
      param(Supplies)
    do
      warehouse_count(WCt),
      sum(Supplies[Cust, 1..WCt]) $>= Demand
    ).
```

So we stipulate that the sum of the supplies from each warehouse does
not exceed its capacity and the sum of supplies to each customer meets or
exceeds its demand.

Finally, we define the cost expression which is the sum of the resulting
transportation costs:

```
cost_expr(Supplies, CostExpr ) :-
    transport_expr(Supplies, TransportExpr),
    CostExpr $= TransportExpr.

transport_expr(Supplies, sum(TExprList)) :-
    transport_costs(TransportCosts),
    ( foreachelem(TCost, TransportCosts),
      foreachelem(Qty, Supplies),
      foreach(TExpr, TExprList)
    do
      TExpr = TCost*Qty
    ).
```

Notice the use of = to construct the expression **TExpr**.[3] If we denote by $S_{C,W}$ the decision variable representing the amount of goods supplied to customer C from warehouse W, the constraints generated by ECL^{i}PS^e are as follows:

$$S_{1,1} + S_{1,2} + S_{1,3} \geq 400,$$
$$S_{2,1} + S_{2,2} + S_{2,3} \geq 200,$$
$$S_{3,1} + S_{3,2} + S_{3,3} \geq 200,$$
$$S_{4,1} + S_{4,2} + S_{4,3} \geq 300,$$

$$600 \geq S_{1,1} + S_{2,1} + S_{3,1} + S_{4,1},$$
$$500 \geq S_{1,2} + S_{2,2} + S_{3,2} + S_{4,2},$$
$$600 \geq S_{1,3} + S_{2,3} + S_{3,3} + S_{4,3}.$$

Additionally all the variables are constrained to be positive. The expression minimised by ECL^{i}PS^e is:

$$5 * S_{1,1} + 4 * S_{1,2} + 1 * S_{1,3} +$$
$$3 * S_{2,1} + 3 * S_{2,2} + 2 * S_{2,3} +$$
$$4 * S_{3,1} + 2 * S_{3,2} + 6 * S_{3,3} +$$
$$2 * S_{4,1} + 4 * S_{4,2} + 4 * S_{4,3}.$$

The optimal solution returned by ECL^{i}PS^e for this problem instance is 1800.0:

```
[eclipse 10]: transport(Supplies, Cost).

Supplies = []([](0.0, 0.0, 400.0),
              [](0.0, 0.0, 200.0),
              [](0.0, 200.0, 0.0),
              [](300.0, 0.0, 0.0))
Cost = 1800.0
Yes (0.00s cpu)
```

---

[3] This is not a numerical equation, but simply a clearer way of writing:

```
( foreachelem(TCost, TransportCosts),
  foreachelem(Qty, Supplies),
  foreach(TCost*Qty, TExprList)
do
  true
)
```

14.6 The linear facility location problem

Recall that the facility location problem has a decision variable associated with each potential warehouse location. This is a binary variable, with 0 representing that the location is *not* chosen, and 1 that it *is* chosen, for an open warehouse. These binary decision variables make the problem harder to solve. (In fact, the class of facility location problems is NP-hard.)

To model this problem in ECL^{i}PS^e we introduce, in addition to the transportation problem data and variables:

- a new data item generated by `setup_costs/1`; its argument is a list of numbers, one for each potential warehouse location, for example

  `setup_costs([100,800,400]).`

- a list `OpenWhs` of Boolean variables, one for each potential warehouse location.

The data structures are now initialised by the following modified `init_vars/2` predicate:

```
init_vars(OpenWhs, Supplies) :-
    init_openwhs(OpenWhs),
    init_supplies(Supplies).

init_openwhs(OpenWhs) :-
    warehouse_count(WCt),
    length(OpenWhs, WCt),
    OpenWhs :: 0.0..1.0,
    integers(OpenWhs).
```

The key extensions to the transportation problem are in the constraints on how much goods can be supplied to a customer from a warehouse, and an extension to the cost function. Consider first the modified supply constraints with the amended constraints on the supply from each warehouse:

```
supply_cons(OpenWhs, Supplies) :-
    capacity_cons(Supplies, OpenWhs),
    demand_cons(Supplies).

capacity_cons(Supplies, OpenWhs) :-
    capacities(Capacities),
    ( count(WHouse, 1, _),
      foreach(OpenWh, OpenWhs),
```

```
    foreach(Cap, Capacities),
    param(Supplies)
do
    cust_count(CustCt),
    Cap*OpenWh $>= sum(Supplies[1..CustCt, WHouse])
).
```

So if the warehouse WHouse is not chosen, then the corresponding OpenWh variable is 0. The constraint ensures that in this case the sum of all the supplies from this warehouse is 0. However, if the warehouse WHouse *is* chosen, then OpenWh = 1 and the constraint reduces to the one used in the previous section.

This way of handling Boolean variables, such as OpenWhs, is standard in mixed integer programming. The constraint M*Bool $>= Expr is called a 'big M' constraint. Our big M constraint is:

```
Cap*OpenWh $>= sum(Supplies[1..CustCt, WHouse]).
```

This example is especially interesting as, by choosing M equal to the capacity Cap of the warehouse, we have created a constraint that does two things at the same time. If the warehouse is not chosen, it precludes any supply from that warehouse, and if the warehouse is chosen, it restricts its total supply to be no more than the capacity of the warehouse.

The second extension of the transportation problem model is an additional argument in the cost function, which is now defined as follows:

```
cost_expr(OpenWhs, Supplies, Cost) :-
    setup_expr(OpenWhs, SetupExpr),
    transport_expr(Supplies, TransportExpr),
    Cost $= SetupExpr+TransportExpr.

setup_expr(OpenWhs, sum(SExprList)) :-
    setup_costs(SetupCosts),
    ( foreach(OpenWh, OpenWhs),
      foreach(SetupCost, SetupCosts),
      foreach(SExpr, SExprList)
    do
      SExpr = OpenWh*SetupCost
    ).
```

(The transport_expr/2 predicate is defined in the previous section.) So the cost variable Cost is now constrained to be equal to the sum of the setup costs of the chosen warehouses plus the resulting transportation costs:

```
Cost $= SetupExpr+TransportExpr.
```

We encode now the facility location problem similarly to the transportation problem:

```
warehouse(OpenWhs, Supplies, Cost) :-
    eplex_solver_setup(min(Cost)),
    init_vars(OpenWhs, Supplies),
    supply_cons(OpenWhs, Supplies),
    cost_expr(OpenWhs, Supplies, Cost),
    eplex_solve(Cost),
    return_solution.
```

The problem instance defined by the example data items above yields the following result:

```
[eclipse 11]: warehouse(OpenWhs, Supplies, Cost).

OpenWhs = [1, 0, 1]
Supplies = [](([](0.0, 0.0, 400.0),
               [](0.0, 0.0, 200.0),
               [](200.0, 0.0, 0.0),
               [](300.0, 0.0, 0.0))
Cost = 2700.0
Yes (0.00s cpu)
```

If the integrality constraints on the Boolean variables are dropped, the optimal cost Cost improves to 2570.0.

14.7 The non-linear facility location problem

The non-linear facility location problem has the same data and decision variables as the previous problem, except that now the capacity of each warehouse is a decision variable instead of being given as input data.

The cost of setting up a warehouse, in this non-linear version of the warehouse problem, includes not only a standard (initial) setup cost, but also an extra cost proportional to the square root of the capacity of the warehouse. This extra cost reflects the fact the larger warehouses cost more, but the cost does not go up linearly with the capacity of the warehouse: larger warehouses are effectively cheaper per unit capacity.

Just as the non-linear facility location problem is an extension of the original facility location problem, the solution is an extension of the original facility location solution. This is a nice feature of constraint programming, and contrasts with traditional modelling and optimisation formalisms.

As for the non-linear problem discussed in Section 14.4, the program for solving the non-linear warehouse problem uses not only the **eplex** library but also the **branch_and_bound** library.

The definition of the main predicate for the non-linear facility location problem combines the structure of the predicate **nonlin/2** of Section 14.4 with that of **warehouse/3** of Section 14.6.

```
nlwarehouse(OpenWhs, Capacities, Cost) :-
    Cost :: 0.0..inf,
    eplex_solver_setup(min(Cost),
                       Cost,
                       [],
                       [new_constraint, deviating_bounds]),
    init_vars(OpenWhs, Supplies, Capacities, SqrtCaps),
    supply_cons(OpenWhs, Supplies, Capacities),
    cost_expr(OpenWhs, Supplies, SqrtCaps, Cost),
    minimize(nlsearch(Capacities, SqrtCaps), Cost),
    return_solution,
    eplex_cleanup.
```

The waking conditions, or 'triggers', on the linear solver ensure it is activated whenever

- a new linear constraint is added to the problem, or
- a bound on a variable becomes tightened so as to exclude its linear optimal value from the previous activation of the linear solver.

The second trigger **deviating_bounds** is newly introduced here. It can avoid a lot of unnecessary calls to the solver which the simpler trigger **bounds** would have made.

The decision variables are initialised as before, but this time we introduce two new lists of variables, **Capacities** and **SqrtCaps**:

```
init_vars(OpenWhs, Supplies, Capacities, SqrtCaps) :-
    init_openwhs(OpenWhs),
    init_supplies(Supplies),
    init_capacities(Capacities, SqrtCaps).
```

Capacities and **SqrtCaps** are, of course, the warehouse capacity variables, and a corresponding list of variables which will, eventually, be instantiated to the square root of the warehouse capacities. The square roots are

needed only for the cost expression. The newly introduced predicate
init_capacities/2 is defined as follows:

```
init_capacities(Capacities, SqrtCaps) :-
    warehouse_count(WCt),
    length(Capacities, WCt),
    length(SqrtCaps, WCt),
    total_demand(CapUPB),
    SqrtCapUPB is sqrt(CapUPB),
    Capacities :: 0.0..CapUPB,
    SqrtCaps   :: 0.0..SqrtCapUPB,
    ( foreach(Cap, Capacities),
      foreach(SqrtCap, SqrtCaps)
    do
      add_linear_cons(Cap, SqrtCap)
    ).
```

```
total_demand(CapUPB) :-
    demands(Demands),
    CapUPB is sum(Demands).
```

So we stipulate that the upper bound on the capacity variables is the total
demand from all the customers – this is the largest warehouse capacity that
could ever be needed.

The add_linear_cons/2 predicate, originally described in Section 14.4,
posts a set of linear constraints that approximate the square root relation.

The next program section posts the problem constraints:

```
supply_cons(OpenWhs, Supplies, Capacities) :-
    capacity_cons(Supplies, OpenWhs, Capacities),
    demand_cons(Supplies).
```

```
capacity_cons(Supplies, OpenWhs, Capacities) :-
    total_demand(BigM),
    ( count(WHouse, 1, _),
      foreach(OpenWh, OpenWhs),
      foreach(Cap, Capacities),
      param(Supplies, BigM)
    do
      cust_count(CustCt),
      Cap           $>= sum(Supplies[1..CustCt, WHouse]),
```

```
BigM*OpenWh $>= sum(Supplies[1..CustCt, WHouse])
).
```

(The demand_cons/2 predicate is defined in Section 14.5.) Since the capacity Cap is now a variable, the expression Cap*OpenWh is no longer linear, and therefore it cannot be used in a linear constraint, as in the capacity_cons/2 predicate in the previous section. Instead, the constraint

```
Cap $>= sum(Supplies[1..CustCt, WHouse])
```

stating that there is sufficient capacity in the warehouse to meet the supply commitment is added separately from the constraint

```
BigM*OpenWh $>= sum(Supplies[1..CustCt, WHouse])
```

stating that a non-zero supply is only possible from an open warehouse.

The cost expression is defined largely as before, except that the auxiliary setup_exp/3 predicate now includes a subexpression involving the square root of the warehouse capacity:

```
cost_expr(OpenWhs, Supplies, SqrtCaps, Cost) :-
    setup_expr(OpenWhs, SqrtCaps, SetupExpr),
    transport_expr(Supplies, TransportExpr),
    Cost $= SetupExpr+TransportExpr.

setup_expr(OpenWhs, SqrtCaps, sum(SExprList)) :-
    setup_costs(SetupCosts),
    ( foreach(OpenWh, OpenWhs),
      foreach(SqrtCap, SqrtCaps),
      foreach(SetupCost, SetupCosts),
      foreach(SExpr, SExprList)
    do
      SExpr = (OpenWh+SqrtCap*0.1)*SetupCost
    ).
```

The value 0.1 in the expression (OpenWh+SqrtCap*0.1)*SetupCost selects the balance between the fixed setup cost and the non-linear cost related to capacity. Experimentally this particular choice of coefficient leads to an interesting optimisation behaviour. Any other coefficient could be used here instead.

Up to now no constraint has been imposed to ensure that SqrtCap is indeed the square root of the chosen warehouse capacity. This relationship is enforced by the following nlsearch/2 predicate:

```
nlsearch(Capacities, SqrtCaps) :-
    ( too_different(Capacities, SqrtCaps, Cap, SqrtCap) ->
      make_choice(Cap),
      add_linear_cons(Cap, SqrtCap),
      nlsearch(Capacities, SqrtCaps)
    ;
      return_solution
    ).

too_different(Capacities, SqrtCaps, Cap, SqrtCap) :-
    get_pair(Capacities, SqrtCaps, Cap, SqrtCap),
    eplex_var_get(Cap,     solution, CapVal),
    eplex_var_get(SqrtCap, solution, SqrtCapVal),
    abs(sqrt(CapVal)-SqrtCapVal) $>= 1e-5.

get_pair([X | _], [Y | _], X, Y).
get_pair([_ | TX], [_ | TY], X, Y) :-
    get_pair(TX, TY, X, Y).
```

The predicate **too_different/4** checks through the warehouse capacities
Cap and the associated square root variables SqrtCap until it finds a pair
for which the value of SqrtCap, held internally in the linear solver, is more
than ϵ (here 1e-5) apart from the square root of the linear solver's value for
Cap.

If it finds such a pair, it returns it and makes a search choice by calling the
make_choice/1 predicate defined in Section 14.4, subsequently imposes the
new (better) linear approximation of the square root function, and continues
the search by invoking **nlsearch/2** again.

Whilst the naive linear approximation described earlier works, the rate
at which the algorithm converges to the optimal solution is poor. Faster
convergence is achieved by sharpening the linear approximation. A more
precise approximation is

$$(SqrtMax - SqrtMin)/(Max - Min) \leq (SqrtX - SqrtMin)/(X - Min).$$

It holds because the function $\sqrt{X}$ is concave, so in the interval between
the current lower bound Min of X and its upper bound Max the square
root of X cannot fall below the straight line joining $\sqrt{Min}$ and $\sqrt{Max}$. This
can be expressed as a linear constraint in the form:

$$(SqrtMax - SqrtMin) * (X - Min) \leq (SqrtX - SqrtMin) * (Max - Min).$$

We therefore add this linear constraint to the definition of
`add_linear_cons/2`:

```
add_linear_cons(X, SqrtX) :-
    eplex_var_get_bounds(X, Min, Max),
    SqrtMin is sqrt(Min), SqrtMax is sqrt(Max),
    SqrtX $>= SqrtMin, SqrtX $=< SqrtMax,
    SqrtX*SqrtMin $=< X,
    SqrtX*SqrtMax $>= X,
    (SqrtMax-SqrtMin)*(X-Min) $=< (SqrtX-SqrtMin)*(Max-Min).
```

If each `SqrtCap` variable is sufficiently ($< \epsilon$) close to its `Cap` variable, then
the search terminates and we have a solution. The variables are instantiated
to their values in the linear solver, and `nlsearch/2` succeeds. The minimisation, however, continues because `nlsearch/2` was originally invoked from
the call

```
minimize(nlsearch(Capacities, SqrtCaps), Cost).
```

Only when `nlsearch/2` fails does the branch and bound minimisation routine finally terminate successfully.

The non-linear facility location problem is solved thus in ECL^{i}PS^e:

```
[eclipse 12]: nlwarehouse(OpenWhs, Capacities, Cost).
Found a solution with cost 3944.3710282197303
Found a solution with cost 3903.40269486325
Found no solution with cost
                         3574.3828982755144 .. 3902.40269486325

OpenWhs = [1, 0, 1]
Capacities = [500.0, 0.0, 600.0]
Cost = 3903.40269486325
Yes (0.06s cpu)
```

This program scales up in a reasonable way. For a set of benchmarks
with 10 warehouses and 50 customers the program typically finds a solution
quickly and proves optimality in about 20 seconds.

14.7.1 Multiple Solvers

Finally, let us mention that if both `ic` and `eplex` are loaded, then some
constraints become ambiguous. For example `X $>= 0` is both an `ic` and
an `eplex` constraint. In this case it is necessary to explicitly qualify each

constraint goal that could be ambiguous, specifying which solver should handle it, thus:

```
ic: (X $>= 2)
```

or

```
eplex: (X $>= 2).
```

Unambiguous constraints, such as X #>= 2 do not need to be qualified.

Here is a simple program that can run with both solvers loaded:

```
test(X, Y) :-
    ic: (X $>= 2),
    Y #>= X.
```

14.8 Summary

In this chapter we introduced the **eplex** solver that allows us to solve linear and non-linear constraints on integers and reals. We discussed in turn:

- the limitations of the **ic** library,
- the **eplex** library: constraint syntax and facilities,
- handling of integrality and its use to solve satisfiability problems,
- repeated **eplex** solver waking (within a branch and bound search).

Then we illustrated these techniques by considering three, gradually more complex, problems: a transportation problem, a (linear) facility location problem and a non-linear version of the facility location problem.

In the process we introduced the following built-ins:

- **eplex_solver_setup/1**, to set up the **eplex** solver,
- **eplex_solve/1**, to invoke the **eplex** solver,
- **eplex_var_get/3**, to extract information about solver variables,
- **eplex_get/2**, to extract information about the solver state,
- **integers/1**, to impose integrality constraints in **eplex**, so that the internal **eplex** branch and bound search will be used,
- **eplex_var_get_bounds/3**, to extract the bounds of an **eplex** variable,
- **eplex_solver_setup/4**, to set up the **eplex** solver with trigger conditions for repeated waking,
- **eplex_cleanup/0**, to close the **eplex** solver, and kill its associated delayed goals.

14.9 Exercises

Exercise 14.1 A company produces two types of products T1 and T2, which requires the following resources to produce each unit of the product:

Resource	T1	T2
Labour (hours)	9	6
Pumps (units)	1	1
Tubing (m)	12	16

The amounts of profit per unit of products are: T1 : 350, T2 : 300.

They have the following resources available: 1566 hours of labour, 200 pumps, and 2880 metres of tubing.

  (i) Write a program to maximise the profit for the company, using `eplex` as a black box solver. Write a predicate that returns the profit and the values for T1 and T2.
 (ii) What program change is required to answer this question: what profit can be achieved if exactly 150 units of T1 are required?
(iii) What would the profit be if fractional numbers of products could be produced?

Exercise 14.2 Explore the behaviour of the program solving the non-linear facility location problem and presented in Section 14.7 with different:

  (i) linear approximations
      Add the following linear approximations one by one to determine their effect on the search performance:

      • SqrtX $>= SqrtMin and SqrtX $=< SqrtMax,
      • SqrtX*SqrtMin $=< X and SqrtX*SqrtMax $>= X,
      • (SqrtMax-SqrtMin)*(X-Min) $=< (SqrtX-SqrtMin)*(Max-Min).

 (ii) setup costs
      Try the following setup costs:

      • SExpr = (OpenWh+SqrtCap*0.3)*SetupCost,
      • SExpr = (OpenWh+SqrtCap*0.1)*SetupCost,
      • SExpr = (OpenWh+SqrtCap*0.01)*SetupCost.

(iii) trigger conditions
      Add the following trigger conditions one at a time:

- new_constraint,
- bounds,
- deviating_bounds.

(iv) precision

Try varying the allowed difference between `SqrtCapVal` and `sqrt(CapVal)` using:

- 10,
- 1,
- 1e-5.

Solutions to selected exercises

Exercise 1.1

```
[eclipse 1]: X = 7, X = 6.

No (0.00s cpu)
[eclipse 2]: X = 7, X = X+1.

No (0.00s cpu)
[eclipse 3]: X = X+1, X = 7.

No (0.00s cpu)
[eclipse 4]: X = 3, Y = X+1.

Y = 3 + 1
X = 3
Yes (0.00s cpu)
[eclipse 5]: Y = X+1, X = 3.

Y = 3 + 1
X = 3
Yes (0.00s cpu)
```

Exercise 1.2

```
[eclipse 1]: book(X, apt), book(X, Y), Y \= apt.

X = constraint_logic_programming
Y = wallace
Yes (0.00s cpu)
```

Exercise 1.3

```
[eclipse 1]: Z = 2, q(X).

Z = 2
X = X
Yes (0.00s cpu)
```

```
[eclipse 2]: Z = 2, q(Z).

Z = 2
Yes (0.00s cpu)
[eclipse 3]: Z = 2, q(X), Y = Z+1.

Z = 2
X = X
Y = 2 + 1
```

Exercise 1.4

```
[eclipse 1]: p(Behold), q(Behold).

Behold = [prolog, works, for, solving(problems), among, others]
Yes (0.00s cpu, solution 1, maybe more) ? ;

No (0.00s cpu)
```

Exercise 1.5

The first solution is obtained twice, by splitting Xs into [] and Xs or into Xs and
[]. In each case, by appending Xs to [] or [] to Xs we get back Xs. The following
modified definition of rotate/2 removes the possibility of such redundancies:

```
rotate(Xs, Ys) :- app(As, Bs, Xs), Bs \= [], app(Bs, As, Ys).
```

Exercise 2.1

The result is X=0, Y=0.

Exercise 2.2

The first procedure call fails, while the other two succeed.

Exercise 2.3

```
app(X1, X2, X3):
    begin
      begin new Ys;
        X1 = []; X2 = Ys; X3 = Ys
      end
    orelse
      begin new X,Xs,Ys,Zs;
        X1 = [X | Xs]; X2 = Ys; X3 = [X | Zs];
        app(Xs, Ys, Zs)
      end
    end
```

Exercise 3.1

```
[eclipse 1]: X is 7, X is 6.

No (0.00s cpu)
```

```
[eclipse 2]: X is 7, X is X+1.

No (0.00s cpu)
[eclipse 3]: X is X+1, X is 7.
instantiation fault in +(X, 1, X)
Abort
[eclipse 4]: X is 3, Y is X+1.

Y = 4
X = 3
Yes (0.00s cpu)
[eclipse 5]: Y is X+1, X is 3.
instantiation fault in +(X, 1, Y)
Abort
```

Exercise 3.2

```
[eclipse 1]: Z is 2, q(X).

Z = 2
X = X
Yes (0.00s cpu)
[eclipse 2]: Z is 2, q(Z).

Z = 2
Yes (0.00s cpu)
[eclipse 3]: Z is 2, q(X), Y is Z+1.

Z = 2
X = X
Y = 3
Yes (0.00s cpu)
[eclipse 4]: Z = 2, inc(X), X = 2.
instantiation fault in +(X, 1, Z) in module eclipse
Abort
[eclipse 5]: X = 2, inc(X), Z = 2.

X = 2
Z = 2
Yes (0.00s cpu)
```

Exercise 3.3

An example is the query min(1+1, 3, Z). For the first program it yields the answer Z = 1+1 and for the second program the answer Z = 2.

Exercise 3.4

Assume the declarations

```
:- op(500, yfx, have).
:- op(400, yfx, and).
```

The following interaction with ECL^{i}PS^e provides the answers.

```
[eclipse 1]: have(and(she,he), luck) = she and he have luck.

Yes (0.00s cpu)
[eclipse 2]: have(they, and(and(time,money),luck)) =
             they have time and money and luck.

Yes (0.00s cpu)
```

Exercise 3.5

Here is a possible declaration that ensures that has_length/2 is properly defined and queries such as [a,b,c] has_length X+1 are correctly parsed:

```
:- op(800, xfy, has_length).
```

Exercise 4.1

Here is one possible solution.

```
len(X, N) :-
    ( integer(N) ->
      len1(X, N)
    ;
      len2(X, N)
    ).

len1([], 0) :- !.
len1([_ | Ts], N) :- M is N-1, len1(Ts, M).

len2([], 0).
len2([_ | Ts], N) :- len2(Ts, M), N is M+1.
```

Exercise 4.2

This exercise illustrates a subtlety in using cut. Consider the query add(a, [a], [a,a]). For the first program it yields the answer 'No' and for the second program the answer 'Yes'.

Exercise 4.3

```
while(B, S) :-
    ( B ->
      S,
      while(B, S)
    ;
      true
    ).
```

Exercise 5.1

Here is one possible solution.

```
vars(Term, []) :- atomic(Term), !.
vars(Term, [Term]) :- var(Term), !.
vars([H|T], VarList) :- !,
    vars(H, L1),
    vars(T, L2),
    app(L1, L2, VarList).
vars(Term, VarList) :-
    Term =.. [_|Args],
    vars(Args, VarList).
```

Exercise 5.3

Here is one possible solution.

```
subs(Input, _X, _Term, Input) :- atomic(Input), !.
subs(Input, X, Term, Term) :- var(Input), X == Input, !.
subs(Input, _X, _Term, Input) :- var(Input), !.

subs(Input, X, Term, Output) :-
    Input =.. [F|Args],
    subslist(Args, X, Term, ArgsOut),
    Output =.. [F|ArgsOut].

subslist([], _X, _Term, []).
subslist([Head|Tail], X, Term, [Output|OutputList]) :-
    subs(Head, X, Term, Output),
    subslist(Tail, X, Term, OutputList).
```

Exercise 7.1

```
( foreach(V,List),
  fromto(0,This,Next,Count)
do
  (nonvar(V) -> Next is This+1 ; Next = This)
).
```

Exercise 7.2

```
( foreachelem(El,Array),
  fromto(0,This,Next,Count)
do
  (nonvar(El) -> Next is This+1 ; Next = This)
).
```

Exercise 7.3

Here is one possible solution.

```
select_val(Min, Max, Val) :-
    ( count(I,Min,Val),
      fromto(go,_,Continue,stop),
      param(Max)
```

```
do
  ( Continue = stop
  ;
    I < Max, Continue = go
  )
).
```

This is an example where the recursive encoding (provided in the **SELECT** program from Figure 3.2) is, perhaps, easier to follow.

Exercise 7.4
(count(I,K,L) do Body) is equivalent to
(L1 is L+1, fromto(K,I,M,L1) do M is I+1, Body).

Exercise 8.1

```
setval(c,0),
( foreachelem(El,Array)
do
  ( var(El) -> true ; incval(c) )
),
getval(c,Count).
```

Exercise 8.2
Here is one possible solution.

```
all_solutions(Query, _List) :-
    setval(sols,[]),
    Query,
    getval(sols,Old),
    append(Old,[Query],New),
    setval(sols,New),
    fail.
all_solutions(_, List) :-
    getval(sols,List).
```

Exercise 8.3
Here is one possible solution.

```
naive_search2(Vars,Vals) :-
    ( foreach(V,Vars),
      count(Indent,0,_),
      param(Vals)
    do
      setval(first,true),
      member(V,Vals),
      ( getval(first,false) -> nl_indent(Indent) ; true ),
      write('v'), write(Indent), write(' = '),
      write(V), write('\t'),
      on_backtracking(setval(first,false))
    ).
```

```
nl_indent(N) :-
    nl,
    ( for(_I,1,N) do write('\t') ).

on_backtracking(_).
on_backtracking(Q) :-
    once(Q),
    fail.
```

('\t' stands for the TAB symbol.)

Exercise 9.1

The following solve/1 predicate does the job:

```
solve(A) :-
    solve(A, true, Susp),
    write_susp(Susp).

write_susp(true) :- !.
write_susp((A,B)) :-
    nl, writeln('Delayed goals:'),
    write_susp1((A,B)).
write_susp1((A,B)) :-
    ( B = true -> true ; write_susp1(B) ),
    write('\t'), writeln(A).
```

We have then for example:

```
[eclipse 1]: solve((suspend:(2 < Y + 1), suspend:(X > 3))).

Delayed goals:
        suspend : (2 < Y + 1)
        suspend : (X > 3)

Y = Y
X = X
Yes (0.00s cpu)
```

Exercise 9.2

In the solution below the predicate diff_list/2 is defined by a double recursion using the auxiliary predicate out_of/2.

```
diff_list([]).
diff_list([E1|Tail]):-
    out_of(E1, Tail),
    diff_list(Tail).

out_of(_, []).
out_of(E1, [E2|Tail]):-
    E1 $\= E2,
    out_of(E1, Tail).
```

Exercise 9.3

The following modification of the `constraints/2` predicate does the job:

```
constraints(QueenStruct, Number) :-
    ( for(I,1,Number),
      param(QueenStruct,Number)
    do
      QueenStruct[I] :: 1..Number,
      ( for(J,1,I-1),
        param(I,QueenStruct)
      do
        subscript(QueenStruct,[I],Qi),
        subscript(QueenStruct,[J],Qj),
        Qi $\= Qj,
        Qi-Qj $\= I-J,
        Qi-Qj $\= J-I
      )
    ).
```

We get then a substantial speed up w.r.t. the original solution, for example:

```
[eclipse 1]: queens(X, 8).

X = [](1, 5, 8, 6, 3, 7, 2, 4)
Yes (0.02s cpu, solution 1, maybe more) ?
```

Exercise 9.4

Here is one possible solution.

```
filter([], [], unsat).
filter([H | T], [H | Rest], Sat) :-
    var(H), !, filter(T, Rest, Sat).
filter([0 | T], Rest, Sat) :- !,
    filter(T, Rest, Sat).
filter([1 |_], [], sat).

test_cl(List) :-
    filter(List, Rest, Sat),
    ( Sat = sat      -> true ;
      Rest = [Var|_] -> suspend(test_cl(Rest), 2, Var->inst)
    ).
```

Exercise 9.5

Here is one possible solution.

```
ordered(List) :-
    ( fromto(List,[X|Successors],Successors,[]),
      fromto([],Predecessors,[X|Predecessors],_RList)
    do
      ( ground(X) ->
        cg(X, Predecessors, Successors)
      ;
```

```
            suspend(cg(X,Predecessors,Successors),2,X->inst)
      )
   ).

cg(X, Predecessors, Successors) :-
   check_gap(X, <, Successors),
   check_gap(X, >, Predecessors).

check_gap(_, _, []) :- !.
check_gap(X, Comp, [Y|Rest]) :-
   var(Y), !,
   check_gap(X, Comp, Rest).
check_gap(X, Comp, [Y|_]) :-
   comp(X, Comp, Y).

comp(X, <, Y) :- X < Y.
comp(X, >, Y) :- X > Y.
```

In this program as soon as an element X of the input list becomes instantiated, it is checked using the call cg(X, Predecessors, Successors) against its nearest instantiated predecessor and its nearest instantiated successor. Thanks to these checks the query ordered(List) detects a failure if the input list contains two integers in the wrong order.

Exercise 10.1

```
[eclipse 1]: X #= 7, X #= 6.

No (0.00s cpu)
[eclipse 2]: X #= 7, X #= X+1.

No (0.00s cpu)
[eclipse 3]: X #= X+1, X #= 7.

No (0.00s cpu)
[eclipse 4]: X #= 3, Y #= X+1.

X = 3
Y = 4
Yes (0.00s cpu)
[eclipse 5]: Y #= X+1, X #= 3.

Y = 4
X = 3
Yes (0.00s cpu)
```

Exercise 11.1
Here is one possible solution.

```
queens(Queens, Number):-
   length(Queens, Number),
```

```
Queens :: [1..Number],
constraints(Queens),
labeling(Queens).

constraints(Queens):-
    noHorizontalCheck(Queens),
    noDiagonalCheck(Queens).

noHorizontalCheck(Queens):-
    diff_list(Queens).

noDiagonalCheck([]).
noDiagonalCheck([Q | Queens]):-
    noCheck(Q, Queens, 1),
    noDiagonalCheck(Queens).

noCheck(_, [], _).
noCheck(Q, [Q1 | Queens], I):-
    Q $\= Q1-I,
    Q $\= Q1+I,
    I1 is I+1,
    noCheck(Q, Queens, I1).
```

The constraints dealing with the diagonals are generated using an auxiliary predicate **noCheck/3**. Given a variable (a queen) Q, and a list of variables **Queens** representing the list of the queens to the right of Q, the query **noCheck(Q, Queens, 1)** generates the constraints stating that the queen Q does not attack along a diagonal any queen from **Queens**. Assuming **Queens = [X1, ..., Xk]**, this is done by generating the constraints

```
Q $\= X1 - 1, Q $\= X1 + 1, ..., Q $\= Xk - k, Q $\= Xk + k.
```

First the constraints Q $\= X1 - 1, Q $\= X1 + 1 are generated. The recursive call of **noCheck/3** deals with the remaining constraints. The second argument of **noCheck/3** becomes the tail of the list, here **[X2, ..., Xk]**, and the third one gets incremented by 1. The recursion terminates when the list becomes empty.

The use of the **length/2** built-in allows one to call **queens/2** with the first argument uninstantiated.

Exercise 11.2

The solution below depends crucially on the constraint **sum(List) #= N**. This constraint holds since for any N-digit number we have $\sum_{i=0}^{9} occ(i) = N$, where $occ(i)$ is the number of occurrences of the digit i in the number.

```
solve(List) :-
    N is 10,
    length(List,N),
    List :: 0..9,
    sum(List) #= N,
    labeling(List),
    correct(List).
```

```
correct(List) :-
    ( foreach(El,List),
      count(I,0,_),
      param(List)
    do
      occ(I, List, El)
    ).

occ(I, List, Count) :-
    ( foreach(El,List),
      fromto(0,This,Next,Count),
      param(I)
    do
      (El = I -> Next is This+1 ; Next = This)
    ).
```

The predicate occ/3 is actually present in ECL^{i}PS^e as the occurrences/3 built-in in the ic_global library. For a solution using this built-in see www.eclipse-clp. org/examples/magicseq.ecl.txt.

Exercise 11.3
Here is one possible solution.

```
solve(X) :-
    N is 10,
    dim(X,[N]),
    dim(Y,[N]),
    subscript(X,[7],6),
    ( for(I,1,N),
      param(X,Y,N)
    do
      X[I] :: 1..N,
      ( for(J,1,I-1),
        param(I,X)
      do
        X[I] $\= X[J]
      ),
      ( I >= 2 ->
        Y[I] $= X[I]-X[I-1],
        Y[I] :: [3,-2]
      ;
        true
      )
    ),
    ( foreacharg(I,X) do indomain(I) ).
```

Exercise 12.1
For the first problem the **continue** strategy is much better than **restart** strategy, while for the second problem the converse holds. Further, labeling(List) performs well for the first problem, while for the second problem it is much better

to use `search(List,0,first_fail,indomain,complete,[])`. We have for example:

```
[eclipse 1]: prob1(List, Max),
             bb_min(labeling(List),
                    Max,
                    bb_options{strategy:continue}).

[...]
List = [7, 5, 3, 1, 0, 2, 4, 6, 8]
Max = 530
Yes (6.48s cpu)

[eclipse 2]: prob1(List, Max),
             bb_min(labeling(List),
                    Max,
                    bb_options{strategy:restart}).

[...]
List = [7, 5, 3, 1, 0, 2, 4, 6, 8]
Max = 530
Yes (87.19s cpu)

[eclipse 3]: prob2(List, Max),
             bb_min(search(List,0,first_fail,indomain,complete,[]),
                    Max,
                    bb_options{strategy:restart}).

[...]
List = [14, 12, 10, 8, 6, 0, 1, 2, 3, 4, 5, 7, 9, 11, 13, 15]
Max = 468
Yes (1.57s cpu)

[eclipse 4]: prob2(List, Max),
             bb_min(search(List,0,first_fail,indomain,complete,[]),
                    Max,
                    bb_options{strategy:continue}).

[...]
List = [12, 13, 10, 8, 6, 2, 3, 0, 1, 4, 5, 7, 9, 11, 14, 15]
Max = 468
Yes (104.27s cpu)

[eclipse 5]: prob2(List, Max),
             bb_min(labeling(List),
                    Max,
                    bb_options{strategy:restart}).

[...]
List = [12, 13, 10, 8, 0, 1, 2, 3, 4, 5, 6, 7, 9, 11, 14, 15]
Max = 468
```

```
Yes (3326.68s cpu)
```

Exercise 12.2

Here is one possible solution.

```
domination(N,Min) :-
    dim(Board,[N,N]),
    matrix_to_list(Board, Vars),
    Vars :: 0..1,
    sum(Vars) $= Min,
    ( multifor([Row,Col],[1,1],[N,N]),
      param(Board)
    do
      covered(Row, Col, Board)
    ),
    minimize(labeling(Vars),Min),
    print_board(Board).

covered(Row, Col, Board) :-
    ( foreachelem(X,Board,[I,J]),
      fromto([],This,Next,AttackList),
      param(Row,Col)
    do
      ( attack(Row,Col,I,J) -> Next = [X|This] ; Next = This )
    ),
    sum(AttackList) $>= 1.

attack(R,C,I,J) :-
    R =:= I ; C =:= J ; R-C =:= I-J ; R+C =:= I+J.

matrix_to_list(Board, List) :-
    ( foreachelem(El,Board),
      foreach(Var,List)
    do
      Var = El
    ).

print_board(Board) :-
    ( foreachelem(El,Board,[_,J])
    do
      ( J =:= 1 -> nl ; true ),
      write(' '), write(El)
    ).
```

The call covered(Row, Col, Board) checks that the list of fields that attack the square [Row,Col] (constructed in the variable Attacklist) contains at least one queen (using the constraint sum(AttackList) $>= 1).

Exercise 12.3

Here is one possible solution with a sample input problem.

```
% problem(Nr, SquareSize, TileSizes)
```

```
problem(1, 10, [7,6,5,4,3,2,1]).

squares(ProblemNr, Bs, Xs, Ys, Min) :-
    problem(ProblemNr, Size, Sizes),
    squares(Size, Sizes, Bs, Xs, Ys, Min).

squares(Size, Sizes, Bs, Xs, Ys, Waste) :-
    ( foreach(X,Xs),
      foreach(Y,Ys),
      foreach(B,Bs),
      foreach(S,Sizes),
      param(Size)
    do
      B :: 0..1,
      Sd is Size-S+1,
      [X,Y] :: 1..Sd
    ),
    waste_expr(Size, Sizes, Bs, Waste),
    no_overlap(Bs, Xs, Ys, Sizes),
    capacity(Bs, Xs, Sizes, Size,Waste),
    capacity(Bs, Ys, Sizes, Size,Waste),
    append(Xs,Ys,XYs),
    append(Bs,XYs,Vars),
    minimize(search(Vars, 0, smallest, indomain, complete, []),
             Waste).

waste_expr(Size, Sizes, Bs, Waste) :-
    ( foreach(S,Sizes),
      foreach(B,Bs),
      foreach(Used,UsedList)
    do
      Used #= B*S*S
    ),
    Waste #= Size*Size - sum(UsedList),
    Waste #>= 0.

no_overlap(Bs, Xs, Ys, Sizes) :-
    ( foreach(B,Bs),
      fromto(Xs,    [X|XXs], XXs, []),
      fromto(Ys,    [Y|YYs], YYs, []),
      fromto(Sizes, [S|SSs], SSs, [])
    do
      ( foreach(X1,XXs),
        foreach(Y1,YYs),
        foreach(S1,SSs),
        param(B,X,Y,S)
      do
        no_overlap(B, X, Y, S, X1, Y1, S1)
      )
```

```
        ).

no_overlap(B, X1, Y1, S1, X2, Y2, S2) :-
    B #=<
    (X1+S1 #=< X2 or X2+S2 #=< X1 or Y1+S1 #=< Y2 or Y2+S2 #=< Y1).

capacity(Bs, Cs, Sizes, Size,Waste) :-
    ( for(Pos,1,Size),
      foreach(W,Ws),
      param(Bs,Cs,Size,Sizes)
    do
      ( foreach(C,Cs),
        foreach(B,Bs),
        foreach(S,Sizes),
        param(Pos),
        fromto(Sum,S*Bool*B+Sum1,Sum1,0)
        do
        ::(C, Pos-S+1..Pos, Bool)
      ),
      W #= eval(Size)-Sum,
      W #>= 0
    ),
    Waste #= sum(Ws).
```

Here ::/3 is the reified form of the variable declaration built-in ::/2 (see Subsection 9.4.4). We have then for example:

```
[eclipse 3]: squares(1, Bs, Xs, Ys, Min).
Found a solution with cost 100

[...]

Found a solution with cost 45

Bs = [0, 0, 1, 1, 1, 1, 1]
Xs = [1, 1, 1, 1, 6, 9, 1]
Ys = [1, 1, 1, 6, 1, 1, 10]
Min = 45
Yes (6.58s cpu)
```

Bibliographic remarks

Chapter 1

The unification problem was introduced and solved in Robinson [1965]. The MARTELLI–MONTANARI unification algorithm was introduced in Martelli and Montanari [1982]. The use of unification for computing is due to Kowalski [1974]. The concept of a pure Prolog was popularised by the first edition of Sterling and Shapiro [1994].

Chapter 2

The language $\mathcal{L}_0$ defined in Section 2.2 and the translation of pure Prolog into it is based on Apt and Smaus [2001], where it is shown that this language supports declarative programming. The declarative interpretation of $\mathcal{L}_0$ programs is closely related to the so-called *Clark completion* of logic programs introduced in Clark [1978], further discussed for example in Apt and van Emden [1982].

The equivalence between the declarative interpretations of pure Prolog programs and $\mathcal{L}_0$ programs w.r.t. successful queries follows from the results of Apt and van Emden [1982] that compare the least Herbrand model of a logic program with the models of Clark completion.

Chapter 4

O'Keefe [1990] discusses in detail the proper uses of the cut. Sterling and Shapiro [1994] provides an in-depth discussion of various meta-interpreters written in Prolog. Apt and Turini [1995] is a collection of articles discussing the meta-programming in Prolog.

Chapter 6

This chapter draws on material from Apt [2003]. The *SEND + MORE = MONEY* puzzle is due to H. E. Dudeney and appeared in England, in the July 1924 issue of *Strand Magazine*. The representation of the *SEND + MORE = MONEY* puzzle and of the n-queens problem as a CSP is discussed in Van Hentenryck [1989].

According to Russell and Norvig [2003] the eight queens problem was originally published anonymously in the German chess magazine *Schach* in 1848 and its generalisation to the n-queens problem in Netto [1901]. The coins problem is discussed in Wallace, Novello and Schimpf [1997].

Chapter 7
The iterators in ECL^{i}PS^e are designed and implemented by Joachim Schimpf. In Schimpf [2002] an early version of the iterators and their implementation in ECL^{i}PS^e is described. It is shown in Voronkov [1992] that in logic programming appropriately powerful iterators have the same power as recursion. The `fromto/4` is an example of such an iterator. The `QUEENS` program given in Figure 7.8 of Section 7.6 is modelled after an analogous solution in the Alma-0 language of Apt et al. [1998]. The summary of the iterators is based on the ECL^{i}PS^e user manual, see `www.eclipse-clp.org/doc/bips/kernel/control/do-2.html`.

Chapter 8
The credit-based search was introduced in Beldiceanu et al. [1997]. The limited discrepancy search is due to Harvey and Ginsberg [1995].

Chapter 10
The illustration of the constraint propagation for Boolean constraints by means of the full adder example is from Frühwirth [1995]. The use of the *SEND + MORE = MONEY* puzzle to discuss the effect of constraint propagation is from Van Hentenryck [1989, page 143]. The details of the constraint propagation mechanisms implemented in the `sd` and `ic` libraries are discussed in Chapters 6 and 7 of Apt [2003].

Chapter 11
Exercise 11.2 is originally from Van Hentenryck [1989, pages 155–157].

Chapter 12
The use of constraint logic programming to solve Sudoku puzzles can be traced back to Carlson [1995]. Various approaches to solving them based on different forms of constraint propagation are analysed in detail in Simonis [2005]. Exercise 12.2 is from Wikipedia [2006]. Exercise 12.3 is a modified version of an exercise from `www.eclipse-clp.org/examples/square_tiling.pl.txt`.

Chapter 13

The first comprehensive account of solving constraints on reals based on constraint propagation is Van Hentenryck [1997] where a modelling language `Numerica` is introduced. The Reimer's system is taken from Granvilliers [2003]. The `MORTGAGE` program was originally discussed in Jaffar and Lassez [1987]. Exercise 13.3 is taken from Monfroy, Rusinowitch and Schott [1996].

Chapter 14

The facility location problem is a standard problem in operations research, see, e.g., Vazirani [2001].

Bibliography

K. R. APT
[2003] *Principles of Constraint Programming*, Cambridge University Press, Cambridge, England. Cited on page(s) 320, 321.

K. R. APT, J. BRUNEKREEF, V. PARTINGTON AND A. SCHAERF
[1998] Alma-0: An imperative language that supports declarative programming, *ACM Toplas*, 20, pp. 1014–1066. Cited on page(s) 321.

K. R. APT AND J. SMAUS
[2001] Rule-based versus procedure-based view of logic programming, *Joint Bulletin of the Novosibirsk Computing Center and Institute of Informatics Systems, Series: Computer Science*, 16, pp. 75–97. Available via http://www.cwi.nl/~apt. Cited on page(s) 320.

K. R. APT AND F. TURINI
[1995] eds., *Meta-logics and Logic Programming*, The MIT Press, Cambridge, Massachusetts. Cited on page(s) 320.

K. R. APT AND M. VAN EMDEN
[1982] Contributions to the theory of logic programming, *Journal of the ACM*, 29, pp. 841–862. Cited on page(s) 320.

N. BELDICEANU, E. BOURREAU, P. CHAN AND D. RIVREAU
[1997] Partial search strategy in CHIP, in: *Proceedings of the Second International Conference on Meta-Heuristics*. Sophia-Antipolis, France. Cited on page(s) 321.

I. BRATKO
[2001] *PROLOG Programming for Artificial Intelligence*, International Computer Science Series, Addison-Wesley, Harlow, England, third edn. Cited on page(s) xiii.

B. CARLSON
[1995] *Compiling and Executing Finite Domain Constraints*, PhD thesis, Uppsala University and SICS. Cited on page(s) 321.

K. L. CLARK
[1978] Negation as failure, in: *Logic and Databases*, H. Gallaire and J. Minker, eds., Plenum Press, New York, pp. 293–322. Cited on page(s) 320.

A. COLMERAUER
[1990]   An introduction to Prolog III, *Communications of the ACM*, 33, pp. 69–
         90. Cited on page(s) x.

A. COLMERAUER AND P. ROUSSEL
[1996]   The birth of Prolog, in: *History of Programming Languages*, T. J. Bergin
         and R. G. Gibson, eds., ACM Press/Addison-Wesley, Reading, Mas-
         sachusetts, pp. 331–367. Cited on page(s) x.

M. DINCBAS, P. V. HENTENRYCK, H. SIMONIS, A. AGGOUN, T. GRAF AND
         F. BERTHIER
[1988]   The constraint logic programming language CHIP, in: *Proceedings of
         the International Conference on Fifth Generation Computer Systems*,
         Tokyo, pp. 693–702. Cited on page(s) xi.

T. FRÜHWIRTH
[1995]   Constraint Handling Rules, in: *Constraint Programming: Basics and
         Trends*, A. Podelski, ed., LNCS 910, Springer-Verlag, Berlin, pp. 90–
         107. (Châtillon-sur-Seine Spring School, France, May 1994). Cited on
         page(s) 321.

M. GARDNER
[1979]   *Mathematical Circus*, Random House, New York, NY. Cited on page(s)
         108.

L. GRANVILLIERS
[2003]   RealPaver User's Manual, Version 0.3. `http://www.sciences.`
         `univ-nantes.fr/info/perso/permanents/granvil/realpaver/src/`
         `realpaver-0.3.pdf`. Cited on page(s) 322.

G. H. HARDY
[1992]   *A Mathematician's Apology*, Cambridge University Press, Cambridge,
         England, reprint edn. Cited on page(s) 251.

W. D. HARVEY AND M. L. GINSBERG
[1995]   Limited discrepancy search, in: *Proceedings of the Fourteenth Inter-
         national Joint Conference on Artificial Intelligence (IJCAI-95); Vol.
         1*, C. S. Mellish, ed., Morgan Kaufmann, Montréal, Québec, Canada,
         pp. 607–615. Cited on page(s) 321.

C. A. R. HOARE
[1962]   Quicksort, *BCS Computer Journal*, 5, pp. 10–15. Cited on page(s) 49.

J. JAFFAR AND J.-L. LASSEZ
[1987]   Constraint logic programming, in: *POPL'87: Proceedings 14th ACM
         Symposium on Principles of Programming Languages*, ACM, pp. 111–
         119. Cited on page(s) xi, 322.

J. JAFFAR, S. MICHAYOV, P. J. STUCKEY AND R. H. C. YAP
[1992]   The CLP($\mathcal{R}$) language and system, *ACM Transactions on Programming
         Languages and Systems*, 14, pp. 339–395. Cited on page(s) xi.

R. KOWALSKI
[1974]   Predicate logic as a programming language, in: *Proceedings IFIP'74*,
         North-Holland, New York, pp. 569–574. Cited on page(s) ix, 320.

A. MACKWORTH

[1977]   Consistency in networks of relations, *Artificial Intelligence*, 8, pp. 99–118. Cited on page(s) x.

A. MARTELLI AND U. MONTANARI

[1982]   An efficient unification algorithm, *ACM Transactions on Programming Languages and Systems*, 4, pp. 258–282. Cited on page(s) 320.

E. MONFROY, M. RUSINOWITCH AND R. SCHOTT

[1996]   Implementing non-linear constraints with cooperative solvers, in: *Proceedings of the ACM Symposium on Applied Computing (SAC '96)*, ACM Press, New York, NY, USA, pp. 63–72. Cited on page(s) 322.

U. MONTANARI

[1974]   Networks of constraints: fundamental properties and applications to picture processing, *Information Science*, 7, pp. 95–132. Also Technical Report, Carnegie Mellon University, 1971. Cited on page(s) x.

E. NETTO

[1901]   *Lehrbuch der Combinatorik*, Teubner, Stuttgart. Cited on page(s) 321.

R. O'KEEFE

[1990]   *The Craft of Prolog*, The MIT Press, Cambridge, Massachusetts. Cited on page(s) 320.

C. H. PAPADIMITRIOU AND K. STEIGLITZ

[1982]   *Combinatorial Optimization: Algorithms and Complexity*, Prentice-Hall, Englewood Cliffs, NJ. Cited on page(s) 278.

J. ROBINSON

[1965]   A machine-oriented logic based on the resolution principle, *J. ACM*, 12, pp. 23–41. Cited on page(s) ix, 320.

S. RUSSELL AND P. NORVIG

[2003]   *Artifical Intelligence: A Modern Approach*, Prentice-Hall, Englewood Cliffs, NJ, second edn. Cited on page(s) 321.

J. SCHIMPF

[2002]   Logical loops, in: *Proceedings of the 2002 International Conference on Logic Programming*, P. J. Stuckey, ed., vol. 2401 of Lecture Notes in Computer Science, Springer-Verlag, pp. 224–238. Cited on page(s) 321.

H. SIMONIS

[2005]   Sudoku as a constraint problem, in: *Proceedings of the Fourth International Workshop on Modelling and Reformulating Constraint Satisfaction Problems*, B. Hnich, P. Prosser and B. Smith, eds. Sitges, Spain. Cited on page(s) 321.

L. STERLING AND E. SHAPIRO

[1994]   *The Art of Prolog*, The MIT Press, Cambridge, Massachusetts, second edn. Cited on page(s) xiii, 320.

I. SUTHERLAND

[1963]   *Sketchpad, A Man-Machine Graphical Communication System*, Garland Publishing, New York. Cited on page(s) x.

P. VAN HENTENRYCK

[1989]   *Constraint Satisfaction in Logic Programming*, The MIT Press, Cambridge, Massachusetts. Cited on page(s) xi, 321.

[1997]   *Numerica: A Modeling Language for Global Optimization*, The MIT Press, Cambridge, Massachusetts. Cited on page(s) 322.

V. V. VAZIRANI

[2001]   *Approximation Algorithms*, Springer-Verlag, Berlin. Cited on page(s) 322.

A. VORONKOV

[1992]   Logic programming with bounded quantifiers, in: *Logic Programming and Automated Reasoning—Proc. 2nd Russian Conference on Logic Programming*, A. Voronkov, ed., LNCS 592, Springer-Verlag, Berlin, pp. 486–514. Cited on page(s) 321.

M. WALLACE, S. NOVELLO AND J. SCHIMPF

[1997]   ECL^{i}PS^e: A platform for constraint logic programming, *ICL Systems Journal*, 12, pp. 159–200. Cited on page(s) 321.

WIKIPEDIA

[2006]   Eight queens puzzle. Entry http://en.wikipedia.org/wiki/Queens_problem in Wikipedia. Cited on page(s) 321.

Index

./2, 81
//, 42
1e-n, 261
::/2, 164, 186, 189
;/2, 62
</2, 47
=../2, 82
=/2, 18
=:=/2, 47
=</2, 47
==/2, 78
=>/2, 160
>/2, 47
>=/2, 47
',',/2, 60
->/2, 62
=\=/2, 47
\==/2, 78
#</2, 166
#=/2, 166
#=</2, 166
#>/2, 166
#>=/2, 166
#\=/2, 166
$</2, 162
$=/2, 162
$=</2, 162
$>/2, 162
$>=/2, 162
$\=/2, 162
&=/2, 186
&\=, 186
!/0, 65
abs/1, 42
alldifferent/1, 196, 241
and/2, 160
append/3, 24
arg/3, 81
atom/1, 77
atomic/1, 77
bb_min/3, 248
  delta option, 248
  factor option, 248

strategy:continue option, 251
strategy:dichotomic option, 251
strategy:restart option, 251
char_code/2, 116
clause/2, 69
compound/1, 77
count/3, 111
decval/1, 146
delete/5, 217
dim/2, 121
div/2, 42
dynamic, 70
eplex_cleanup/0, 288
eplex_get/2, 281
eplex_solve/1, 280
eplex_solver_setup/1, 280
eplex_solver_setup/4, 287
eplex_var_get/3, 281
eplex_var_get_bounds/3, 286
eval/1, 174
exclude/2, 199
fail/0, 65
fix/1, 128
flatten/2, 241
for/3, 115
foreach/2, 111
foreacharg/2, 120
foreachelem/2, 122, 123
fromto/4, 124
functor/3, 80
fx, 55
fxx, 54
fxy, 54
fy, 55
get_domain_as_list/2, 208
get_max/2, 206
get_min/2, 206
getval/2, 146
ground/1, 77
halt/0, 17
incval/1, 146
indomain/1, 209
indomain/2, 219

Printed in the United States
by Baker & Taylor Publisher Services